FEMINIST LEGAL ACTIVISM IN INDIA

This open access book examines the work of feminists engaging with legislative lobbying and strategic litigation in their fight for equality and self-determination.

Across the world, feminists engage in legal activism. This book showcases the ways in which feminists in India have been particularly successful in their legal interventions such as legislative lobbying and strategic litigation.

The book looks at eight national campaigns for law reform waged by the protagonists of the Indian women's movement between the 1970s and today, addressing sexual assault, domestic violence and family law, among other issues. Using interviews and other primary source materials, it illustrates how women's rights activists and feminist lawyers think about the law and how they work to make the law more gender-just. The book develops a multi-faceted approach to understanding feminist legal activism and shows how activists' strategies, constitutional rights, the responsiveness of courts and parliaments, and socio-cultural factors impact the outcome of legal activism.

Feminist Legal Activism in India

Tanja Herklotz

•HART•
OXFORD • LONDON • NEW YORK • NEW DELHI • SYDNEY

HART PUBLISHING

Bloomsbury Publishing Plc

Kemp House, Chawley Park, Cumnor Hill, Oxford, OX2 9PH, UK

1385 Broadway, New York, NY 10018, USA

Bloomsbury Publishing Ireland Limited, 29 Earlsfort Terrace, Dublin 2, D02 AY28, Ireland

HART PUBLISHING, the Hart/Stag logo, BLOOMSBURY and the Diana logo are trademarks of Bloomsbury Publishing Plc

First published in Great Britain 2026

Also: Berlin, Humboldt-Universität zu Berlin, Juristische Fakultät, dissertation, 2021, title: Streets and Courtrooms: Feminist Legal Activism in India

The publication of this work was supported by the Open Access Publication Fund of Humboldt-Universität zu Berlin and the Dr Giesing Stiftung.

A catalogue record for this book is available from the British Library.

A catalogue record for this book is available from the Library of Congress.

Library of Congress Control Number: 2026936533

ISBN: HB: 978-1-50998-568-5
ePDF: 978-1-50998-570-8
ePub: 978-1-50998-569-2

Typeset by Compuscript Ltd, Shannon

For product safety related questions contact productsafety@bloomsbury.com

To find out more about our authors and books visit www.hartpublishing.co.uk. Here you will find extracts, author information, details of forthcoming events and the option to sign up for our newsletters.

ACKNOWLEDGEMENTS

This book grew out of my doctoral dissertation, completed at Humboldt-Universität zu Berlin in 2021, and it bears the imprint of many conversations and forms of support that accompanied me throughout the years of research and writing.

First and foremost, I wish to express my profound gratitude to Philipp Dann, who supervised this doctoral project with rigorous and encouraging guidance. I am thankful for the many conversations that situated this project within the broader debates in comparative constitutional and socio-legal research, and for the opportunity to learn from the intellectually stimulating environment he created at the Chair for Public Law and Comparative Law. I also wish to thank Philipp Dann and the members of his team for their valuable feedback during doctoral colloquia and for the exchanges of ideas which significantly shaped the direction of the research.

I am also deeply indebted to Susanne Baer, who served as the second supervisor of the project, for her thoughtful and valuable critique of my work and for being an inspiring example of a feminist critical legal scholar.

This book is based in part on empirical research conducted during several research visits to India. I am sincerely grateful to the feminist activists, lawyers, and individuals in Delhi, Mumbai, and Bengaluru who agreed to be interviewed and generously shared their time, experiences, and expertise. They remain anonymous in this book. Yet, I wish to express that it has been a privilege to speak with them and learn from them. Their openness and willingness to engage in thoughtful discussion were essential to the analysis presented here. I hope that this book does justice to their insights.

I am further grateful to all the feminist organisations and women's and human rights groups that allowed me to attend meetings and activities, shared materials with me, and helped me better understand how feminist legal activism works. Thanks are due to the All India Democratic Women's Association, the All India Progressive Women's Association, the Alternative Law Forum, Awaaz-e-Niswaan, Bharatiya Muslim Mahila Andolan, the Lawyers Collective Women's Rights Initiative, Majlis Legal Centre, Partners for Law and Development, Saheli and Vimochana.

The numerous struggles against the injustices of a patriarchal system that I discovered through my research have deeply moved me. I would like to dedicate this book to all activists who oppose discrimination and fight for the protection and realisation of human rights.

During my time in India, I benefitted greatly from the intellectual environments provided by several universities and research institutions, including Ambedkar University, Azim Premji University, the Centre for the Study of Developing Societies, the Centre for Women's Development Studies, Jawaharlal Nehru University, Jindal Global Law School, the National Law School of India University, the Tata Institute for Social Sciences, the University of Delhi and the University of Mumbai. These institutions allowed me not only to attend workshops and lectures and access libraries, but also offered opportunities for scholarly exchange that enriched the project in meaningful ways. I am grateful to all those individuals who welcomed me so generously, took the time to have conversations with me, and contributed to making my research visits both productive and inspiring. I owe special thanks to Aparna Chandra, Radhika Chitkara, Kalindi Kokal, Jhuma Sen, Rukmini Sen, and Arun Thiruvengadam.

I also wish to thank Shailaja Bajpai, whose home became a second home to me during several research visits to Delhi, and whose hospitality, guidance and generosity made my visits not only productive but also enjoyable and memorable.

I had the opportunity to present and discuss the ideas and arguments of this research with other scholars at conferences of the Law and Society Association, the Socio-Legal Studies Association, the Law and Development Research Network, and the Netzwerk Recht und Gesellschaft, the South Asia Legal Studies Workshop at the University of Wisconsin-Madison, and on several other occasions. I thank the organisers, other panellists, and the audience for their critical feedback and discussions. Other sources of intellectual inspiration were my research stays at the Center for the Study of Law and Society at UC Berkeley, the School of Law at the University of Warwick, and several visits to SOAS University of London and the conversations with excellent scholars at these institutions. Special thanks are due to Martin Lau and Werner Menski.

The research and writing of this book were made possible through the financial support of the Elsa Neumann Scholarship by the State of Berlin and Humboldt-Universität's Caroline von Humboldt Scholarship. Research trips abroad, and conference participation have been funded by the German Academic Exchange Service (DAAD) and the German Association for Asian Studies (DGA). Humboldt-Universität's Open Access Fund and the Dr Giesing Foundation provided funding for the Open Access publication. I am grateful for this support and for the recognition of the project that it represents.

I would also like to express my sincere thanks to Kate Whetter and Joanne Choulerton from Hart Publishing for their professional support throughout the publication process. Their guidance, responsiveness, and careful attention to detail greatly facilitated the transformation of the manuscript into its final form.

Finally, I wish to thank Sebastian Cacean, who supported me at every stage of this journey in more ways than I can possibly count.

CONTENTS

ABBREVIATIONS

AIDWA	All India Democratic Women's Association
AIMPLB	All India Muslim Personal Law Board
AIPWA	All India Progressive Women's Association
AIWC	All India Women's Conference
BJP	Bharatiya Janata Party
BMMA	Bharatiya Muslim Mahila Andolan
BNS	Bharatiya Nyaya Sanhita
CEDAW	Convention on the Elimination of All Forms of Discrimination against Women
CEW	Committee for the Empowerment of Women
CrPC	Code of Criminal Procedure
EPW	Economic and Political Weekly
FIR	First information report
HMGA	Hindu Minority and Guardianship Act
HSA	Hindu Succession Act
IDA	Indian Divorce Act
IEA	Indian Evidence Act
IPC	Indian Penal Code
JWP	Joint Women's Programme
LCI	Law Commission of India
LEAF	Women's Legal Education and Action Fund (Canada)
LGBTIQ	Lesbian, Gay, Bisexual, Transgender, Intersex and Queer
n.d.	no date
NCW	National Commission for Women
NGO	Non-governmental organisation

NOW	National Organization for Women (USA)
PIL	Public interest litigation
PLD	Partners for Law and Development
PWDVA	Protection of Women from Domestic Violence Act
UCC	Uniform Civil Code
UDHR	Universal Declaration of Human Rights
WARLAW	Women's Action Research and Legal Action for Women
WIA	Women's India Association

TABLE OF CASES

India

Canada

Colombia

Germany

Israel

South Africa

United States

International Tribunals

1

Introduction

I. Feminist Legal Activism in India

The law is an ambivalent tool from the viewpoint of the marginalised. On the one hand, it serves to stabilise existing power hierarchies, on the other, it may be used to challenge and change those very hierarchies – if the marginalised succeed in using the law's promises to emancipate themselves and to have a say in the process of law-making and law-interpretation.

Feminist legal struggles around the world have done just that. Women's rights activists across the globe oppose discriminatory and paternalistic laws, and they fight for their right to equality and self-determination. They send petitions to parliaments and litigate cases in court to strive for gender equality. In doing so, they have obtained great victories – but also severe defeats. But what determines whether a campaign for legal change fails or succeeds? Is it the rights that constitutional or international law provides, the movement's strategies, the composition of parliaments and courts that activists address, or cultural and societal factors?

This book is interested in the outcomes of feminist legal activism. Its central question is: In which areas, by which means, and under which conditions are feminist activists successful with their campaigns for legal change? I tackle this question by looking at feminist legal activism in India. The decision to focus on India draws on the fact that the Global South is still neglected in feminist legal studies, scholarship on law and social movements and – despite a 'southern turn' (Dann, Riegner, Bönnemann, 2020, 2024; Dann 2023) in the last years – potentially even in comparative law. Yet to understand complex causal relations between society and the law, we must look beyond the usual suspects of countries in the Global North. The Indian case, for example, alludes to the impact of the socio-cultural context, especially the role of religion and legal culture, on the outcome of feminist activism. It points to the limits and potentials of feminist legal interventions in a plurilegal system where the state frequently 'outsources' decisions about law reform and dispute resolution to other societal actors.

An early example of a study comparing (feminist) legal activism in India with its counterparts in selected countries in the Global North is Charles Epp's book *The Rights Revolution* from 1998. Epp stated that compared with women's movements in Canada, the US and the UK, the Indian women's movement had been reluctant to strategically use the courts in its fight for gender equality (Epp, 1998). According to Epp, Indian litigants and their lawyers had acted 'entirely independently of any larger strategy' and without the support or coordination of women's groups (Epp, 1998, p 106). Indian women's organisations, in Epp's opinion, were weak because they lacked professionalisation and competed against each other (Epp, 1998, p 107). Accordingly, Epp argued, Indian women's rights activists achieved almost no success in bringing about a 'rights revolution'.

This book takes a fresh look at feminist legal activism in India, thereby painting a contrasting picture to Epp's evaluation. I show that Indian feminists build on a long history of legal activism and that, in several cases, they have succeeded with their demands for legal change. Individual women, feminist lawyers and women's groups have indeed worked strategically and collaboratively to bring about successes, not only for themselves and their clients but also for women at large.

I arrive at this assessment by taking a more holistic look at legal activism. Other than Epp's study, this book not only considers developments at the Supreme Court but also points to the successes of feminist legal activism at other levels. Change did not only occur through pathbreaking precedent by the Supreme Court (although that is also there) but also through new legislation and high court judgments. One goal of the book is, therefore, to de-centre the Indian Supreme Court from the academic discourse around legal change to a certain extent – by pointing to the Parliament and the High Courts as other important locales of legal change and by shedding light on the protagonists who initiated the reform processes in the first place: women's groups, feminist lawyers, and activists.

Furthermore, a lot has happened since the publication of Epp's book in the late 1990s. In the 1990s and 2000s, several feminist legal organisations were founded to provide 'legal inputs to the women's movement' (Lawyers Collective, n.d.-a). These are organisations of trained feminist lawyers representing women in court to bring about landmark cases. In addition, around the same time, women began to set up religious women's organisations to counter those religious groups exclusively led by men and to push for advancing the rights of religious minority women living under religious family law. Both sets of organisations are crucial in understanding the developments of legal activism in India.

This book follows feminist legal activism in eight specific campaigns for legal change led by Indian feminist activists between the 1970s, when the second wave of the Indian women's movement emerged, and the 2010s. By way of process tracing, it depicts how selected feminist demands 'travelled' in the process of legal change: from being articulated in women's groups or at feminist conferences via their broader dissemination through media, letters to the Parliament, ministries or the Indian Law Commission to being debated in Parliament and enacted in laws or via petitions to court that impacted judgments.

To gather data on these campaigns I visited nine women's organisations: the All India Democratic Women's Association (AIDWA), the All India Progressive Women's Association (AIPWA), the Lawyers Collective Women's Rights Initiative, Partners for Law and Development (PLD) and Saheli in Delhi, Majlis Legal Centre, Awaaz-e-Niswaan and the Bharatiya Muslim Mahila Andolan (BMMA) in Mumbai and Vimochana in Bengaluru. In addition, I conducted research at women's studies centres at universities and other research institutes, met with feminist academics, and attended seminars and conferences at Ambedkar University, the Centre for Women's Development Studies, the Centre for the Study of Developing Societies, Jawaharlal Nehru University and the University of Delhi in Delhi, at Jindal Global Law School in Sonipat, at the Tata Institute for Social Sciences and the University of Mumbai in Mumbai, and at Azim Premji University and the National Law School of India University in Bengaluru.

During my visits to the various organisations and institutions, I collected primary sources on the women's movement, such as reports, memos, pamphlets, and newsletters produced by feminist activists and women's groups. In addition, I used the sources provided by the (online) Feminist Law Archives of PLD and the archives of the journals *Economic and Political Weekly* (EPW), *Manushi* and *Kali's Yug*. I also drew on publications in journals of women's/ gender studies, the websites and newsletters of women's groups and studied autobiographical accounts of women's rights activists. Furthermore, I attended movement-related activities, including conferences, seminars, discussion groups and informal gatherings. In addition, I conducted 15 semi-structured expert-interviews with activists from the nine women's groups mentioned above, between 2015 and 2019. My interview questions concerned activists' evaluation of family law and the laws on violence against women, the groups' way of working, in particular with regard to legal activism, their self-assessments of success or failure in campaigns and explanations for these.

In addition to engaging with primary sources from and about the Indian women's movement, I also studied primary sources on law-making processes and court cases. These included constitutional and parliamentary debates, reports by the Indian Law Commission and by parliamentary standing committees, legislative Bills and Acts, court petitions and judgments.

II. Legislative Lobbying and Litigation

I understand feminist legal activism as feminist attempts to approach law-making or law-interpreting institutions to push for legal or doctrinal change. Hence, two central forms of legal activism – and these are what this book focuses on – are legislative lobbying and strategic litigation.[1]

Legislative lobbying (sometimes also called 'advocacy') refers to an attempt by social movement actors and activists to impact the legislator (the government, ministries, parliamentarians). Actors who use this form of activism might aspire to bring about either the enactment of a new law or the amendment of an existing law by deletion or replacement of a specific provision that is deemed to be unfit. In some instances, activists may also campaign against the passing of a Bill that they regard as retrograde/reactionary.

[1] Beyond these two forms, activities of feminist legal activism also include interactions with other – state and non-state – institutions, such as the police or religious dispute settlement bodies, to impact how these actors interpret and apply legal norms.

Litigation refers to individuals' or groups' deliberate use of the courts to obtain favourable judgments. This might happen at the constitutional or supreme courts with the power to undertake judicial review, in the lower courts, which play essential roles in (re)interpreting and implementing legislation, or regional and international courts, which deal with human rights violations. The aim of activists could be for the court to declare a particular law unconstitutional or otherwise invalid, or set a positive precedent by interpreting a norm in a specific way or by using a new legal concept.

Much (Indian and international) scholarship on (comparative) constitutional law has focused on the courts as the central actors in bringing about legal and social change. Ran Hirschl (2007, p 1) coined the term 'juristocracy' to describe how countries worldwide have experienced a shift of power from representative institutions to judiciaries, creating a situation in which courts 'have become increasingly important, even crucial, political decision-making bodies'. This increased importance of the courts has resonated with an increased scholarly interest in the role of courts as political actors and motors of social change (Tate & Vallinder, 1995; Sieder, Schjolden, & Angell, 2005; Gargarella, Roux, & Domingo, 2006; Gauri & Brinks, 2008; Bonilla Maldonado, 2013) and in social movements', interest groups' and cause lawyers' attempts to use the courts strategically to advance their goals (Epp, 1998; Manfredi, 2004; Sarat & Scheingold, 2001, 2004, 2006; Cichowski, 2007; Collins, 2008).

In India, the perception of a strong Supreme Court, protecting the rights of the marginalised and compensating for a dysfunctional Parliament, has been particularly powerful. Feminist lawyer and activist Indira Jaising even terms the Indian Supreme Court the 'most powerful court in the world' (Jaising, 2011, p 257). In contrast with this view of a powerful Supreme Court, commentators regard the Indian Parliament as relatively weak – ineffective or even dysfunctional, a place of 'rowdiness and disorder' where theatrics replace debate (D Kapur & Mehta, 2006, p 29). Also, the picture of the activist Indian Supreme Court does not extend to the Indian High Courts.

The Supreme Court's image as a powerful institution stems from the high times of Public Interest Litigation (PIL) in the 1980s, but has somewhat endured, even though the Supreme Court has a different political outlook today than it did then and even though the Court's landmark decisions might not have been representative of the Court even then. Yet, as Rosenberg, Krishnaswamy and Bail (2019, p 1) point out:

> There is a widely held belief among Indian academics, political and civil society activists, and public-spirited citizens that the Indian Supreme Court is both capable and uniquely structured to help the relatively disadvantaged. The broad scope of rights granted by the Indian Constitution and the relative institutional independence of the Indian Supreme Court bolster this optimistic view of the Court. This view also draws support from the perceived inability of the Indian political system to respond to chronic denials of human rights. Political infighting, corruption, inert bureaucracies, and an ossified yet resilient cultural system render the political system structurally incapable

> of decisive and progressive social change. In contrast, the Indian Supreme Court is free from these constraints.

In this light, one could assume that Indian feminists have been more successful in advancing gender equality by approaching the Supreme Court than by approaching either the Parliament or the High Courts. This book shows that this is not the case. The campaigns I engage with demonstrate that, firstly, the Indian Parliament has played a crucial role in bringing about legal change concerning women's rights. Secondly, it was frequently the High Courts and not the Supreme Court that struck down discriminatory laws and kick-started significant law reforms by pushing the Parliament to intervene, while the Indian Supreme Court refrained from declaring blatantly discriminatory laws unconstitutional.

III. Areas of Intervention

From the 1970s until today, Indian feminist activists and women's rights groups have tackled a broad spectrum of legal and social issues. Early campaigns addressed rape and dowry violence. They were followed by campaigns against amniocentesis use for sex determination and sex-selective abortion, (domestic) violence, and sexual harassment in the workplace. Activism also included the topics of sexuality and reproductive rights, women's health, the portrayal of women in the media, pornography, women's economic rights and women's political participation.

This book focuses on eight national campaigns waged by Indian feminist activists between the 1970s and the early 2010s. My focus thereby lies on two broad areas: a) marriage and the family; and b) violence against women. In the area of *marriage and the family*, I analyse the campaigns (1) for a Uniform Civil Code and reforms in (2) Christian, (3) Hindu, and (4) Muslim personal law. In the area of *violence against women*, I assess the campaigns for reforms regarding the laws on (5) rape, (6) dowry-related violence, (7) domestic violence, and (8) sexual harassment in the workplace.

All eight campaigns had country-wide participation, lasted for several years or decades, and gathered significant media attention. I understand a 'campaign' here as the cumulation of protest events, lobbying and litigation activities that attempt to achieve the goal of legal change – even though the activities that are part of a campaign may not be coordinated or planned by the same group of individuals and even though different feminist protagonists may frame their goals and demands in slightly different terms. To say that these were overarching feminist campaigns is not to say that there was only one uniform feminist position on the issue in question. Chapter two will elaborate that, although scholarship often speaks about *the* Indian women's movement and although many feminist activists see themselves as part of *a* movement, feminist activism is heterogeneous and includes a variety of different actors and standpoints. Yet, despite this heterogeneity, there have been widely shared demands on several issues, resulting in joint campaigns for specific law reforms.

I focus on the two different legal fields – *marriage and the family* and *violence against women* – because contrasting feminist activism in these fields is particularly fruitful. The comparison shows that the legal or constitutional lens alone is not decisive for a campaign's chances of success. Although from a constitutional law viewpoint, Indian family law may seem the easier target for legal change, since it clearly contains gender-discriminatory regulations, Indian feminists were more successful with their activism in the area of violence against women. Let me elaborate on this.

Indian family law is based on a system of religious 'personal laws' in which different religious norms apply to people with different religious affiliations. The legal rules in each of these sets of religious laws were – and to some extent still are – discriminatory against women (Parashar, 1992; MacKinnon, 2006; Parashar & Dhanda, 2008; Agnes, 2011a, 2011b). Existing family law provisions regularly granted women lesser rights than men, thereby explicitly using sex as a criterion for difference. For example, Christian inheritance law provided less inheritance for daughters than sons. Muslim divorce law granted husbands extensive divorce rights, while wives' divorce rights were limited. Hindu law gave fathers greater guardianship rights than mothers. Such regulations violate not only the general principle of equality in Article 14 of the Indian Constitution but also the more specific prohibition of discrimination on the grounds of sex in Article 15(1). Given that the Indian legislature is bound by the fundamental rights chapter in the Indian Constitution (Article 13) and that the Indian higher judiciary enjoys the power of judicial review, feminist legal activism against these norms, if looked at through the constitutional lens, would appear promising.

In the area of violence against women, the constitutional argument for reform was more difficult. Here, the discrimination against women was not de jure, but rather de facto. It rarely resulted from the legal norms themselves and more often from the social and institutional structures in which these norms operated (R Kapur & Cossman, 1996; Baxi, 2014; Basu, 2015; Satish, 2016). Statutes in criminal and civil law that dealt with violence against women were usually formulated in a gender-neutral manner or even treated women preferentially. In doing so, however, they often drew on gendered stereotypes of women as weak and lacking sexual agency. Feminists also regarded the norms as insufficient or inadequate to tackle societal realities of gender-based violence. In practice, cases of sexual assault rarely resulted in convictions. Furthermore, women who reported assault and brought cases before a court were often confronted with gendered stereotypes and biases in the (male dominated) state institutions.

Indeed, feminist legal scholarship (starting with MacKinnon, 1979), the jurisprudence of several constitutional courts,[2] and norms of international law (especially the Convention on the Elimination of All Forms of Discrimination

[2] See for example the Canadian Supreme Court in *Andrews v Law Society of British Columbia*, [1989] 1 SCR 143 (Can).

Against Women (CEDAW)) have understood gender-based violence and sexual harassment as violations of the principle of equality, arguing that equality provisions do not merely disallow differentiation but prohibit discrimination or hierarchisation. According to this understanding, the law must actively respond to societal realities and discriminating structures so as not to perpetuate inequalities. The norms in the Indian Constitution are open to such an interpretation. In addition to Article 15(1)'s prohibition of discrimination on the grounds of sex, Article 15(3) allows the state to make 'special provision' for women in the form of affirmative action to help mitigate historical disadvantage. A look at other constitutional provisions also indicates the Constitution's transformative potential (Bhatia, 2019). The Indian Supreme Court, too, has – albeit sporadically – applied a substantive understanding of the Constitution's equality principle.[3] These are valuable approaches that feminists could use in their campaigns concerning violence against women. However, both the international and the Indian jurisprudence that goes in this direction primarily stems from more recent years. This substantive understanding of equality was certainly not shared during the earlier feminist campaigns that I engage with here in the 1970s, 1980s, and 1990s and is still not the dominant viewpoint in today's jurisprudence. Instead, the Indian judiciary has focused on formal equality (R Kapur, 2016; Bhatia, 2019) and interprets the prohibition of sex discrimination in a restrictive manner.[4]

Thus, from a constitutional law viewpoint, it would appear easier for feminist activists and women's groups to achieve legal success regarding family law and harder regarding violence against women. Yet, as this book shows, the opposite is the case. The success of feminist campaigns in family law remained limited. Despite decades of campaigning for reforms in family law, activists failed with several of their demands. In other cases, courts and the Parliament brought about reforms, but in a watered-down manner, only several years or decades down the line of campaigning and often without reference to gender equality. In the area of violence against women, however, feminists achieved significant successes. They brought about several legislative reforms in a relatively short time. In some cases, such as in the case of the law on domestic violence, the legislature even adopted verbatim large parts of the legislative proposals drafted by women's rights organisations.

If the constitutional lens alone does not help us understand and explain feminist success with legal activism, then other factors must be decisive. To elaborate on these factors, looking at different dimensions of feminist legal activism is helpful.

[3] Chapter 3 will provide examples.

[4] In several judgments, the Indian courts ruled that a violation of Article 15(1) only occurred if sex was used as a criterion of difference in the law. Measures that discriminate indirectly and are linked to social criteria were not regarded as unconstitutional, even if these social criteria were based on gendered stereotypes. Chapter 3 will engage with this topic in more detail.

IV. Four Dimensions of Legal Activism

This book proposes a frame of analysis that considers four dimensions of (feminist) legal activism, each containing a range of impact factors. In carving out these factors, I rely on scholarship on feminist legal activism worldwide. Chapter three elaborates on the frame of analysis and provides several examples. In short, I distinguish between the following four dimensions.

The first dimension is that of *rights*. It assesses the preconditions for legal change that constitutional and international human rights law create. These include equality and anti-discrimination provisions. However, other provisions that serve women (say, women's dignity) and conflicting fundamental rights (such as the rights of the foetus or of religious groups) are also influential.

The *activism* dimension includes success factors internal to the social movement, such as its strength (membership, expertise, unity, etc) and strategies. This dimension includes how feminist groups and activists frame their demands for law reform, what locales and tactics they use, and with whom they build alliances. For example, in the Indian case, direct attacks on religion-based family law were far less successful than campaigns invoking non-discriminatory readings of religious texts and campaigns involving religious communities' spokespersons.

Thirdly, *state institutions* as the receptors of change, most notably the judiciary and the Parliament, are important for understanding the outcomes of feminist legal activism. This includes factors such as the partisanship of state institutions, the representation of women in Parliament and the courts, women's policy agencies and the state's international obligations. For example, the fact that the Indian National Commission for Women often does not have a particularly feminist approach towards pressing social and legal issues made it difficult for feminist activists to use this actor in their fight for gender equality. Also, India's formal reservations relating to CEDAW reduced the importance of that international treaty in family law and limited feminists in their argumentation.

These three dimensions, however, cannot fully explain why the movement has been so much more successful in its campaigns concerning violence against women than in those concerning family law. After all, the movement worked with similar means in both areas, and the institutional and legal contexts were similar too. A crucial fourth dimension is thus *society*. It focuses on the socio-cultural factors that impact feminist activism. These could be public opinion and media coverage, counter-mobilisation, the role of religion, and legal culture. For example, media-effective protests such as demonstrations and vigils in front of the court and activists' use of print media and, later, social media made it difficult for the Parliament and the courts to ignore the women's movement's concerns. On the other hand, counter-mobilisation by religious and anti-feminist groups hindered the success of feminist activism.

V. Success in Legal Activism

Success in the context of this study means a positive response by the legislature or the judiciary to the feminist reform campaigns. There are cases where it is obvious that the campaign has been successful. If feminist activists suggest a law reform and draft model legislation, and the Parliament then passes this law as suggested by feminist groups, this is an example of a successful campaign. If a women's group litigates a case against a discriminatory legal provision and the Supreme Court declares it unconstitutional, they can also be called successful. In most cases, however, the story is more complex. Interest groups or social movements striving for legal change rarely achieve 100 per cent of their goals. Instead, if activists succeed in having the Parliament take up their demands, their reform suggestions often get watered down in the law-making process. Even a court case that a women's group has won might turn out to be a Pyrrhic victory because the judgment is so infused with gender stereotypes that it can hardly be counted as a success from a feminist viewpoint.

On the other hand, a lost case in court might still contain favourable precedent. Furthermore, to have one's case heard at the Supreme Court may stimulate public discussion on an issue, generate media coverage, increase widespread awareness (including by law-makers), broaden mobilisation on the topic and exert political pressure, which may bring the movement closer to its goal. Morton and Allen (2001, pp 65–66) point out that while winning the dispute is the priority for the litigant, it is often secondary for women's groups intervening in the case. Instead, intervening women's groups might focus on eliciting a favourable precedent providing 'new legal resources with which to win future political battles'. Also, '[a]n interest group whose case is heard by the Supreme Court acquires a certain legitimacy as the "representative" of the interests involved in the case' – legitimacy which might buy the actors 'access to decision makers, not just judges but also legislators and civil servants' (Morton & Allen, 2001, p 83). Ratna Kapur (2016, p 750) therefore, advises us to 'take a step back and examine what has been lost when we experience a victory in the courtroom, as well as what has been won when we experience a defeat'.

Scholarship that attempts to provide more nuanced understandings of 'success' in feminist legal activism evaluates which specific feminist arguments the court took up in its decisions (Manfredi, 2004), whether the judgment provides for new legal resources and what indirect effects judgments have had, ie whether the case led to the elimination or change of a law or administrative practice (Morton & Allen, 2001).

A second challenge in assessing feminist success is proving that the passing of a favourable law or judgment did in fact result from the feminist campaign, ie proving causality between feminist activism and legal change. Indeed, '[t]he realized agenda of a social movement cannot simply be regarded as its outcome without demonstrating that the movement made it happen' (Kolb, 2007, p 23). Here, the method of process tracing helps to establish causal chains from an interest group's campaign to the campaign's outcomes (Dür, 2008). This involves scrutinising all stages of a campaign for law reform: activists' articulation of demands, their attempts to influence decision-makers (members of the government, the ministries or the Parliament or judges), the decision-makers' responses to these influence attempts, the degree to which the feminist demands are reflected in the legal effects and the feminist statements of (dis)satisfaction with the outcome.[5]

As described above, this book traces the feminist demands and their way into the law. I carved out these demands by analysing primary sources, including writings by women's rights organisations, individual activists, feminist scholars and journalists, as well as statements made at women's conferences or meetings. I then followed these demands through various forms of activism, including street campaigns or attempts at litigation. I assess how they were taken up in parliamentary debates and how they ultimately found or could not find their way into new legislation or landmark judgments.

I evaluate the level of the feminist campaign's success by considering the following aspects: I assess whether in response to the feminist campaign the Parliament passed a law that is substantially close to what the movement aimed at or whether the courts gave a judgment that provides a favourable precedent from a feminist point of view. If that is the case, I also analyse to what degree feminist demands are reflected in the law or judgment. Notably, different degrees of attainment of objectives are possible: feminists may reach all, some or none of their goals. Where feminists did not obtain a law or a judgment, I assessed how far into the law-making process they made it and whether the failed campaigns had indirect effects later.

In doing so, I not only compare feminist demands articulated in primary sources with judgments and legislative acts but also consider the discourses that preceded or followed the making of these legal outcomes – in parliamentary debates, recommendations by the Indian Law Commission, reports by parliamentary standing committees, Bills that did not make it into legal acts, media discourses, etc. I also assess how participants in the law-making process, Bills' statements of 'objects and reasons' and judgments reason their decisions. This allows me to see where law-makers and judges take up feminist arguments, concepts or terminology and where they subscribe to gender stereotypes and misogyny. Lastly, I consider the time elapsing between the first articulation of a feminist demand and the legal change as a factor in determining the degree of a campaign's success.

Thus, at the end of each analysis of the eight campaigns, I will not only be able to say how successful a campaign was but will also point to the factors that impacted the campaign's outcome. I do this by placing the eight campaigns in their

[5] At the same time, it is important to note that legal change is seldom brought about by only one factor. It is typically a complex mix of factors that impacts decisions in law-making processes, including the political context, socio-economic situation, international pressure, public opinion, etc. Social movements can, however, engage with and use these factors to their advantage.

historical, political and societal context and by linking them to the success factors depicted above. In addition, the juxtaposition between the different campaigns will allude to the factors that were decisive for the campaign's success or failure.

At this point, it might be helpful to state what this book does *not* attempt to do. This book is concerned with whether and how the Indian women's movement has brought about legal change; in other words, it focuses on the responsiveness of the legislator and the judiciary to feminist campaigns. I do *not* assess whether or not this legal change has translated into social change, ie whether new laws or progressive court decisions brought about at the initiative of the women's movement have been implemented adequately on the ground and positively changed the people's lives.

The question of how legal change translates into social change is complex, and much has been written about it. Most prominently, Rosenberg (1991) found in the context of the US that except for scenarios where there exists a small set of unusual enabling conditions, judicial decisions aimed at helping the disadvantaged sections of society, by themselves, were unable to achieve the widespread change for which these decisions are celebrated. For the Indian case, Rosenberg, Krishnaswamy, and Bail (2019) have collected empirical studies on whether (and if so, under what conditions) decisions by the Indian Supreme Court have improved the lives of the relatively disadvantaged. The Indian system has several advantages that other systems, including the US one, lack: the broad sweep of rights provided by the Indian Constitution, the procedural improvisations by the Court's PIL jurisprudence, the Court's *suo moto* jurisdiction and its structural independence from the other branches of the state (Rosenberg, Krishnaswamy, et al, 2019). Ultimately, the case studies assembled by Rosenberg et al demonstrate that the Indian Supreme Court emerges as 'an effective agent of progressive social change' when certain conditions pertain: (1) the Court monitors its judgments, (2) the national government is supportive of the judgment, and (3) civil society/ the public pressurises bureaucrats to implement the decision (Rosenberg, Bail & Krishnaswamy, 2019, pp 355–56). In short, what this shows is that legal reforms *can* matter.

This understanding that legal change can bring about social change under certain circumstances is shared by many activists I spoke with. As I will show in Chapter two, many feminist activists believe in the power of law, which drives their activism. At the same time, they are realistic about what to expect from the law. Decades of experience and some degree of frustration with the limited application of the laws on the ground have given them an understanding of the law's limits. And yet, Indian feminist activists have not rejected the law, but rather seen it as one tool, albeit a crucial one, among others. As one activist, for instance, told me:

> A large population of poor, rural, tribal women, will have no access to this law, which we are fighting for. But law also makes a statement. It makes a statement on [the] gender question, it may be making a statement on [the] Dalit question, it will be making a statement on human rights. So that statement has to be there, that recognition of an issue, of a problem (Activist at Saheli, interview with the author on 29 September 2014).

The notion of the 'statement' points to the fact that laws also have important symbolic functions. But it is not only that. Law reform can under certain conditions also be a starting point in a broader process for social change, and feminist activists play an important role in this broader process. Chapter six will elaborate on this and point to the importance of legal culture in implementing new laws and progressive judgments on the ground.

This study speaks about 'women' and 'men' in a manner that some readers might find problematically binary and unidimensional. After all, the actors of feminist struggles include people of all genders. And feminist campaigns do not only concern the rights of women, but of all those suppressed by a patriarchal system, including trans, intersex, non-binary and queer people. Yet I chose to speak about 'women' (rather than for instance 'womxn'), 'women's rights' and the 'women's movement'. The reason for this decision is that the activists used these terms in the campaigns I focus on in this study (many of which date back to the 1970s and 1980s). They identified as 'women' and themselves as part of the 'women's movement'. Their activism was primarily concerned with cis women.[6] It was only from the mid-1990s onwards that the rights of the LGBTIQ community began to play a more central role in the Indian women's movement (Sen, 2014, p 337), albeit in other campaigns than the ones I address here, most importantly in the campaign against Section 377 of the Indian Penal Code.[7] Hence, changing the terminology to make it more inclusive would mean adding an aspect in retrospect that was not there at the time of feminist activism that I engage with, and would therefore not provide an accurate picture.

VI. Structure of the Book

Chapter two introduces the reader to feminist legal activism in India, placing the emergence and development of Indian feminism in the broader historical, political, and social context.[8] I show how feminists first impacted the constitution-making process and later realised women's constitutional rights by lobbying the legislature and approaching the judiciary. I place a particular focus on the constitutionally enshrined conflict between religious freedom and women's rights – a conflict that plays out in a specific way in many countries of the Global South

[6] Urvashi Butalia (2017) critically reflects upon the early decades of Indian feminism, stating: 'Trans men and women were very far from the movement. Our battles focused on sexual violence, dowry, marriage laws, sexual harassment at the workplace, equal wages for equal work and health. Sexuality and sexual identities? We stayed away from them'.

[7] Section 377 of the Indian Penal Code criminalised sexual acts 'against the order of nature' and was used to prosecute people engaging in oral and anal sex, along with homosexual activity.

[8] An earlier version of Chapter 2 has been published in the journal *World Comparative Law* in 2023 (Herklotz, 2023a).

and that confronts feminist activists with challenges that their counterparts in the Global North might not face in the same way.

Chapter three engages with the question of what makes feminist legal activism successful. It tackles this question by zooming out from India and looking at scholarship on feminist legal activism worldwide, in countries of the Global North and South. Assessing numerous examples of successful and unsuccessful feminist endeavours to bring about legal change in various countries allows me to develop an analytical framework that I later apply in the case studies in Chapters four and five. The proposed framework looks at four different dimensions of feminist legal activism, and points to multiple success factors. These factors include provisions in a country's constitution, its statutory norms or international human rights on gender equality, anti-discrimination, human dignity and rights claims competing with women's rights (*rights*), the strength and strategies of the social movement (*activism*), powers of the judiciary and access to justice, the composition and partisanship of state institutions, women's policy agencies and the state's international obligations (*state institutions*) and public opinion, media, counter-mobilisation, the role of religion, and aspects of legal culture (*society*).

Chapters four and five then focus on India again. I apply the success factors framework developed in Chapter three to two different focus areas. In Chapter four, I analyse feminist legal activism around religion-based family law, particularly the feminist campaigns for a Uniform Civil Code and reforms to Christian, Hindu, and Muslim personal law.[9] For each campaign, I set out what triggered the feminist campaign, how individuals and women's groups strategically pursued their goals and what the legal outcomes of the campaign were. I then explain the feminists' successes and failures. For instance, I reconstruct the stories of feminist activists who regularly phoned the Law Ministry to bring about changes in Christian divorce law, and of a Muslim woman who successfully approached the Supreme Court to ban unilateral instant divorces. I show that from a constitutional law viewpoint, individuals and women's groups had good chances of success in this area. Yet, their actual success remained limited.

Chapter five analyses feminist legal activism in the area of gender-based violence. I look at the campaigns for reforms of the laws related to rape, dowry violence, domestic violence, and sexual harassment in the workplace. Among other examples, I narrate the story of activists who rallied in front of police stations and court buildings to bring about change in the laws on dowry violence and the incident of a female army officer who convinced the courts that unwanted touching of a sexual nature was not merely an insult to her 'modesty', but in fact sexual harassment. I demonstrate that, although from a constitutional law point of view,

[9] The sections of Chapter 4 engaging with the court cases initiated by Mary Roy, Githa Hariharan and Shayara Bano have previously been published in a chapter titled 'Armed with the Constitution: Feminist Litigation on Indian Family Law' in Siddharth de Souza's and my book *Mutinies for Equality: Contemporary Developments in Law and Gender in India* (Herklotz, 2021).

the chances of success were not very high in this area, the feminist activists and women's groups were successful in all four campaigns.

Chapter six summarises the book's key findings. It points out that some success factors examined more closely in Chapter three were particularly important in the Indian scenario: the movement's strategies, public opinion and media coverage, religious counter-movements, and legal culture. The chapter also links the topic of feminist legal activism in India to current developments under the Modi government, and in the context of growing Hindu nationalism, it points to the phenomenon of shrinking spaces for civil society and the creation of a climate of fear for religious minorities.

2

A Century of Indian Feminist Activism

How did feminist legal activism in India emerge, and how did it develop over time? Who are the protagonists, and how do they work? What potential and what limits do activists see in using the law as a tool for social change? Which institutions do they revert to when making their claims?

This chapter elaborates on these questions. I explain how early forms of feminist activism emerged, how feminists impacted the constitution-making process, and how they realised women's constitutional rights by holding the legislature accountable to the Constitution and demanding that the judiciary declare laws unconstitutional if they violated women's fundamental rights. This historical overview shows that one conflict of values was particularly present: the conflict between religious freedom and women's rights.

The chapter begins by looking back to the late nineteenth and early twentieth centuries, to the predecessors of feminist constitutional activism: endeavours to broaden women's rights as a part of social reform and forming women's groups when India was a British colony. Section II looks at feminist activism around and during the constitution-making process after independence. Section III describes the new wave of feminist activism that emerged in the late 1970s out of disillusion with the constitutional reality. Section IV engages with the means activists use to hold the state accountable to the constitutional promise of equality, most importantly, legislative lobbying and strategic litigation. Section V demonstrates how feminist actors work 'on the ground' to make equality a reality for women.

This chapter draws on scholarship from women's and gender studies, Indian legal history, and socio-legal studies, as well as first-hand material, including Constituent Assembly debates, published and unpublished material by women's organisations, autobiographical accounts of women's rights activists, and interviews with activists.

I. Laying the Foundations: Feminist Legal Activism in the Late Nineteenth and Early Twentieth Centuries

It is impossible to identify a clear starting point for feminist activism in India. History provides several examples of individual women who fought against oppressive societal structures. However, a more organised movement for broadening women's rights in India began in the nineteenth century.

A. Social Reforms

The social reform movement in the nineteenth century aimed for women's societal 'uplift', primarily through the abolition of certain practices that were prevalent among the Hindu community and through women's education. These practices included *sati* (the immolation of Hindu widows on the funeral pyres of their deceased husbands), child marriage, and the restriction of remarriage for widows. Two aspects of the social reform movement are especially remarkable. Firstly, while a few women's associations were established at the end of the nineteenth century (A Basu, 1995), the social reform movement, by and large, was initiated and carried out by men.[1] Secondly, in its attempt to end societal evils or 'primitive' practices, the movement was closely linked to the civilising mission of the British colonisers.[2]

The social reform movement successfully brought about several new statutes, including the Hindu Widows' Remarriage Act of 1856, the Age of Consent Act of 1891, and the Child Marriage Restraint Act of 1929. These Acts bettered the situation for girls and women to a limited extent (the age of consent to sexual intercourse for girls, for instance, was raised from 10 to 12) but were far from providing formal (let alone substantive) equality. Instead, the reform attempts had a paternalistic and protectionist approach and were oriented towards 'progress' rather than gender equality (Forbes, 1996, p 30). The reforms aimed to achieve a 'world where women would be educated and free from some of the worst customs of the society' but where women would still be devoted to the home and the family (Forbes, 1996, pp 27–28).

The social reform movement nevertheless somewhat changed the societal structures. It expanded the 'appropriate activities' for women and the 'appropriate arena' in which women could move (Forbes, 1996, p 28). By the end of the nineteenth century, several educated, articulate, mobile 'new women' were increasingly involved in public activities (Forbes, 1996, p 28).

B. Political Participation

This broadening of women's possibilities led to a second phase of women's rights activism that emerged in the early twentieth century. Several groups of well-situated women formed organisations to debate women's legal and societal situations critically. In 1917, women in Madras established the Women's India Association (WIA). In 1926, the National Council of Indian Women was founded, followed a

[1] Raja Ram Mohan Roy and Ishwar Chandra Vidya Sagar, for instance, played a key role in the reforms.

[2] Indira Jaising argues that reforms usually took place when two factors were fulfilled: the practice in question was regarded as 'primitive' and there was an (alleged) initiative among the community for reform, so that it could be claimed that the reforms were not imposed on the Indian people, but rather grew out of an autochthonous demand for reform (Jaising, 2005a, p 325).

year later by the All India Women's Conference (AIWC). Together, these groups served as networks of communication, mobilisation, and protest (Keating, 2011). They challenged the exclusion of women from the public sphere and redefined women as equal to men. Key demands were women's education, a reform of Hindu family law and women's right to vote (John, 2005, p 108; R Sen, 2014, p 520). Muslim women also organised themselves. They founded the All-India Muslim Women's Conference in 1907, the Anjuman-e-Khwateen-Deccan in 1919, and numerous smaller groups that served as fora for critical discussion (Keating, 2011).

In stark contrast to the social reform movement, which focused on 'protective legislation', this second phase of activism concentrated on equal rights for women. The earlier discourse on women's 'uplift' was replaced by an increasing reliance on formal equality, not only in the so-called 'public sphere' of women's suffrage and constitutional rights but also in the 'private' sphere of the family (R Kapur, 2005b, p 157).

As a result of the campaigns by these groups, Madras and Bombay granted women voting rights in 1920 and 1921, respectively. Other provinces followed, and, in 1947, after its independence from the United Kingdom, the Indian state granted 'universal' suffrage to adult women and men (still excluding certain groups of people from the right to vote, such as non-residents, people of 'unsound' mind, criminal offenders and people below the age of 21).

The government also reacted to the feminist demands to reform Hindu family and inheritance law. Throughout the 1930s, the AIWC passed a series of resolutions that demanded a right to divorce for Hindu women and women's equal rights to property and inheritance, and that condemned polygamy and marriages between older men and minor girls (A Basu & Ray, 1990, pp 46–47). In reaction to this agitation, in 1941, the government appointed the Hindu Law Committee to examine Hindu family law from a gendered perspective (A Basu & Ray, 1990, p 49). It would take another 15 years, however, for the legal reforms to be enacted.

C. Women in the Independence Movement

Indian women also participated in the movements related to the Indian nation-building process – the non-cooperation movement of 1920–21, the civil disobedience movement of 1930–31, and the Quit India Movement of 1942. Though the main feature of these movements was the anti-colonial struggle and not women's rights, women generated a sense of power and realised their strength through their participation (A Basu, 1995). Furthermore, their activism contributed significantly to drawing women out of the 'private' realm of the home and provided them with opportunities to participate in public events (Desai, 2006). In addition, some leaders of women's organisations engaged actively in the national movement and used their access to the male leadership to press for feminist claims (Dhingra, 2022, p 36). Nationalism and women's rights were also linked in the debates around topics such as the Uniform Civil Code (UCC), as I will show in Chapter four. The struggle for independence terminated successfully when, on 15 August 1947, India was declared a sovereign and democratic nation-state.

II. Drafting the Constitution

A. Women in the Constituent Assembly

A Constituent Assembly was established and met from 1946 to 1949 to create a constitution for the independent nation. The Assembly had 299 members, 15 of whom were women. Yet, even though women were strongly underrepresented in the Assembly, they made their voices heard.

Several of the women members of the Constituent Assembly were affiliated with the WIA or the AIWC (Devenish, 2019) and used their position in the Assembly strategically to point to women's discrimination and make feminist demands. Hansa Mehta, president of the AIWC in 1946, used her position as a member of the Constituent Assembly to point out how

> [t]he average woman in this country has suffered now for centuries from inequalities heaped upon her by laws, customs and practices … There are thousands of women today who are denied the ordinary human rights (Hansa Mehta, Constituent Assembly Debates (Proceedings), Volume I, 19 December 1946[3]).

Mehta used the Assembly as a forum to rearticulate some of the AIWC's demands, calling for 'social justice, economic justice, and political justice' (ibid.) At the same time, the women members of the Constituent Assembly made it clear that they 'have never asked for privileges', such as reserved seats, quotas, or separate electorates (ibid). Instead, their focus lay on formal equality and an idea of a 'sexless citizen' (Devenish, 2019).

Women's organisations also used the constitution-making process to push their agendas. In 1945, the AIWC drafted an 'Indian Woman's Charter of Rights and Duties' – a document to educate women, raise awareness and impact the constitution-making process – and sent it to the interim Indian and provincial governments in 1946 (Devenish, 2019). By claiming equal rights and opportunities for women and challenging the constructed division between the public and the private, the Charter sought to 'rewrite the social contract for a democratic and independent India' (Devenish, 2019).

B. Religion vs Women's Rights

A controversial topic in the debates of the Constituent Assembly regarded balancing the right to religious freedom and gender equality. Rajkumari Amrit Kaur, for

[3] The Constituent Assembly debates are available at: https://www.constitutionofindia.net/constitution-assembly-debates/.

instance, argued – albeit unsuccessfully – in favour of defining religious freedom in a narrow sense as granting freedom to 'worship' rather than 'practise' religion (Jha, 2008, p 340). In her opinion, a right to 'practise' religion would be stacked against women and Dalits[4] because the infringement of women's and Dalits' rights was in fact part of the practice of several religions in India (Jha, 2008, p 340). Hansa Mehta called for the 'abolition of purdah', ie the seclusion of women from public observation through a requirement that women wear concealing clothing. Purdah, in her view, was 'an inhuman custom', and she argued that '[a]ny evil practised in the name of religion cannot be guaranteed by the Constitution' (Hansa Mehta, Constituent Assembly Debates (Proceedings), Volume XI, 22 November 1946).

Women members of the Constituent Assembly also stressed the gender-discriminatory character of other religious practices but hoped that these would ultimately vanish even without constitutional regulation. G Durgabai, for example, held that a provision prohibiting the practice of *devdasi* (the dedication of lower caste women to temples for sexual exploitation) was unnecessary. While the practice, in her words, was an 'evil' and a 'bad practice … in the name of religion', the existing 'relics of that system' would, in her view 'disappear' over time (G Durgabai, Constituent Assembly Debates (Proceedings), Volume VII, 3 December 1948).

A central debate concerned religion-based family law. For many members of religious communities, the personal laws of Hindus, Muslims, Christians, and Parsis were an essential aspect of religious identity and thus worthy of protection (especially after the inter-religious violence that occurred during partition). At the same time, the personal laws of all religious communities discriminated against women.

Women members of the Constituent Assembly rearticulated a demand for a Uniform Civil Code. Interestingly, however, they did not frame this demand in terms of gender equality but rather in terms of national identity. Hansa Mehta, for example, stated: 'We have too many personal laws in this country and these personal laws are dividing the nation today. It is therefore very essential if we want to build up one nation to have one Civil Code'. Nevertheless, in their demand for a UCC, the women stressed that the envisioned Code should include 'progressive' laws providing for gender equality. Hansa Mehta held that

> the Civil Code that we wish to have must be on a par with, or in advance of, the most progressive of the personal laws in the country. Otherwise, it will be a retrograde step and it will not be acceptable to all (Hansa Mehta, Constituent Assembly Debates (Proceedings), Volume XI, 22 November 1949).

Renuka Ray called for a constitutional clause explicitly stating that religious family and inheritance laws must not discriminate on the grounds of sex. She stated:

> I think it is necessary to have an explicit provision that social laws of marriage and inheritance of the different communities shall not also have any disabilities attached to them on grounds of caste or sex. It is, of course, true that the right of equality includes this but

[4] Dalits represent the lowest stratum in the Hindu caste system. They are placed outside the four social classes (varna) of the caste hierarchy and experience oppression, marginalisation and discrimination.

> there may be different interpretations and much confusion, and I therefore appeal to the House to have a proviso to explain this (Renuka Ray, Constituent Assembly Debates (Proceedings), Volume VII, 9 November 1948).

In the final constitutional document, these demands to curtail religion were, however, only included to a minimal extent, as the next sub-section will show.

C. Passing the Constitution

The Indian Constitution was adopted in November 1949 and came into effect on 26 January 1950. Articles 14 and 15 provide for equality before the law and non-discrimination. Article 15(2) stipulates that the non-discrimination provision also applies to certain private actors, such as shops, restaurants and hotels. Article 15(3) allows the legislature to take measures of positive discrimination for women and children. Article 39, a non-binding directive principle, urges the state to secure for men and women alike an adequate means of livelihood and equal pay for equal work. Article 51A(e) makes it a fundamental duty of every citizen 'to renounce practices derogatory to the dignity of women'. Article 42 directs the state to make provision for maternity relief.

On the other hand, religious freedom, or more precisely, 'the right freely to profess, practice and propagate religion', is protected in Article 25(1). This right is subject to 'public order, morality and health' and other fundamental rights. Article 26 guarantees religious denominations the right 'to establish and maintain institutions for religious and charitable purposes' and 'to manage its own affairs in matters of religion'. Article 44, a non-binding directive principle, urges the state to implement a Uniform Civil Code.

Evaluating these provisions from a feminist viewpoint, one might say that the drafters of the Constitution could have gone further in providing for gender equality (Dhingra, 2022, p 33). For instance, while allowing the legislature to provide for measures of positive discrimination, the Constitution generally draws on an understanding of formal, not substantive, equality. Provisions such as the one on maternity leave recognise that women bear the burden of reproductive labour but those provisions might, at the same time, reinforce conservative gender roles. Furthermore, the word 'only' in Article 15's prohibition of discrimination has led to case law that ironically did not see discrimination in cases where the law discriminated against women on the grounds of sex as well as other grounds, thereby ignoring the phenomenon of intersectional discrimination.[5] Furthermore, while

[5] For example, in *Air India v Nergesh Meerza* (1981) the Supreme Court upheld a regulation requiring female flight attendants of a government-owned airline to retire if they got married within four years of being employed, while the condition was not imposed on their male counterparts. The judgment concluded that Article 15 prohibited a discrimination 'only' on the ground of sex, but did not prohibit a discrimination 'on the ground of sex coupled with other considerations' (such as the marital status) and therefore saw no violation of that provision – a reasoning that received much criticism (Sood, 2008; Jaising, 2013; Kapur, 2016).

making religious freedom subject to other fundamental rights, the Constitution does not curtail the rights of religious groups more explicitly in order to prevent discrimination against women. And while the drafters of the Constitution *did* see the need to establish a National Commission for Scheduled Castes and Scheduled Tribes (Article 338), no separate institutions or policies were envisaged to engage with gender equality. It was only in 1992 that the National Commission for Women was established.

Nevertheless, in 1950, when it came into force, the Constitution seemed a progressive and transformative document that would mark the beginning of a new societal order. With a right to equality being established by the Constitution, the reform of Hindu Law on its way, and the UCC as a declared constitutional goal, feminists in the early 1950s could proudly look at their achievements and be hopeful for women's futures. The pre-constitutional feminist activism thus somewhat came to an end. Many long-established women's organisations, such as the AIWC, reoriented themselves as primarily social organisations, running schools and hostels or providing work opportunities for women (I Sen, 2012, p 523). Vina Mazumdar (in an interview with S Rai, 2007, p 106), a member of the First Committee on the Status of Women, recalls this optimistic spirit of the time as follows:

> The first generation beneficiaries of the equality clauses of the Constitution which included people like us who walked into jobs, whether in the Government or in academia, never felt discriminated against or unwelcome or unequal. We were too snooty to participate in organizations of women because we were having a high old time being accepted as equal by men.

This optimistic spirit, however, would not last for very long.

III. Posters and Petitions: Post-Independence Feminist Activism

By the mid-1960s, the optimistic mood articulated by Vina Mazumdar turned into discontent. The transformative potential of the Constitution seemed not to have translated into reality. A 'new wave of nationwide unrest' (I Sen, 2012, p 522) emerged, and many women were part of the agitations.

High unemployment, poverty, land disputes, caste-based tensions, and ecological degradation made many people feel that the state had 'failed to deliver' (I Sen, 2012, p 522). 'New social movements' mushroomed in multiple forms to demand the protection of the constitutional rights of vulnerable groups (Omvedt, 1993; Ray & Katzenstein, 2005, pp 5–6). It was against this backdrop that a new wave of feminism emerged. Initially, it was not primarily feminist topics that triggered women's engagement but other issues, like social inequality, the caste system, the displacement of indigenous people and a struggle for workers' and peasants' rights (Chandhoke, 2011, p 174). Women's groups that formed in these years often grew out of, and overlapped with, other movements or organisations, such as university-based formations, trade unions and splinter groups of political parties (Agnihotri, 2001).

Some women entered the movement rather 'by accident', like Ruth Vanita (2011, p 22), who recalls:

> [I] met Madhu Kishwar ... who suggested that we form a women's group. Although I thought women's issues might be a diversion from [the] proletarian struggle, I agreed, and we formed the group by telling friends who seemed likely to be interested. So I entered the women's movement, without knowing there was one.

In the mid-1970s, three aspects fuelled this emerging activism and contributed to making the topic of gender (in)equality more salient. The first one was the publication of the report of the Committee on the Status of Women in India in 1974, which showed that while middle-class women's entry into education had expanded after independence, the condition of the vast majority of women had deteriorated since the 1950s (Committee on the Status of Women in India, 1974). The second aspect was the mass atrocities against women committed during the state of emergency (1975–77),[6] including mass sterilisations and custodial violence, that came to light after the emergency was lifted (Kannabiran, 2010; Patel & Khajuria, 2016, p 4). The third aspect was the United Nations' proclamation of the International Women's Year in 1975 following the World Conference on Women in Mexico City.

A. Second Wave Feminism

By the late 1970s and early 1980s, women's rights groups had emerged in various parts of the country. This new wave of feminism (sometimes called the second wave, following the first feminist wave of the early twentieth century) pointed out that Indian women had still not achieved formal equality in many areas of life, particularly in family law. But unlike their predecessors of the pre-independence days, the new feminism also articulated demands for substantive equality, addressing women's subordination and oppression in a patriarchal society and the misogynist behaviour of state institutions (Kumar, 1993, pp 105–6; R Kapur, 2005b, p 158).

(i) Themes

One aspect feminists engaged with was the discriminatory provisions in family and inheritance law. Although the Constitution envisioned a family law reform via a Uniform Civil Code, no such code had been passed. Moreover, the reform

[6] The state of emergency was declared for a 21-month period from June 1975 to March 1977 by Prime Minister Indira Gandhi, citing internal and external threats to the country. The period, during which the PM ruled by decree, was marked by political repression, suspension of civil liberties, and widespread human rights violations.

of Hindu personal law had turned out to be cumbersome. Progressive reform suggestions had met with heavy opposition from, among others, the then President, Rajendra Prasad. Eventually, the reforms were passed in a watered-down version, which ameliorated the situation for women but did not achieve many feminist goals (Kumar, 1993, p 97). Furthermore, the laws of the Christian, Muslim and Parsi communities, which also discriminated against women, were undergoing no reform. In addition, it was difficult to challenge discriminatory personal law provisions in the courts. The Bombay High Court in 1952, in *State of Bombay v Narasu Appa Mali*, had even given a judgment commonly interpreted as stating that personal laws could not be tested against the Constitution.[7] After all, Renuka Ray's anxiety that the constitutional right to equality would not suffice to have courts declare discriminatory provisions and practices among religious personal law unconstitutional, turned out to be justified.

Alongside the nexus between law and religion, gender-based violence was a central topic in feminist activism. One of the primary triggers for feminist protests and the formation of women's groups was the Supreme Court's decision in the *Mathura* case of 1978 (*Tuka Ram and Another v State of Maharashtra*), which I will deal with in more detail in Chapter five. The Court had acquitted two police officers accused of having raped a minor girl named Mathura on the compound of a police station, arguing that since there were no visible marks of injury on the girl's body and no signs of struggle, no rape had occurred. Mathura's case provoked national campaigns around the issue of custodial rape and demands for reforms of the laws on rape (Katzenstein, 1989, p 62; R Sen, 2014, p 335). 'Mathura had transformed us into feminists', stated Nandita Gandhi (2011) later. The case also led to the founding of several women's groups, including the Forum Against Rape (later re-named the Forum Against Oppression of Women) in Bombay, Saheli ('friend') in Delhi (Gangoli, 1996; Murthy & Dasgupta, 2011, p 46). Saheli (1984a) later described the founding of the organisation as follows:

> On 8th March, 1980 many of us marched together demanding the reopening of the Mathura rape case … It was at this point of the women's movement in Delhi, that some of us felt strongly the need for a women's centre. A group of 9 women came together and in August 1981, Saheli, Women's Resource Centre was started in a garage in 10 Nizzamuddin East, New Delhi.

Dowry-related violence was another topic that the early women's movement focused on. 'Dowry deaths' were cases in which young wives were killed at the hands of their husbands or the husband's family members because the latter were dissatisfied with the amount of the dowry that the bride had brought with her. The

[7] Read in context, the paragraph where the Court holds that personal laws were not 'laws in force' within the purview of Article 13 of the Constitution, leads to the assumption that the Court meant only *uncodified* personal laws. Later the Supreme Court held that personal laws 'must be consistent with the Constitution lest they become void under Article 13 if they violated fundamental rights'; see *C Masilamani Mudaliar and Others v The Idol of Sri Swaminathaswami Thirukoli*, Supreme Court of India, 30 January 1996.

death of Tarvinder Kaur in 1979, a 24-year-old woman who had been burnt alive by her in-laws, caught particular attention and produced protests against dowry and dowry-related murders (Agnihotri & Mazumdar, 1995, p 56; Butalia, 2005, p 332). Women's groups like Mahila Dakshata Samiti ('committee for women's protection') and Stree Sangharsh ('women's struggle') were very vocal about the issue of dowry-related violence.

Another topic that came up as a feminist issue in reaction to a specific event was *sati*. While the practice of widow burning had already been banned during British rule (see the Bengal Sati Regulation of 1829), incidents of *sati* still occurred in some regions. In 1987, in Rajasthan, the 18-year-old Roop Kanwar died on the funeral pyre of her husband – the voluntariness of this act being unclear – while thousands of people watched, some of them chanting slogans glorifying *sati* (Kumar, 1993, p 173; Agnihotri & Mazumdar, 1995). The incident provoked a public outcry that went far beyond the women's movement, especially in urban centres. Questions of choice and autonomy, individual rights, societal pressure, tradition, culture and group identity arose in the debate (R Sen, 2014, p 335).

Mathura, *Tarvinder Kaur* and *Roop Kanwar* became reference points for the women's movement. The women's names were linked to feminist debates about violence and hierarchies, misuse of power, caste-based biases and distorted understandings of morals and culture. These were the issues that the new women's movement focused on and that feminist activists addressed when they demanded that the law intervene.

The women's movement addressed these themes in street protests – a central aspect of the early activism. The feminist writer Urvashi Butalia, in an interview with the podcast 'Intersectional Feminism – Desi Style', remembers how exhilarating this experience was:

> There were things that we were fighting. And there was protests on the streets. And we were organising those protests. We were joining them. It was actually the most exciting, the most exhilarating, sometimes dangerous thing, because we also got attacked by the police. We got beaten up by the police. All those kind of things also happened. (Feminism in India, 2021).

(ii) Organisation

Women's rights activism took different forms of organisation. A defining feature of the new women's movement was the autonomous groups that formed in the late 1970s and early 1980s. These groups declared themselves independent from party affiliation, rejected hierarchies and attempted to build a decentralised structure with a collective responsibility for leadership (Gandhi & Shah, 1992). They also rejected funding from the government or donor agencies, which meant that funding had to come through individual donations, expenses had to be modest, and members largely worked on a voluntary basis (Saheli, 2006a).

Part of the groups' work was to provide support structures and counselling for women who had experienced violence or sought a divorce (Kumar, 1993, p 143; Butalia, 2005, p 340). Furthermore, the groups conducted discussions, workshops, and conferences, produced leaflets, and spread their messages through street play performances. Beginning in 1980, the various autonomous groups met regularly at National Conferences, where several hundred, sometimes several thousand, women came together to discuss current topics.[8] Some of these conferences produced joint resolutions with demands towards politics and society and an agenda for feminist activism.

Apart from the autonomous groups, party-affiliated mass-membership women's organisations, which campaigned for women's rights as a part of their broader political aims, emerged in the 1980s. For instance, the All India Democratic Women's Association – the women's wing of the Communist Party of India (Marxist) – was set up 'to remove all discrimination between man and woman, to fight for democracy, equal rights and emancipation of women, in a society free from exploitation' and '[t]o struggle for the implementation of all legal and constitutional rights for women' (All India Democratic Women's Association, n.d.).

Complementing women's activism 'on the ground', women's studies centres provided '[t]he other arm of the women's movement' (Desai, 2006, p 68). The first such centre was the Research Unit on Women's Studies, initiated by the SNDT Women's University, Bombay in 1974 (Desai, 2006, p 68). Other independent or university-based centres followed, also as a reaction to the 'Towards Equality' report by the Committee on the Status of Women in India (Juyal, 2005, pp 19–20; R Menon, 2011, p xx).

To disseminate feminist ideas, women also created feminist journals and magazines. One of the early magazines was *Manushi* ('humanity'), founded by Madhu Kishwar and Ruth Vanita in 1978. The journal, among other aspects, reported cases of the Indian higher judiciary concerning women's rights and demanded legal change in several areas of law. Feminists also used the journal *Economic and Political Weekly* (*EPW*) as a forum to articulate their thoughts and demands. *EPW*'s section 'Review of Women's Studies' served as a space where feminist authors regularly wrote on issues concerning women, often regarding developments in the legal sphere. In 1988, the Centre for Women's Development Studies brought out the first women's studies journal in India, *Samya Shakti* (later renamed *The Indian Journal of Gender Studies*), which occasionally featured articles on gender and law.

Over the years, feminist activism has diversified, and more specialised subgroups have emerged. Two forms of such specialised groups are of particular importance for the context of this book: religious women's groups, placing a focus on the reform of family law; and women's legal organisations. The next two sub-sections shall elaborate what they are and how they work.

[8] The first national conference took place in Mumbai in 1980. It was followed by conferences in Mumbai (1985), Patna (1987), Calicut (Kozhikode) (1990), Tirupati (1994), Ranchi (1997) and Kolkata (2006).

B. Gender Equality and Religion

From the mid-1980s onwards, feminist scholars and women's rights activists began to criticise the fact that the early Indian women's movement was predominantly led by urban middle- or upper-class Hindu women, while poor women or women belonging to minorities (like Muslim, Dalit or tribal women) were not adequately represented, and their interests fell somewhat outside of the visual range. Scholars and activists took up concepts of intersectionality (Crenshaw, 1989, 1991) to demand that feminism focus on the complex interplay between gender and religion or gender and caste (Agnes, 1986).

One trigger for a critical rethinking of feminist demands had been the *Shah Bano* case from 1985, in which the Indian Supreme Court decided to grant a Muslim woman, Shah Bano, maintenance under a secular legal provision (Section 125 Code of Criminal Procedure, 1973), even though traditional Muslim family law does not recognise post-divorce maintenance rights beyond the three months *iddat* period[9] (*Mohamed Ahmed Khan v Shah Bano Begum*). The judgment led to an outcry among the Muslim community, and Shah Bano came under so much pressure that she eventually gave up the maintenance the Court had approved for her (Gangoli, 2007, p 41; N Menon, 2012, p 153). The case showed how minority women often found themselves in a situation where they had to choose between the conflicting political agendas of the women's movement and their community. In an attempt to undo the judgment, the government in 1986 passed the Muslim Women (Protection of Rights on Divorce) Act, which stipulated that a divorced Muslim woman shall only be entitled to maintenance payments during the *iddat* period.

It was in the aftermath of this case that the specific challenges that minority women faced received more attention and that feminist activists became critical of Hindu dominance in the Indian women's movement. Flavia Agnes, for instance, herself a Christian, modified a slogan that had earlier been used by Black feminists in the United States – 'All the women are White, All the Blacks are Men, But some of Us are Brave' (Hull et al, 1982). Agnes (1986, p 12) held: 'This statement is applicable to Minority women in India as well. We could very well rephrase the slogan and say: "All Women are Hindus, All Minorities are Men, But Some of us are Brave"'. Later, US scholar and civil rights advocate Kimberlé Crenshaw (1989) would coin the term 'intersectionality' to describe the cumulative effect of multiple forms of discrimination.

In India, Muslim and Dalit women and other individuals founded new groups to address intersectional discrimination and scholarship engaged with the specific situation and demands of these groups (Moon & Pawar, 2008; Narain, 2008; Irudayam, Mangubhai, & Lee, 2011; Hong Tschalaer, 2017). Islamic feminism emerged as one significant arm of feminism with a set of new organisations to speak

[9] The period under Muslim law during which a divorced or widowed woman may not yet remarry.

up for the rights of Muslim women, to provide counselling for Muslim women, and to suggest reforms to Muslim family law (Vatuk, 2008b; Schneider, 2009). One such organisation was the Mumbai-based Awaaz-e-Niswaan ('voice of women'), founded in 1987. Later, other organisations followed, such as the Bharatiya Muslim Mahila Andolan ('Indian Muslim women's movement' (BMMA)), founded in 2007. In their call for gender equality, Muslim women's organisations draw on different sources, including the Quran, the Indian Constitution and international human rights law. BMMA, for instance, stresses its belief in equality, human rights and justice as 'enshrined in the Holy Quran as well as the Constitution of India' (Bharatiya Muslim Mahila Andolan, 2015).

A central goal of these organisations was the reform of religion-based personal laws. Their activism was also part of a shift regarding feminist positions on personal laws, which occurred in the 1990s and which I will engage with in more detail in Chapter four: a shift from a demand for a Uniform Civil Code towards other reform suggestions that would leave the personal law system in place.

C. Feminist Lawyers

A second type of group that emerged in the 1990s was women's legal organisations. These were groups of trained lawyers pushing for gender equality using the tools of the law: bringing cases before the courts and suggesting concrete law reforms.

The Mumbai-based Majlis Legal Centre (Majlis – meaning 'association'), an all-women team of lawyers and social activists, for instance, was set up in 1991 by Flavia Agnes. Agnes had experienced domestic violence herself and published her story in an autobiography (Agnes, 2014 [1984]) before she founded the organisation. Majlis seeks to ensure that 'the rights of individual women are protected by providing legal counseling, legal representation and innovative legal strategies' (Majlis, 2020).

The organisation Women's Action Research and Legal Action for Women (WARLAW), founded in 1994 by Rani Jethmalani, was focused on international law and was set up to force the government to take action on its commitments under the Convention on the Elimination of All Forms of Discrimination Against Women (CEDAW).

The Lawyers Collective Women's Rights Initiative (Lawyers Collective) was founded in 1998 to provide 'legal inputs to the women's movement' (Lawyers Collective, n.d.-a). It is headed by Indira Jaising, who worked as a cause lawyer to foster women's rights throughout the 1980s and 1990s. It describes itself as 'a group of Lawyers with a mission to empower and change the status of marginalised groups through the effective use of law, and an engagement in human rights advocacy, legal aid and litigation' – a mission that is 'based on the belief that law is an instrument of social change and can be used in different ways to further the constitutional and human rights of women' (Lawyers Collective, n.d.-b).

1998 was also the founding year of Partners for Law and Development, 'a legal resource group pursuing the realisation of social justice and equality for women', which began its work by conducting legal research and doing community work and today focuses primarily on monitoring the implementation of laws and identifying gaps in the justice system (Partners for Law in Development, n.d.). Except for WARLAW, these organisations remain active today.

Legal organisations work through different avenues. They pursue 'policy level interventions', seeking to 'ensure that no discriminatory laws against women are passed' (Majlis, 2020, p 2) and fight for law reforms where statutory law contains gender discriminatory provisions. Some also pursue litigation through individual representation in the lower courts or public interest litigation in the regional High Courts and the Supreme Court. Some organisations offer training programmes for students, law enforcement agencies, policy-makers, and local communities, and they publish books and brochures on matters of law and gender. Via newsletters or magazines, they inform a larger audience about developments in national and international human rights law and report on important case law.

Besides those women's organisations, the scholarship is central to advancing feminist legal activism. Women's studies centres, feminist conferences and academic journals engaging with women's rights issues are essential places of knowledge production and often link scholarship and activism. Feminist legal scholarship also takes place at law schools – although, in general, law schools remain 'very male spaces' where feminist viewpoints are marginalised (Ballakrishnen & Samuel, 2021, p 128). The Indian Feminist Judgements Project, for example, writes alternative judgments for landmark cases, thereby revealing 'how cases could (and should) have been decided from a feminist perspective' (Chandra, Sen, & Chaudhary, 2021, p 262), thereby aspiring to be 'a blueprint for alternative feminist futures of juridical practices and critical lawyering' (Chandra et al, 2021, p 261). The project understands itself as 'not only a form of scholarship but a political, socio-legal movement' (Chandra et al, 2021, p 262). Feminist legal scholarship also takes place outside the Indian law schools. It is pursued by academics who teach, research, and publish in departments other than Law or at foreign universities, or by independent researchers without a formal university affiliation (Ballakrishnen & Samuel, 2021).

Activists working in the legal field have prominently described their passion for their work and their motivation to work for a cause. Indira Jaising (2011, p 335), for instance, describes how cause lawyers like her believed that they 'were in a profession that had a social function, that was not just another business'. And elsewhere she states:

> as a lawyer, I believed my main task was to struggle for social and economic rights of the marginalized as we were still a country defined by poverty and undeserved want. The Constitution promised to the marginalized a life of equality. The work was exciting, and the Constitution proved very useful for our fights (Jaising, 2025, p 75).

IV. From the Streets to the Courtrooms: Claiming Women's Rights Through Multiple Avenues

Demands for legal change featured in several of the feminist campaigns, demonstrations, conferences and discussions. But how exactly do women's groups and feminist lawyers activate the law in their campaigns? How do they use the Indian Constitution to push for reforms? This section looks at two strategies: campaigns for law reforms via the legislature, and strategic litigation in the courts.

A. Campaigns for Law Reform

One method of feminist constitutional activism lies in approaching the legislator to replace discriminatory laws, arguing that these laws violate the constitutional equality provisions in Articles 14 and 15 or other provisions in the Constitution. Legislative lobbying happens through protests or other forms of public statements criticising the provisions in question. It may also occur through attempts to directly influence government or legislature members or active participation in the legislative process. Activities that Indian activists and women's groups have used include the coordination of campaigns or demonstrations demanding the abolition of discriminatory laws, the organisation of seminars and conferences to discuss the need for law reform, publications in print and online media, TV and social media, and the writing of legislative draft Bills to be submitted to the government, the Law Ministry, the Ministry of Women and Child Development, and parliamentarians. Feminists have also served as experts on parliamentary standing committees or in consultations with the National Commission for Women or the Law Commission of India.

In pursuing this activism, feminists have focused on the Indian Parliament (and more specifically, the lower house, the Lok Sabha ('assembly of the people'),[10] the Law Commission and the National Commission for Women as addressees of feminist lobbying.

In the Indian Parliament ordinary Bills may be introduced in either of the houses as a government Bill, if introduced by a minister, or as a private member's Bill, if introduced by another Member of Parliament. They become law once they have gone through three readings, been passed by both houses and received the assent of the President (Article 111 of the Constitution). Feminists may thus attempt to impact law-making either by influencing the government or individual

[10] Besides the Lok Sabha, the upper house of Parliament, the Rajya Sabha ('states' assembly') represents the States. The States also maintain individual Parliaments. The Union is, however, the 'centre of gravity' of Indian federalism (Dann, 2011, p 166), holding much more power than the States. The legislative competence of the Union and the States are regulated in three different lists in Schedule VII to the Constitution.

ministers to introduce a particular law reform, to impact Members of Parliament to introduce a private members Bill or to impact parliamentarians at large to vote on a Bill in a certain manner.

One institution within the Parliament that has sought to improve the status of women explicitly is the Parliamentary Committee for the Empowerment of Women (CEW). Jointly constituted by the Lok Sabha and Rajya Sabha in 1997, this standing committee is the only committee dominated by women MPs. The CEW is tasked with considering the reports by the National Commission for Women and examining and reporting on government measures related to women's empowerment. In practice, however, the CEW 'occupies a marginal position in Parliament' (SM Rai & Spary, 2019, p 211) and suffers from a lack of visibility, presumably because, unlike other committees, it is not affiliated with ministerial portfolios (SM Rai & Spary, 2019, p 228). In fact, much of the high-profile legislation relating to women's equality has not passed through the CEW but through other committees affiliated with specific ministerial portfolios, such as the Committee on Personnel, Public Grievances, Law and Justice (SM Rai & Spary, 2019, p 225). Many women's groups know very little or nothing about the Committee, even when they are actively involved in legislative advocacy (SM Rai & Spary, 2019, p 234). Others are sceptical about the CEW's ability to bring about change (SM Rai & Spary, 2019, p 212).

In preparing legislative processes the Law Commission of India (LCI) plays a crucial role. The establishment of this institution, which is empowered to recommend legislative reforms, dates back to colonial times: The first Law Commission was established in 1834. The first Law Commission of independent India was established in 1955 (Law Commission of India, n.d.). Since then, 23 Commissions have been appointed, each with a three-year term. The Law Commission has, to date, submitted 289 reports to the Parliament, each dealing with a specific area of law. Many of these reports have influenced the legislative process to a significant extent; some have been cited by the Supreme Court and commissions such as the Justice Verma Commission, which I will deal with in Chapter five. For the women's movement, the LCI has been a 'key institution' (R Sen & Mandal, 2015, p xiv). In their attempts to bring about law reforms, feminists and women's groups have not only tried to influence the Law Commission and impact its reports but have also used the Commission's recommendations for advocacy at the level of other state actors (R Sen & Mandal, 2015, p xiv).

The National Commission for Women (NCW) is another organ of importance for feminist activists attempting to engender legal change. It was established in 1992 as an autonomous body to monitor and influence state policies with regard to women (see the National Commission for Women Act, 1990). The need for such an autonomous commission was first articulated in the 'Towards Equality' report by the Committee on the Status of Women in India (1974). According to the National Commission for Women Act, 1990, the NCW has the power to 'investigate and examine all matters relating to the safeguards provided for women under the Constitution and other laws' (Section 10(1)(a)). It shall present to the government annual reports with recommendations for legislative measures (Section 10(1)(b), (c) and (d)). It may also call for special studies or investigations into specific problems arising out of discrimination and atrocities against women (Section 10(1)(g)). Women's organisations and women's studies centres play a central role here, as the NCW can ask them to provide such reports. The Act also allows the Commission to fund 'litigation involving issues affecting a large body of women' (Section 10(1)(f)). The Commission has also intervened in court cases to support litigation initiated by women's groups.

From the viewpoint of women's groups and feminist activists, however, the Commission has several shortcomings. Feminists have held that the Commission cannot be fully independent as long as its members are nominated by the central government (Saheli, 2014b). They further argued that with every new Chairperson, the focus of the NCW has changed, resulting in no coherent work or programme (Arya, 2010, p 24). Feminists have further bemoaned that the Commission's reports are not taken seriously by the government (the absence of a time limit for the government to respond to the recommendations aggravates this problem) and have argued that, in practice, the Commission's members lack an understanding of women's rights issues and are 'distanced' from women's organisations (Arya, 2010, p 42; Saheli, 2014b). Yet, despite better alternatives, in their campaigns for law reforms, many women's groups have tried to use the NCW strategically to push their agenda (Arya, 2010, p 46).

B. Strategic Litigation

A second avenue of feminist legal activism is strategic litigation. Herein, feminists approach the higher judiciary arguing that a particular law violates fundamental rights of the Constitution and must, therefore, be struck down. In doing so they benefit from the fact that the Supreme Court and the High Courts have granted themselves the power to undertake judicial review over legislative action and to strike down laws that violate fundamental rights.[11]

Women's groups, feminist lawyers and activists have thereby benefitted from the possibility of Public Interest Litigation (PIL),[12] especially the Supreme Court's relaxation of the rules on standing. In PIL cases, the individual or group approaching the Supreme Court or the High Court does not have to claim a violation of their own rights; it suffices that there is an interest of the wider public in the

[11] While the courts have not been entirely clear about the question of where they draw this power from, a plausible argument is that Article 13 of the Constitution (read with the power of the judiciary recognised under Articles 32 and 226) implies the judiciary's power to strike down such laws (Thiruvengadam, 2017, p 104).

[12] Public interest litigation is not regulated in the Constitution, although Article 32 provides a basis for it. Rather, it was 'invented' by the Supreme Court at a moment of reconfiguration of Indian political life in the aftermath of the state of emergency in the mid-1970s (Bhuwania, 2014, p 314 et seq.).

case. While the PIL system has been criticised for different reasons,[13] it certainly provides advantages for women's rights groups and feminist lawyers.

Apart from filing cases in the name of disadvantaged groups, women's groups and lawyers may also use the avenue of litigation by supporting individual claimants who have filed cases in their own names. They act as amicus curiae, or they provide expert opinions.

Some feminist lawyers have described their job as a cause lawyer as alienating and cumbersome. Indira Jaising (2011, p 355) narrates how she and other cause lawyers often felt like 'outsiders', for whom 'there was no place … in the judicial system'. She explains:

> I chose to represent those who had no legitimacy in society and that lack of legitimacy rubbed off on me. We were the outcastes of the profession. I believe that my status as an outcaste made me fight for a place in the profession, and it has been a successful fight (Jaising, 2011, p 368).

And yet, she also strongly believed in courts as 'a space where law can be used as an instrument of social change for women' (Jaising, 2022) and thought of herself as someone who could set this instrument of change into motion: by impacting legal thinking, legal culture and jurisprudence. She states:

> I believe in the transformative role of the courts, which is why I chose to pursue cases that raise important social reformation questions like the rights of hawkers, women's right to inherit property, the right of the mother as the natural guardian in child custody cases, the unconstitutionality of Triple *Talaq*, compensation for the victims and survivors of the Bhopal Gas disaster, rights of pavement dwellers, and women vegetable vendors of the Self-Employed Women's Association (Jaising, 2022).

And elsewhere she states:

> Many like me … found ourselves included in the adventure of building a democratic and just legal culture. Those were exhilarating times. We were engaged in the process

[13] Commentators have criticised that the courts regularly overstep the boundaries of separation of powers (Sathe, 2002). In scenarios where the Indian higher judiciary grants itself the power to 'initiate a case on any public issue on its own, appoint its own lawyer, introduce its own machinery to investigate the issue and then order its own solutions to the issue at the level of the entire state', warns Bhuwania (2017, p 106), the actual petitioner would become an 'increasingly redundant figure' (Bhuwania, 2017, p 39). Other scholars have bemoaned a shift in the ideology of the Supreme Court. The Court, it is argued, has turned away from its earlier constituency of the poor and the marginalised to follow a neo-liberal path. While earlier the Supreme Court was concerned with the rights of bonded labourers, incarcerated 'undertrials', child labourers, migrant workers or women in custody, and it invited and collaborated with social movements, social activists, socially committed academics and investigative journalists, from the late 1990s onwards, this was no longer the case (Ramanathan, 2002). The Supreme Court's jurisprudence, it is argued, is biased 'in favor of the state and development, in favor of the rich and against workers, in favor of the urban middle-class and against rural farmers, and in favor of a globalitarian class and against the distributive ethos of the Indian Constitution' (Rajagopal, 2007, p 158). PIL, in some cases, is used as 'a means to target those populations living on the margins of legality' (Bhuwania, 2017, p 9).

> of rewriting the history of the court. We were exposed to great judges. I realised that there was something in the nature of law which made it susceptible to being shaped and moulded to become something new (Jaising, 2011, p 355).

For feminist activists and women's groups, the goal of strategic litigation, either by filing their own cases or by supporting others' cases, is to establish precedents on 'issues that are of importance to the women's movement' (Activist at Lawyers Collective, interview with the author on 14 October 2014). Such litigation is based on a view of the judiciary as a vehicle to bring about legal (and social) change and a perception of the feminist lawyers or women's groups as a driving force to get this vehicle set in motion.

Litigation may also accompany campaigns for law reform. As I will show later with the example of the reform of Christian divorce law, feminist activists may use lobbying and litigation in parallel, and the two routes may reinforce each other.

V. Securing Rights on the Ground

Legislative lobbying and strategic litigation are only two forms of legal activism in which women's groups, feminist lawyers and activists engage. Both strategies have limitations and they can only bear fruit if they are implemented on the ground.

A. The Limits of Law Reforms

Even if feminists obtain victories at the level of the legislature or the judiciary, reformed laws and case law do not necessarily lead to a change in behaviour patterns among people working in state institutions, such as the police, or among society at large. One activist at the women's group Vimochana ('liberation'), for instance, told me: 'law cannot bring about change as such … No matter what law you bring, changing the mindsets of people here is extremely difficult' (interview with the author on 1 March 2016). Yet, as I pointed out in Chapter one, many feminist activists still regarded law reforms as a crucial first step in the larger fight for gender equality.

Feminist activists also point to the problem that judges at the level of the lower courts do not necessarily follow the progressive case law that has been passed in the High Courts or the Supreme Court. 'No landmark case shakes the world', said one activist at Majlis, because there is no guarantee that other judges will necessarily follow these landmark cases (Interview with the author on 29 December 2015). A judge dealing with a particular case 'may not [even] refer to a judgment that just came a month before, and [instead] give his own judgment', she continued (ibid). To some extent, this may be because judges in lower courts are not aware of the latest case law (ibid). But judges might also not 'see value in strengthening the rights of vulnerable groups', as another activist suggested (Activist and writer in Delhi, interview with the author on 14 April 2015).

Yet, we know from scholarship that landmark judgments help disadvantaged social groups foster rights consciousness, which in turn allows them to further their agenda in interactions with the state (McCann, 1994; Roychowdhury, 2021). Several activists saw their role in advancing this process of translating landmark cases into everyday law. A favourable judgment by the higher judiciary, as the activist at Majlis put it, can only have an effect if 'you take it down' to the level of lower courts and '[l]et this judgment come every day' (Activist at Majlis, interview with the author on 29 December 2015). For these reasons, a large part of feminist activism also takes place in the lower courts.

B. Everyday Litigation

Despite its limits, many activists understand legal change via legislative reforms or case law by the higher judiciary as 'an introductory gambit' (S Basu, 2015, p 19) to advance women's societal situation. If law reforms are to be successful, they must be adequately implemented. In the words of an activist at Majlis:

> It's that ground level hard work that one needs to do rather than saying: 'It's very difficult to do this so let's just change the law and believe that it'll trickle down later' (Activist at Majlis, interview with the author on 19 March 2015).

One form of this important 'ground level work' that some women's groups pursue is representing women in the lower courts. I speak about 'everyday litigation' in this context, a form of litigation that accompanies the above-mentioned strategic litigation. Everyday litigation happens in the district and sub-district courts and in specialised courts, like family courts, where women's organisations seek to 'secure the rights of individual women' and to introduce 'a culture of women's rights within the precincts of courtrooms' (Agnes, 2006, p 25).

Women's organisations that pursue litigation at the lower and family court level are usually approached directly by individual women who seek help and who may know about the organisations' work through referrals from former clients, media, community-based organisations, or the police (Majlis, 2020, p 7). The members of the organisation then discuss the case at hand with the client and decide on how to proceed with it. One activist explained this procedure as follows: 'We try to judge whether it's worth it for her or not to go to court' (Activist at Lawyers Collective, interview with the author on 14 October 2014). In maintenance cases, for instance, there may be circumstances where the lawyers might suggest not filing a court case: 'If the husband is missing or if he is not earning anything, then there is no sense in filing a maintenance application. So then she may very well be wasting her time' (ibid). If the organisation, together with the client, decides that a court case makes no sense, the members of the organisation may still offer legal consultation or social support. Majlis, for instance, provides legal consultation to over 1000 women in one year, of whom only around 100 opt to approach the courts (Majlis, 2020, p 7).

If the women's organisations and their clients decide to approach the courts, the organisations assist the women by 'walking the legal journey with them' (Majlis, 2020, p 7). This may include various steps from helping the client file a first information report at the police station, to preparing her for recording statements with the police and the cross-examination in court, arguing in her favour at the various hearings, cross-examining the perpetrator and supporting the client in appeal cases if the outcome of the judgment is unsatisfactory. This work seems to pay out. Majlis prides itself on the fact that whereas before its interventions, the conviction rate in sexual violence cases in Mumbai lay at around 12 to 15 per cent, the organisation achieves convictions in over 60 per cent of the cases it supports (Majlis, 2020, p 13).

The outcome aspired to in these cases is a victory for the client, and not so much a precedent to help other women. Some activists, however, stressed that progressive judgments in lower and family courts may be just as much 'landmark cases' as those judgments that the higher judiciary produces. As one lawyer at Majlis explained:

> In every case that we represent, we are stretching the boundary of law … [F]or example, the first time that we represented a sister against her brother under the Domestic Violence Act, it was a landmark case because the judges had never heard of something like that (Activist at Majlis, interview with the author on 19 March 2015).

'Other lawyers learn from it', she continued, 'They ask you: How are you doing this? Can you help us? And that's how you introduce concepts' (ibid).

Scholarship also shows that engaging in court cases empowers the individual women. Roychowdhury (2021, p 15) states:

> Women who 'ran cases' started believing they deserved what the law promised, a life free of violence where they could exercise a modicum of control over their bodies and material possessions. They began thinking of the law as a strategic field they could engage and manipulate.

Independently of the outcomes of a court case, the women who 'run cases' often gain something through the journey of claiming their rights: confidence in talking to law enforcement officers, the ability to use newfound knowledge to support other women, and confidence to take their lives in their own hands (Roychowdhury, 2021).

VI. Conclusion

We look back at a century of feminist legal activism in India, in which feminist activists, lawyers and women's groups have worked continuously to improve women's legal and societal situation. Feminist activists not only worked to have provisions for gender equality included in the Constitution, but also used these constitutional provisions later to push for gender equality at the legal and societal levels.

When comparing feminist legal activism across time, we see a shift from a demand for formal to substantive equality. We also see a shift from focusing on the legislator as the primary receptor of change to focusing on the courts. This has to do with the fact that feminist lawyers' organisations emerged from the early 1990s onwards. Set up by and staffed with trained lawyers, these organisations have the knowledge and skills to help women win legal battles in everyday litigation but also use strategic litigation to bring about landmark changes in the legal landscape for women.

Another shift that feminist activism saw concerned the engagement with religion and religious laws. While the early women's movement of the 1970s was dominated by Hindu women and, in its demands, focused on the abolishment of religion-based personal laws, Christian and Muslim women's groups that were set up later pursued a different strategy, pointing to the fact that being feminist and being religious were not mutually exclusive. Chapter four will discuss this shift in detail.

Lastly the chapter engaged with feminist positions towards the law as an instrument for social change. While activists are clear that the law is not the only tool needed in the fight against patriarchal societal structures, many still trust this instrument as one crucial factor when pushing for change.

Having provided an overview of how feminist legal activism looks in India, the next chapters will engage with the question as to under which circumstances feminist legal activism is successful. In pointing to potential factors of success, Chapter three will first move away from India to establish an analytical framework that helps in understanding success in feminist legal activism. Chapters four and five will then engage with specific examples in the Indian case to test which success factors have been particularly important there.

3

Success Factors in Feminist Legal Activism

Chapter two has shown that Indian feminists have reverted to the Constituent Assembly, the Parliament and the courts to ask for legal change. While they are aware that new laws do not automatically end women's oppression, they see law reforms as an introductory gambit in the larger struggle for a more egalitarian society. Laws set the standards for what is considered appropriate and inappropriate behaviour. They can be used to hold state institutions and private actors accountable. They may also have an empowering function for marginalised groups.

The question that this chapter seeks to answer is: which factors make feminist attempts at law reforms successful, and which ones hinder their success? The answer to this question is complex, as the factors impacting success in feminist legal activism are manifold and intertwined. This chapter provides a roadmap to understanding success in feminist legal activism by suggesting an analytical framework that distinguishes between four dimensions – rights, activism, state, and society – and systematises various potential impact factors. I derive these impact factors from engaging with scholarship on feminist legal and political activism. In doing so, I also attempt to link different strands of literature that so far stand rather unconnectedly next to each other, including the scholarship on feminist constitutionalism stressing the importance of constitutional design for the advancement of women's rights, the scholarship on legal mobilisation that addresses social movement strategies and political opportunity structures, and the scholarship on legal culture that is interested in cultural factors allowing for legal change.

The *rights* dimension (section I) includes the preconditions for legal change that constitutional and international human rights law create. I address the provisions on equality and anti-discrimination as well as norms on dignity and competing rights claims. The *activism* dimension (section II) encompasses success factors internal to the women's movement (or any other social movement, for that matter), such as its strength and strategies. I look at how feminist groups and activists frame their demands for law reform, which locales and tactics they use, and where and with whom they form alliances. The *state* dimension (section III) refers to the receptors of change, most notably the judiciary and the Parliament. I engage with the powers of the judiciary, the composition and partisanship of state institutions, women's policy agencies and the state's international obligations. Lastly, the *society* dimension (section IV) includes socio-cultural factors that influence legal activism. I address public opinion and media coverage, counter-mobilisation, the role of religion, and aspects of legal culture.

For the purpose of clarity, I engage with each factor individually. However, the various factors are connected and influence each other. The rights provided in a country's constitution, the institutional framework, and the societal context in which a women's movement operates all impact the strategies and tactics that feminist activists choose. At the same time, feminist activism may also shape these institutions and the societal context.

The following sections engage with the four different dimensions to assess feminist legal activism, and list a large variety of factors that may be influential in each. At the end of each section, I refer to the Indian case.

I. Rights

A set of fundamental rights is the first aspect that impacts feminist activism. Rights stemming from national constitutions or similar documents, such as rights Bills or charters, are crucial for successful litigation in supreme and constitutional courts. But constitutional rights can also enhance the legitimacy of demands for law reform that feminists make towards the legislator. Constitutional rights, in the words of Lambert and Scribner, 'provide women's rights advocates with a constitutional anchor for legislative and judicial action and influence the content of legislation and judicial review of laws and policies' (Lambert & Scribner, 2023, p 18). In addition, rights deriving from international or regional human rights documents that the state has signed and ratified allow the state to be held accountable in national, regional, and international courts and add value to attempts at legislative lobbying.

To make a case for women's rights, feminists have used the whole spectrum of constitutional and international human rights, including the right to work and to vote, the right to health, physical integrity, privacy, and autonomy, the freedom of speech, and the freedom of movement. Yet, provisions on equality play a central role and will be addressed here in more detail. In addition, provisions on human or women's dignity have also held potential for feminist activists – an aspect that is not uncontroversial among feminist commentators.

A. Equality and Anti-Discrimination

Scholarship has shown that constitutional provisions recognising gender equality are crucial for civil society actors to hold their governments accountable (Lambert & Scribner, 2020, p 243). Baldez, Epstein and Martin (2006) investigated constitutional sex discrimination litigation in 50 states with and without constitutional sex equality provisions. They found that the presence of sex equality provisions 'significantly increases the likelihood of a court applying a higher standard of law, which in turn significantly increases the likelihood of a decision favoring the equality claim' (Baldez et al, 2006, p 243).

But it is not only important whether a constitution contains equality provisions; *how* constitutions recognise gender equality also impacts the possibilities for and outcomes of feminist legal activism (Lambert & Scribner, 2023, p 16). Provisions based on an understanding of formal equality assume men and women to be equal and seek to create a gender-neutral legal order. They allow women to ask for the same rights as men, which is especially important in areas where women have not yet achieved formal equality, such as in various aspects of family law. However, in countries where the constitution draws on a formal concept of equality, courts have, for instance, struggled to accommodate pregnancy discrimination and affirmative action (Baines & Rubio-Marin, 2005, p 13). In contrast, other constitutions draw on an understanding of women as separate but equal, emphasising respect for women's different reproductive and caregiving roles and seeking to ensure that the law does not treat them worse than men. In systems working with this concept, providing women with rights that men do not enjoy is possible. However, one challenge for these systems has been that legislation often draws on stereotypical understandings of women's roles or treats women in a paternalistic way (Baines & Rubio-Marin, 2005, p 13). Yet again, other constitutions and international human rights law instruments have worked with an understanding of substantive equality and oblige the state to take proactive measures to redress historical discrimination and promote women's full participation in society. Such an account acknowledges women's historical discrimination, and the political, economic, and social barriers that women face in various areas of their lives. It aims to provide equal access to opportunities and equality of outcomes. Such constitutions oblige the state to proactively promote women's full participation in society. They aim to transform social patterns of discrimination 'partly by uncovering the inequalities embedded in gender neutral laws and partly by challenging schemes that differentiate women by offering us only paternalistic benefits' (Baines & Rubio-Marin, 2005, p 14).

Constitutions that draw on concepts of substantive rather than formal equality and that address gender equality in several different contexts throughout the constitutional text have been held to be favourable for feminist activism (Lambert & Scribner, 2020, p 243). For instance, in South Africa and Argentina, feminists have benefitted from the fact that their constitutions draw on a concept of substantive equality and include provisions recognising and seeking to advance gender equality, including through quotas, equal pay for equal work provisions, a principle of non-sexism, the protection of women's bodily autonomy, their reproductive choice and their right to freedom from violence (Lambert & Scribner, 2020, 2023). Feminist activists in these countries view the constitution as a central tool for their legislative and litigation efforts and have found that the specific 'constitutional provisions made it possible to get legislative changes and judicial decisions that they would not have gotten otherwise' (Lambert & Scribner, 2020, p 238). In contrast, in the case of Chile and Botswana, where the constitutions provide for formal equality only, women's rights activists have found it challenging to use the constitution for their aims (Lambert & Scribner, 2020, 2023). While they have successfully fought laws that discriminated against women, activists have not achieved proactive measures to increase women's economic or political power (Lambert & Scribner, 2020, 2023).

In Canada, the Supreme Court established the principle of substantive equality and provided feminist activists with solid ground to push for legal change (Baines, 2005). The Court decided in 1989 that 'every difference in treatment between individuals under the law will not necessarily result in inequality' and that 'identical treatment may frequently produce serious inequality' (*Law Society of British Columbia v Andrews* [1989] 1 SCR 143, 164). Later, the Court affirmed that its decision in *Andrews* had signalled its commitment to substantive equality, and stated that the purpose of the Canadian equality provision was

> to prevent the violation of essential human dignity and freedom through the imposition of disadvantage, stereotyping, or political or social prejudice, and to promote a society in which all persons enjoy equality recognition at law as human beings or as members of Canadian society, equally capable and equally deserving of concern, respect and consideration (*Law v Canada*, [1999] 1 SCR 497 at paragraph 51).

These precedents provided the ground for a remarkable feminist success story, in which women's rights activists won a large number of litigation cases and, step-by-step, expanded women's rights (Manfredi, 2004).

B. Dignity

Feminist activists have also drawn on and benefitted from constitutional provisions on dignity. For instance, feminist campaigns against sexual harassment in the workplace in Spain (Rubio-Marin, 2005) and Germany (Zippel, 2006) successfully argued that workplace harassment violated women's dignity. This strategy differed from the one used by US feminists, where activists argued that sexual harassment violated women's equality but was in line with the position of the EU institutions and several EU Member States (Zippel, 2006) and, therefore, effective in this context.

Several other discourses around women's rights also referred to dignity, and supreme and constitutional courts have taken up this argument to foster women's rights. For instance, the South African Constitutional Court found that a rule of male primogeniture in African customary law entrenched patriarchy and violated women's constitutional guarantees to human dignity and equality (*Bhe v Magistrate, Khayelitsha and Others*, 2004). The Canadian Supreme Court held that the restriction of pornographic material was constitutional because

> [a]mong other things, degrading or dehumanizing materials place women (and sometimes men) in positions of subordination, servile submission or humiliation. They run

against the principles of equality and dignity of all human beings (*R v Butler* [1992] 1 SCR 452).

Similarly, the Supreme Court of Israel has argued that films could legitimately be censored where they were regarded as degrading to the dignity of women (*Station Film Co v Public Council for Film Censorship*, 1994). The US Supreme Court has in the past justified removing restrictions on abortion with the argument that personal decisions about procreation, contraception and family relationships are 'choices central to personal dignity and autonomy' and therefore protected by the Constitution (*Planned Parenthood of Southeastern Pennsylvania v Casey*, 1992). The judgment was, however, overturned by the Supreme Court's decision in *Dobbs v Jackson Women's Health Organization* in 2022. Similar references to women's human dignity were made by the Federal Constitutional Court of Germany, the Supreme Court of Canada and the Constitutional Court of Colombia (Dixon & Nussbaum, 2012).

Feminists have, however, also articulated scepticism towards the use of dignity to further women's rights. Susanne Baer points out that the invocation of women's dignity can have paternalistic tendencies, especially in cases where dignity is understood as 'an honourable way of being in the world' and might be misused as 'a vehicle for problematic expectations antithetical to the variety of ways in which people want to express themselves' (Baer, 2009, p 458). For instance, the Federal German Administrative Court held that women could legitimately be prohibited from exposing themselves to men in 'peep shows' (BVerwGE 64, 274 (1981)). The Court in this decision, according to Baer, found fault with 'a violation of specific morals rather than economic deprivation or sexual violence' and 'regulated' women rather than liberate them (Baer, 2009, p 458).

Baer makes another point to warn against the use of dignity for the protection of women's rights, namely that some jurisdictions understand dignity too narrowly and involve the concept only in extreme situations (Baer, 2009, p 459). In Germany, for example, where the Constitution's dignity provision is a reaction to and renunciation of the atrocities committed during the Nazi regime and World War II, dignity doctrine focuses on atrocities such as genocide, humiliation, torture, and the denial of subjectivity, but leaves out other claims, which look petty in comparison (Baer, 2009, p 459). As the meaning of dignity varies significantly across jurisdictions (McCrudden, 2008), in other places, scholars have found the other extreme to be the case: dignity is used in so inflated a manner that it almost loses its meaning (Baruah, 2020, 2022), a point that I will return to when speaking about the case of India.

C. Competing Rights Claims

An individual's rights are always balanced against the rights of others. Therefore, the recognition of the rights of other groups or individuals can hinder feminist activists' chances of success.

Strong constitutional protection of the rights of the unborn, for instance, can significantly limit women's reproductive rights and thus impair feminist legal activism in this area. The Irish Constitution, for example, until an amendment in 2018, explicitly referred to the 'right to life of the unborn',[1] and courts prioritised this right over other rights (Irving, 2008, pp 202 et seq). In other countries, constitutional courts have upheld restrictions on women's access to abortion by holding that general provisions on the right to life or dignity apply to the foetus too.[2]

Religious communities' rights to govern their community members, protected under the freedom of religion, may also impair feminist legal activism. According to UN Women, 84 per cent of constitutions contain provisions relating to the status of customary or religious law, thereby often sanctioning practices that discriminate against women (UN Women, 2017). Several constitutions display 'claw back clauses' allowing exceptions to non-discrimination provisions in matters of family and inheritance law (UN Women, 2017). Chapter four will refer to the Indian case to show how this can create hurdles for feminist activism.

If constitutions strongly emphasise the family and understand this as a unit consisting of a married heterosexual couple and their children, this may also hinder the success of specific feminist legal campaigns. Lambert and Scribner (2020, p 233), for instance, show that Article 1 of the Chilean Constitution, which singles out the family as 'the fundamental core of society', has hurt the efforts of women's rights advocates.

D. Women's Constitutional Rights in India

In India, Article 13 of the Constitution stipulates that pre- and post-constitutional laws are void if they are inconsistent with the fundamental rights provided under Part III of the Constitution. The fundamental rights include the right to equality and the right to life (Article 21), which is generally interpreted as the right to live with human dignity. They also include the right to freedom of religion (Article 25).

(i) Equality

The constitutional equality provisions in the Indian Constitution hold some potential for feminist activists. Article 14 provides equality before the law. Article 15(1) prohibits the state from discriminating against any citizen 'on

[1] Article 40.3.3. The subsection that read 'the equal right to life of the pregnant woman and the unborn' had been inserted into the Constitution in 1983 through the Eighth Amendment of the Constitution Act. The provision was repealed in 2018 after a campaign by pro-abortion rights groups, members of the medical profession and legal academics and a referendum by the Irish people. The constitutional provision today states: 'Provision may be made by law for the regulation of termination of pregnancy'.

[2] See, for instance, the decisions by the US Supreme Court in *Gonzales v Carhart*, 550 US 124 (2007) or the German Federal Constitutional Court in BVerfGE 39, 1 (1975).

grounds only of religion, race, caste, sex, place of birth'. Article 15(2) extends this prohibition to certain private actors.[3] Article 15(3) allows the state to make special provisions for women. According to MacKinnon (2006, p 189), this latter provision 'recognizes … that sex has been made into a social disadvantage for women' and 'suggests a substantive recognition of women's unequal social status by permitting special provisions to rectify their inequality'.

In order to determine whether a law is in compliance with Article 14, the Supreme Court has developed a 'doctrine of reasonable classification' (or 'classification test'). According to this doctrine, a classification is reasonable and allows for different treatment when it meets two conditions: firstly, it must be founded on an intelligible differentiation that distinguishes persons or things that are grouped together from others left out of the group; and, secondly, the differentia must have a rational relation to the object that is sought to be achieved by the statute in question (*Budhan Choudhry v State of Bihar*, 1954). This means that only those individuals who are similarly situated must be treated the same in law. The Supreme Court thus draws on the concept of formal (not substantive) equality as it equates equality with sameness (R Kapur, 2016, p 745).

With regard to gender equality, Indian jurisprudence has long worked with a 'formal approach' according to which the differential treatment between men and women does not amount to discrimination if it is based on presumed 'natural differences' between the sexes (R Kapur, 2016; Bhatia, 2019, pp 7–13). This reading holds that discrimination 'results only from conscious, hostile intentions of lawmakers' (Bhatia, 2019, p 4). Drawing on the word 'only' in Article 15(1) courts have denied discrimination claims in cases where the classification was drawn along the lines of grounds other than sex (eg pregnancy) and, therefore, did not burden all women but only some women in an indirect manner (Bhatia, 2019, pp 8–9).[4] Furthermore, according to the formal approach, Article 15(3), which allows special provisions for women, is interpreted as an exception to the principle of non-discrimination guaranteed by Article 15(1) and not as a dimension of it (R Kapur, 2016, p 745).

From the mid-1970s onwards, we find examples of judgments moving away from this formal reading towards what Bhatia (2019) calls a transformative approach. This approach differs from the formal approach in significant ways. Most importantly, it 'understands discrimination as a product of social, economic, and cultural structures and institutions that create "patterns of … exclusion"' (Bhatia, 2019, p 4). Furthermore, while not denying that differences between men and women exist, the transformative approach rejects 'the manner in which these differences are often given legal *salience*, as the bases of laws that permit or sanction discrimination' (Bhatia, 2019, p 19). The transformative approach also does not accord such a limiting role to the word 'only' as the formal approach, which means that state action is not exempted

[3] On this rather extraordinary provision prohibiting forms of horizontal discrimination, see Bhatia (2016a).

[4] The formalist reading culminated in the Supreme Court's decision in *Air India v Nergesh Meerza* (1981).

from discrimination claims when it differentiates by reasons other than sex (Bhatia, 2019, p 19). According to Bhatia (2019, p 16) this second judicial tradition found its culmination in *Anuj Garg v Hotel Association of India* in 2008. In this judgment, the Supreme Court struck down a law from 1914 that prohibited women from selling liquor. The Court rejected the argument of the Government of Delhi that the law had been passed to protect women from the hazards of employment in the liquor industry. The Court held that the law in question 'suffers from incurable fixations of stereotype morality and conception of sexual role' (paragraph 44). It further stated that 'Legislation should not be only assessed on its proposed aims but rather on the implications and the effects' (paragraph 44).

There are multiple examples of case law applying a substantive (rather than formal) equality approach, especially in cases regarding caste-based discrimination (Bhatia, 2022), but also in cases concerning gender equality, where the courts '[take] the social context of sex-based disadvantage clearly into account' (MacKinnon, 2006, p 188).[5] For instance, in *T Sareetha v T Venkata Subbaiah* (1983), the High Court of Andhra Pradesh stated that although the Hindu Marriage Act, 1955 makes 'the remedy of restitution of conjugal rights equally available both to wife and husband' and thereby 'it apparently satisfies the equality test', in reality, the remedy is 'used almost exclusively by the husband and is rarely resorted to by the wife' (paragraph 38). Thus, the norm would work 'as an engine of oppression' against married women (paragraph 38). Consequently, the Court also held that, in addition to violating Article 21, Section 9 of the Hindu Marriage Act, which provides for the restitution of conjugal rights, violated Article 14 of the Constitution and would, therefore, have to be struck down – a view that was, however, not followed in later judgments.

However, despite these progressive examples, the transformative approach has certainly not replaced the formal one (yet). Rather, the two approaches 'continue to coexist in an uneasy tension' and courts continue to apply the formal approach, thereby ignoring that seemingly 'neutral' or benign legislative classifications draw on gendered stereotypes (Bhatia, 2019, p 35). Kapur holds that 'the formal approach to equality has been the dominant one within Indian constitutional law', while 'fragments of the substantive approach have from time to time been identifiable' (R Kapur, 2016, p 743).

(ii) Dignity

The word 'dignity' is mentioned three times in the Indian Constitution – in the preamble ('dignity of the individual'), in the directive principles of state policy (children shall have the opportunities to develop 'in conditions of freedom and dignity', Article 39(f)) and in the fundamental duties (duty to 'renounce

[5] For an overview of cases see MacKinnon (2006) and R Kapur (2016). I will deal with some of these cases in detail in Chapters four and five.

practices derogatory to the dignity of women', Article 51A(e)). However, unlike the Constitutions of South Africa, Canada, and Germany, the Indian Constitution does not mention dignity in the chapter on fundamental rights. Yet, the Indian Supreme Court has applied the concept of dignity in adjudicating on fundamental rights, refraining, however, from determining what dignity means and encompasses, and under what circumstances it is violated (Baruah, 2020, 2022). This has led to 'problematic inconsistencies' (Baruah, 2022): judicial decisions speak of dignity both as a right and a value that justifies rights, and both as absolute and limitable by law (Baruah, 2020, 2022). When it comes to women's rights, courts often use women's dignity and equality in a single breath, as I will show in later chapters.

(iii) Competing Rights Claims

Regarding competing rights, the text of the Indian Constitution is promising for women. The Indian Constitution in Article 25 guarantees the right to 'profess, practice and propagate religion' but makes this right subject to other fundamental rights, including the right to equality. According to Indian jurisprudence, only 'essential religious practice' is protected under Article 25 (*Commissioner of Police v Acharya Jagdishwarananda Avadhuta*, 2004). The Constitution's preamble, since 1976, has defined India as a secular state. The Supreme Court has not only held that secularism is part of the basic structure of the Constitution (*His Holiness Kesavananda Bharati Sripadagalvaru v State of Kerala*, 1973) but also that ordinary laws can be tested against the basic structure of the Constitution (*Dr M Ismail Faruqui v Union of India*, 1994). Article 44 of the Constitution holds that the Indian state 'shall endeavour' to secure a Uniform Civil Code, thus drawing on the understanding that religion-based personal laws will eventually be replaced.

In practice, however, equality has often lost out against religious freedom, as I will elaborate in Chapter four. Furthermore, while feminist scholars have argued that religious personal laws contradict the principle of secularism (Jaising, 2005b, p 5), this argument is accepted by neither mainstream scholarship nor the judiciary. Notably, the Indian state has also made significant declarations towards CEDAW, holding that the government is only obliged to eliminate discrimination against women as long as this is 'in conformity with its policy of non-interference in the personal affairs of any community without its initiative and consent' (United Nations, 2006, p 14).

II. Activism

While feminist scholars agree that constitutional rights matter for the success of feminist activism, they also agree that other factors are crucial in realising these rights (Baines & Rubio-Marin 2005; Banda 2005). As Dobrowolsky and

Hart (2003, p 3) contend, 'only constant vigilance and the hard grind of sustained activism ensure that over time textual promises are honoured and … women's lives change for the better' (Dobrowolsky & Hart, 2003). A second set of success factors thus revolves around feminist activism: the characteristics – strength, expertise – of women's movements and the strategies and tactics that feminist groups deploy.

A. Characteristics of a Successful Social Movement

In their demands for legal change, the spokespersons of feminist activism typically speak for a larger women's movement. It is this movement that forms the backbone of feminist legal activism, that provides the 'pressure from below' (Epp, 1998) that ultimately brings about legal change. We know from social movement scholarship that how the movement is constituted significantly impacts the outcome of its campaigns.

One determining factor of a social movement's success is its strength, indicated by its membership, its (financial) resources, the number of social movement organisations participating in it or the number or size of protest events (demonstrations, etc.) (McCammon, Campbell, Granberg, & Mowery, 2001, p 57; Kolb, 2007, pp 39–40). The assumption is that the stronger a movement is, the higher its chances of success. After all, a strong movement is more visible and might be taken more seriously in the political debates around a particular issue.

Comparing legal reforms in the area of violence against women across the globe and locating the drivers of such reform, Htun and Weldon demonstrated that strong and autonomous domestic feminist movements are the most critical factor (Htun & Weldon, 2012; S Laurel Weldon & Htun, 2013). Feminist movements even proved to be a more influential factor than the strength of leftist parties, the proportion of women in government or national wealth (Htun & Weldon, 2012). Epp's comparative study of rights mobilisation in the US, Canada, the UK, and India argued that in contexts with a 'deep and vibrant' support structure for legal mobilisation (lawyers, rights advocacy organisations, and sources of financing), we are more likely to see a 'rights revolution', whereas in contexts where the support structure is 'shallow and weak,' such revolutions will probably fail (Epp, 1998).

However, movement size and visibility alone are not the only, and potentially not even the determining factors. For success, it is also crucial that the movement's members are united in their viewpoints on which topics to choose for their campaign and how to frame the movement's demands. Scholarship shows that movements tend to be successful with their campaigns if the issue they tackle has a high priority on the movement agenda (Lovenduski, Baudino, Guadagnini, Meier, & Sainsbury, 2005, pp 275–78; Haussman & Sauer, 2007) and when they speak with one voice in making demands for legal change

(McBride Stetson, 2001a, p 286). When women's movements are internally fragmented due to tensions between individual groups or conflicts over standpoints and strategies, this diminishes the movement's chances of success. Various scholarship supports this finding, including studies on feminist activism in West Germany (Kamenitsa, 2001), New York City (Merry, Rosen, Levitt, & Yoon, 2010), Morocco (Evrard, 2014) and Bolivia (Goetz & Jenkins, 2018). In the Bolivian case, for instance, a law that sought to strengthen the rights of predominantly female domestic workers was stalled by the initiative of middle-class women who benefitted from domestic work provided by indigenous and lower-class women (Goetz & Jenkins, 2018, pp 725–26).

The expertise of a movement's members can also determine its success in legal activism. This is particularly the case when women's groups use litigation to advance their claims. Scholarship has pointed out that 'repeat players' are more likely to be successful in bringing about change through the courts than those groups and activists with little experience with litigation (Galanter, 1974; O'Connor & Epstein, 1983; Manfredi, 2004; Merry et al, 2010).

Burstein (1991), for instance, shows for the US context that immediately after the enactment of Title VII of the Civil Rights Act of 1964, which prohibited employment discrimination based on 'race, color, religion, sex or national origin', women were less successful than Black people in winning equal employment opportunity disputes, even though women were arguably more disadvantaged in the labour market. This was partly because Black people were better organised and had more experience of using litigation to challenge discrimination than women (Burstein, 1991). However, when in the 1980s, litigation had become a key strategy in women's rights activism in the US, women's groups and feminist lawyers were largely successful with it (George & Epstein, 1991).

Likewise, in Canada, the Women's Legal Education and Action Fund (LEAF) owes its enormous success (at least in part) to its expertise in litigating as a 'repeat player' (Manfredi, 2004, pp 15, 33). LEAF has regularly served as an amicus curiae in cases concerning women's rights since the 1980s. Manfredi (2004) shows that in 83.9 per cent of the cases in which LEAF intervened until the early 2000s, the Supreme Court treated the appellate court ruling as LEAF argued that it should. This is a remarkably high figure, given that the overall success rate of claims made concerning the Canadian Charter of Rights and Freedoms was about 33 per cent over the same period (Manfredi, 2004, p 20). In contrast, Australian feminists could not develop strong litigation organisations – a factor that explains the relatively low success in litigation compared to their Canadian counterparts (Chappell, 2002, p 140).

Expertise also plays a role in legislative lobbying. Again, the example of the US shows that in addition to mass-member organisations such as the National Organization for Women (NOW), it was often specialised groups with technical expertise, such as the Center for Women Policy Studies, and single-issue groups, like the National Abortion Rights Action League, that successfully pushed for law reforms (Freeman, 1975; Gelb & Palley, 1982; Boneparth & Stoper, 1988b).

B. Strategies

Apart from the movement's characteristics, the choice of strategies and tactics is influential in determining the success of law reform campaigns.

(i) Lobbying and Litigation

Speaking about *legal* activism, a central choice for feminist activists and women's groups is whether to approach the legislator or the judiciary.

When lobbying the legislature, feminist activists may choose between outside and inside strategies (McCammon et al, 2001, p 58; Dür & Mateo, 2013, pp 662–63). Outside strategies are directed at the public and aim at mobilising or changing public opinion or the dynamics of a debate. They can take the form of demonstrations, strikes and boycotts, public speeches, and the dissemination of ideas through traditional and social media. Inside strategies aim directly at influencing political decision-makers, such as by sending petitions to legislative and executive organs, attempting to be heard in parliamentary debates, and approaching women's policy agencies as intermediaries who have the power to influence Parliament or government.

When choosing litigation, depending on the judicial system, feminists may be able to choose between directly sponsoring a test case or participating as a third-party intervener (by testifying in court hearings or submitting amicus curiae briefs) in cases that they did not initiate themselves, but in which they have an interest in the outcome.

Whether lobbying or litigation is more effective depends on the specific context in which the feminist groups operate. Women's groups often 'forum shop' for the political institutions that seem most responsive to their claims (Goetz & Jenkins, 2018, p 731). Legislative lobbying, for instance, may be a good choice when there are 'sympathetic insiders' in the government and Parliament (Waylen, 2007) or when informal channels of communication with political decision-makers exist (Guerrero, 2020). Feminists will also revert to legislative lobbying when courts have no judicial review powers (Samuels, 2005, p 20) or the Constitution does not provide for or constitute a strong rights instrument (Chappell, 2002). Furthermore, strategic litigation will not be a viable route in cases where the risks connected to litigation are particularly high, for instance in cases where there exists a high risk of generating a backlash (Guerrero, 2020).

In any case, the choice between lobbying and litigation is usually not an either-or question. Scholarship has shown that movements may increase their chances of success if they draw on a combination of different legal tactics (McCann, 1994; Manfredi, 2004) or a combination of legal and non-legal tactics (Krishnan, 2006, p 577; McCann, 2006, pp 23, 31). The Canadian organisation LEAF, for example, has successfully pursued a holistic strategy in which it combined litigation in the Supreme Court with other legal strategies, including litigation in other courts and submissions to various legislative committees (Manfredi, 2004, p 30). Also, to promote the concept of substantive equality, as a first step preceding litigation, the organisation conducted a broad campaign to disseminate its equality theory in order to gain acceptance by academics, lawyers, and the judiciary (Manfredi, 2004, p 49). For this purpose, LEAF members published articles in law journals, presented papers at conferences and participated in judicial training sessions (Manfredi, 2004, p 49).

(ii) Making Demands and Framing them

Scholarship has indicated that women's movements are more successful if they demand small, step-by-step changes, rather than substantive changes that challenge the system. Hawkesworth, for instance, states that US feminists were most successful when they sought 'incremental reforms the system could handle easily' (Hawkesworth, 1994, p 99 referring to Freeman's work in the 1970s and '80s). Similarly, Gelb and Palley (1982, pp 10–11) stated:

> The broader the goals of a social movement, the more central its focus, and the greater its threat to the status quo, the less likely it is to succeed. Single issue reformist politics that does not threaten displacement of existing power configurations, then may often provide the easiest route to success to emergent groups.

Related to the question of *what* to demand is the question of *how* to make these demands. Scholarship on law and social movements has pointed out that groups and movements are successful when they manage to influence the discourse around a particular issue by framing it in terms that benefit them. 'To frame', in the words of Robert Entman (1993),

> is to select some aspects of a perceived reality and make them more salient in a communicating text, in such a way as to promote a particular problem definition, causal interpretation, moral evaluation, and/or treatment recommendation for the item described.

Frames thus call our attention to particular aspects and direct our attention away from others (Rein & Schön, 1991; Ferree, Gamson, Gerhards, & Rucht, 2002).

As a part of their broader legal strategies, activists have, for instance, successfully transformed debates and added weight to claims by framing 'women's issues' in terms of 'rights' and by using international human rights terminology (McCann, 2006, p 28; Merry et al, 2010; Evrard, 2014). In Colombia, for instance, feminist activism successfully framed abortion as a human right and public health issue rather than a matter of religious doctrine, a frame that significantly impacted public discourse (Reuterswärd, Zetterberg, Thapar-Björkert, & Molyneux, 2011). Feminists also used this frame when they filed a lawsuit at the Colombian Constitutional Court in 2005. Attorney Monica Roa and the organisation Women's Link Worldwide argued that the abortion ban denied women their fundamental right to health and violated women's human rights guaranteed under CEDAW and other international law (Reuterswärd et al, 2011, p 813). This strategy proved successful. In 2006, the Court decriminalised abortion in specific circumstances (Colombia, Constitutional Court, C-355/2006, 10 May 2006). Later, in 2022, the Court legalised abortion on all grounds during the first 24 weeks of pregnancy (Colombia, Constitutional Court, C-055/22, 21 February 2022).

Yet, here again, context decides which is the most promising framing tactic, and feminist activists in different countries may choose different frames to argue for similar aims.[6] Scholarship shows, for instance, that claims for women's universal human rights fare better as a bargaining tool in contexts where the state is receptive towards human rights institutions (Ertürk, 2019, p 21). Where this is not the case, other strategies might be better suited. In some contexts of the Global South, feminist activists are wary of using a discourse of 'rights' because this might be understood as 'Western'/foreign and may produce a backlash from local elites (Nazneen & Hickey, 2019b, p 193).

In some contexts, feminists have found it most promising to advocate for legal reforms by adhering to established gender roles and drawing on conservative or religious norms and values. McCammon et al (2001, pp 64–65) show that suffragettes who campaigned at the State level in the US were more likely to get the vote when they argued that women would use their right to vote to protect their children and their homes. Scholarship has also pointed out that framing a project as 'feminist' or in terms of 'women's rights' may risk triggering conservative backlashes. Sadiqi and Ennaji (2006, p 108), for example, argue in the Moroccan context that women's groups fare better when they frame the specific issue as a 'project of society' rather than a women's project. Similarly, the women's movement in Botswana was more successful in framing its demands in terms of women's 'empowerment' than in terms of women's 'equality' or women's 'rights' (Leslie, 2006, p 134). Women's rights activists in the Gaza Strip (Shehada, 2013, p 29), Yemen (Dahlgren, 2013, pp 67–68), Egypt (Al-Sharmani, 2013, p 78), and Iran (Ertürk, 2019, p 20) adopted a discourse that links women's rights to *Sharia* to claim 'religious legitimacy' for their proposed reforms (Al-Sharmani, 2013, p 79), but challenge conservative interpretations of Islamic law and draw on more egalitarian interpretations.

[6] For instance, while feminists favouring abortion rights in Colombia focused on the right to health, US feminists broadly framed abortion as a matter of women's privacy, and German pro-speakers concentrated on women's self-determination (Ferree et al, 2002, p 127). And while feminists in the US framed sexual harassment as an issue of sex discrimination and drew parallels between sexual harassment and race discrimination, feminists in Germany argued that sexual harassment was primarily a violation of their constitutional rights to sexual self-determination and dignity (Zippel, 2006).

(iii) Confrontational vs Conciliatory Tactics

Feminists have also had to choose between tactics that abide by or that radically challenge conservative ideas about appropriate behaviour. Women's rights activists have repeatedly used tactics to shock and draw media attention to their causes. Between 1903 and 1914, some British suffragettes, for instance, fought with drastic means and militant actions, including 'sporadic acts of violence and arson', thereby displaying 'a remarkable instinct for the propaganda effects of spectacle' (Walters, 2005, pp 78, 80). They smashed shop windows and set public buildings on fire (Walters, 2005, p 80). Suffragettes imprisoned for violent actions protested against the authorities in prison by going on hunger strikes (Walters, 2005, p 83). In Egypt in 1951, suffragettes led by Doria Shafiq publicly unveiled and stormed the Parliament to draw attention to their demand for women's suffrage (Zuhur, 2014, p 30). In 2008 women belonging to the 'Femen' movement in Ukraine and other parts of Europe protested topless. In the northeastern Indian State of Manipur, in July 2004, women demonstrated naked in front of the headquarters of a paramilitary union after a young woman, Thangjam Manorama, had been raped and murdered by the union's personnel (Murthy & Dasgupta, 2011, p 36; Basu, 2015, p 161). The women used their nudity as a symbol of resistance and as a shock tactic, and also challenged victim blaming by holding up a banner stating 'Indian Army, Rape Us!' (Murthy & Dasgupta, 2011, p 36).

But shock tactics do not necessarily work in the movements' favour, as the public response is not always predictable (Zuhur, 2014, p 46). Instead, scholars have held that 'tactful agitation' often serves the purpose of pushing for women's rights better than disruptive or confrontational tactics (Leslie, 2006, p 142). The women's movement in Botswana, for instance, fared better when it shifted its strategies from a disruptive approach (among other things, activists had stormed the passport offices demanding that the government change the citizenship laws) towards more conciliatory measures (Leslie, 2006, pp 91, 134).

(iv) Building Alliances and Learning from Others

Scholarship has further pointed out that women's groups and movements are more successful when they seek coalitions with like-minded organisations, movements, or other allies than when they fight only by themselves (O'Connor & Epstein, 1983; Boneparth & Stoper, 1988b; Manfredi, 2004; Krishnan, 2006).

Scholarship has used the terms 'issue networks' or 'advocacy networks' in contexts where feminist activists cooperated with other players, such as other activists, politicians, or academics, to lobby policy-makers and offer expert advice on particular policy issues (Keck & Sikkink, 1999; Htun, 2003; Reuterswärd et al, 2011). For instance, women's groups working for pay equity in the US successfully formed coalitions with labour unions (Boneparth & Stoper, 1988a, p 12). Likewise, in its fight against sexual harassment, the American women's movement formed coalitions with the civil rights and labour movements (Baker, 2008, p 179). Women's activists fighting for the legalisation of abortion in the US (McBride Stetson, 2001b) and in Latin America (Htun, 2003; Reuterswärd et al, 2011) have sought the support of doctors and population control groups. In South Africa, the Women's National Coalition, an alliance of women academics, politicians, and activists, strategically articulated gender issues during the transition from the Apartheid regime to democracy and significantly impacted the interim Constitution (Waylen, 2007, p 524).

In countries where religious institutions play a vital role, feminist activists have benefitted from close relationships with clerical figures. In Iran, for instance, feminists managed to bring about change in inheritance and criminal law because they engaged with high-ranking clerical figures, who then issued *fatwas* (non-binding legal opinions on an aspect of Islamic law) that influenced the legislatures' response to the feminist demands (Alikarami, 2019, pp 157–58).

Yet, feminist activists have sometimes also found themselves in problematic alliances, which has led to criticism from their peers. For instance, in the US, feminists seeking legislation against pornography stood on the same side as the religious right (Boneparth & Stoper, 1988a, p 12). Similarly, feminists criticising discrimination in the practices of religious or ethnic minorities have had to position themselves vis-à-vis right-wing majoritarian positions. Arguments of 'women's safety' and 'gender justice' are routinely (mis)used by conservative forces to deploy racist, xenophobic or anti-Muslim stereotypes (for the Indian context I will show this in Chapter four). In Germany, for instance, feminism was appropriated in the service of racism and stereotypes against Muslim male refugees in the wake of New Year's Eve 2017 in Cologne, where several women had experienced acts of sexual violence (Hark & Villa, 2017). Scholars have spoken about 'femo-nationalism' to describe the problematic connection between racism and anti-sexist critique (Farris, 2017). Uneasy alliances with supporters of feminist claims who stand in a very different political corner than the feminist activists might also lead to fragmentations among the women's movement and ultimately weaken it.

National women's movements also draw on the experience of women's movements in other countries or collaborate in international or transnational organisations (Ertürk, 2019, p 24). There are several examples of movements copying successful campaigns from their counterparts in other countries.[7]

[7] Early examples here were the feminist campaigns in the 1970s that brought together women to publicly confess that they had had an abortion and demand the right to abortion for every woman. The campaigns started in France with the manifesto of the 343 (*manifeste des 343*) appearing in the Magazine *Le Nouvel Observateur* on 5 April 1971. Among the women who signed the manifesto were Simone de Beauvoir and other intellectuals and media stars. The German campaign, which was signed by 374 women, followed shortly thereafter: On 6 June 1971 the cover of the magazine *Stern* under the headline '*Wir haben abgetrieben*' ('We have had an abortion') incorporated pictures of 28 of the better-known participants. In the US, in its 1972 debut issue, *Ms.* Magazine ran a similar petition with 53 well-known US women declaring that they had undergone abortions. Other examples include feminist activists across the globe organising 'take back the night' marches as a protest against violence, thereby copying a campaign from Philadelphia in 1975 (Gordon, 2014, p 120). The #MeToo campaign, in which women shared experiences with sexist behaviour via social media, is a more recent example of a campaign that was used globally.

(v) Timing

Feminists' decision on *when* to lobby the legislature or initiate a strategic litigation case also impacts their chances of success. Scholarship has shown that it benefits the campaigns when activists use 'windows of opportunity' (Kolb, 2007, p 64; El Masry, 2014, p 111). In Morocco, a change in the political context and the weakening of the Islamist ideology after the 2003 Casablanca bombing helped the feminist project seeking family law reform (Sadiqi & Ennaji, 2006, pp 108–9; Ennaji, 2014). The European women's movement, spearheaded by the European Women's Lobby, used the enlargement of the EU through the integration of three northern countries into the Union as a window of opportunity to include gender equality provisions in the 1997 Treaty of Amsterdam (Helferich & Kolb, 2001).

C. Feminist Activism in India

Chapter two has shown that feminist activism in India has a long tradition and that today's activists stand on the shoulders of their predecessors who have been fighting for women's rights for over a century. While the majority of women's groups do not have particular expertise in the law, there are some hubs of legal expertise. Legal organisations such as the Lawyers Collective or Majlis provide critical analysis of the law, suggest concrete law reforms, and have, in the last 20 to 30 years, gained significant experience in litigation. Religious groups such as BMMA and Awaaz-e-Niswaan have crucial knowledge about religious personal law. They are connected not only to other feminist organisations but also to the Muslim clergy. Both types of groups play a vital role in making demands for law reform, bringing cases before the courts, and giving special impetus to feminist demands. But other women's groups, too, play a critical role. They act as amplifiers of feminist ideas, supporting the demands for legal change, even though they do not engage in the nitty-gritty legal discourse. All these aspects are assets for successful legal activism.

But there are also weaknesses. The fact that the Indian women's movement is rather heterogeneous may provide obstacles, especially when the heterogeneity means that the movement's protagonists have different opinions on prioritising, approaching, and framing specific issues. No organisation acts as a spokesperson for or is representative of the women's movement in India. The movement is polyvocal. Another challenge for feminist activism may be the limited funding with which many women's organisations work.

In terms of strategies, feminist activists – as Chapter two has shown – have used both legislative lobbying and litigation, although litigation began later than lobbying. Overall, Indian feminists have been careful not to be too confrontational with their demands – especially after their experiences with the failed campaign for a Uniform Civil Code, which I will engage with in detail in Chapter four. Instead, like other 'Third World feminists' (Mohanty, 1991), they have often gone through careful deliberation or 'bargaining' processes (Kandiyoti, 1988) and attempted to strike a balance between gender equality and respect for religious sentiments and the local culture (Kalpagam, 2004, p 341; Agnes, 2011b, p xxviii).

III. State Institutions

Success with feminist legal activism, according to this book's understanding, means that state institutions – most notably the Parliament and the courts – respond to feminist demands favourably. Whether this is the case depends not only on how well feminists make their claims but also on the competencies, characteristics, and constraints of the institutions themselves. This section focuses on the judiciary's powers, the composition and partisanship of state institutions, women's policy agencies, and international obligations as influential factors in the success of feminist activism.

The points made here are related to scholarship in political science on 'political opportunity structures' (Kitschelt, 1986; Amenta & Zylan, 1991). The concept of political opportunity refers to 'consistent – but not necessarily formal or permanent – dimensions of the political environment … that provide incentives for collective action by affecting people's expectations for success or failure' (Tarrow, 2011, p 163). Feminist scholars have utilised this concept to explain how political institutions provide openings for and constraints on feminist activism (Banaszak, 1996; Dobrowolsky, 2000; Chappell, 2002). The roles and powers of state institutions and other political actors such as political parties, formal rules and informal procedures about how these institutions make decisions are some dimensions of political opportunities (Banaszak, 1996, pp 30–31) and will be discussed in this section.[8]

A. Powers of the Judiciary and Access to Justice

If feminists opt for litigation as a strategy, factors related to the competencies of the judiciary are central. This regards, first and foremost, whether the judiciary possesses the power to exercise judicial review, ie the power to rule an act of the legislature or executive as unconstitutional. But it also regards rules on standing and access to justice more broadly and funding for litigation.

(i) Standing and Judicial Review

The rules governing standing and class action are central to legal activism (Cichowski & Stone Sweet, 2003; Baines & Rubio-Marin, 2005, p 5; Irving,

[8] I cover other dimensions that some scholarship deems to be part of the political opportunity structure below under the rubric of 'society'.

2008, pp 147–48). Since feminist activists are usually not directly affected by the specific law or state action in question, states allowing individuals or groups to file cases in the public interest and letting third-party actors intervene in court cases to support claimants are beneficial for feminist activists. Also, the likelihood of strategic litigation increases when organisations are granted standing rights (Guerrero, 2020).

Canada, for example, liberalised its rules on standing in the 1970s and 1980s, when it no longer demanded a 'special injury' but allowed citizens to access the courts with constitutional challenges against statutes in cases of a 'generalized grievance' (Cichowski & Stone Sweet, 2003, p 211). The Canadian Supreme Court allows public interest groups to either intervene as a party or to serve as amicus curiae in constitutional cases (Chappell, 2002, p 144). The feminist organisation LEAF has greatly benefitted from this approach. Similarly, the relaxation of the rules of standing in judicial review cases in the UK in the 1980s made it easier for civil rights groups to challenge administrative decisions (Samuels, 2005, p 21).

The situation in Canada and the UK differs significantly from the Australian scenario, where it is tough for individuals or groups to run test cases or intervene in cases as amicus curiae, as Australian law on standing requires a personal, or 'special', interest on the part of the parties to a case (Chappell, 2002, p 145). Consequently, Australian feminists have had a significant disadvantage in gaining access to the court system compared to their Canadian counterparts (Chappell, 2002, p 145).

(ii) Funding for Litigation and Access to Justice

State funding for litigation is another aspect impacting feminist litigation. Even when there are no actual fees to file a case, litigation requires 'resources of time, physical and emotional energy, confidence, and knowledge' (Irving, 2008, p 158). Where individuals or organisations lack time, (legal) knowledge and/or experience in litigation, they need to hire and pay for lawyers or other experts to support them. This is especially the case when asymmetry between the parties exists, such as in cases where women sue their employer or where a constitutional challenge is brought against the state, a party that tends to be 'powerful, well resourced, and intimidating' (Irving, 2008, p 158). State funding for litigation helps in this situation. Chappell's comparative study, for example, shows that feminist activism in Canada benefitted from public funding for litigation, while in Australia, the lack of funding 'has been a crucial factor in feminists' non-engagement in the legal and constitutional realms' (Chappell, 2002, p 143).

Apart from funding, other aspects can contribute to the accessibility of a court and make it easier for feminist activists to file cases. Irving mentions the Constitutional Court of Costa Rica as a positive example in terms of accessibility: 'The court is open 24 hours a day, all year, with one magistrate always on duty. Anyone, regardless of citizenship, age, or other classification can file a case. Legal representation is not required, and there are no filing fees' (Irving, 2008, p 149).

On the other hand, '[r]estrictive time limits for advancing discrimination claims, long court proceedings or high judicial fees can frustrate litigation efforts' (Guerrero, 2020, p 104).

(iii) Judicial Interpretation

The sources and methods that judges use to interpret the Constitution play a central role in the outcome of cases. Many constitutions do not make explicit statements on how judges should interpret constitutional provisions. Some, however, do provide interpretative instructions. The South African Constitution, for instance, requires that when interpreting the Bill of Rights, courts 'must promote the values that underlie an open and democratic society based on human dignity, equality and freedom', 'must consider international law' and 'may consider foreign law' (Article 39(1)).

Scholars working on feminist constitutionalism have stressed that while no single methodology necessarily produces a 'feminist reading' of the Constitution, there are still 'traceable differences in gender impact between methodologies' (Irving, 2008, p 53). Historical originalism, for instance, will often disadvantage women if the Constitution is an old document written when women's subordinate status was accepted as normal (Baines & Rubio-Marin, 2005, p 10; Irving, 2008, p 58). In contrast, the purposive approach and interpretive progressivism are open to new ways of reading constitutional provisions and have historically 'lent much support to those seeking a constitutional meaning consistent with the expansion of rights' (Irving, 2008). Having said that, scholars also stress that progressivism does not always produce progressive results, and originalism will not always be regressive (Irving, 2008, p 60). Instead, we may very well see examples of countries where the original values at the time the Constitution was passed were more progressive than the ones currently prevailing. Thus, context is important.

B. Composition and Partisanship of State Institutions

The composition of the Parliament, the partisanship of the government, and the political/ideological outlook of judges are also factors to be considered when determining the success of feminist legal activism.

(i) Parties in Power

The scholarship suggests that feminist activists are more likely to be successful if left-wing or labour parties are in power than when conservative parties govern (Chappell, 2002, p 175; Weldon, 2002, p 55; Lovenduski et al, 2005, p 278). Regarding some issue areas, this effect is particularly strong. Abortion, for instance, is a partisan issue in many countries, with left or liberal parties favouring broader abortion rights and conservative parties opposing such rights. Conservative parties in power also often limit the scope and resources of women's policy agencies (Sauer, Haussman, & McBride, 2007, p 297) and/or cut back welfare programmes that benefit women (Chappell, 2002, p 35).

Governments play a vital role in selecting judges for constitutional and supreme courts in many systems. They may thus impact the outcome of court cases by selecting judges with a particular political and ideological outlook. Abortion cases in the US Supreme Court, for instance, became more challenging to win when the judges' attitudes regarding abortion were more staunchly conservative because of Republican appointments to the Court (McCammon, Moon, Hearne, & Robinson, 2020, p 237).

Yet, the scholarship has also argued that the obstacles that neo-conservative governments create for realising the goals of women's movements can be 'compensated' for by other factors, such as the representation of women in important positions in the legislature or the judiciary (Bashevkin, 1994), as I will elaborate on now.

(ii) Women in State Institutions

Whether a high number of women in decision-making roles is decisive for a women's movement's success is contested. Weldon's (2002, p 5) comparative study on government responsiveness to the claims of women's movements shows that among the most responsive states were several with very few women in government, and among the least responsive ones were several with a large proportion of women in government. Similarly, Chappel (2002, p 53) argues for the Australian case that the increase in the number of women in Parliament did not lead to significantly more 'women friendly' legislation. Likewise, Nazneen, Hickey and Sifaki (2019) argue that women's presence in formal politics and policy spaces alone does not explain the pace of adopting and implementing domestic violence law. Similarly, regarding women in the courts, some studies have found no significant gender differences in terms of judging (McCormick & Job, 1993; Westergren, 2004).

Other scholars have, however, seen a correlation between a high number of women in Parliament or on the bench and pro-women legislation/ case law, at least concerning some issue areas. The comparative study of five Western European countries by Annesley, Engeli and Gains (2015) found that higher numbers of women in Parliament *did* have an impact on the decisions on costly 'class-based gender equality issues', such as subsidised childcare, parental leave and anti-discrimination in hiring, wages, and pensions, but were irrelevant in decisions about 'status-based issues', such as reproduction, same-sex marriage, and domestic violence. A correlation between the gender of the judge and the outcomes of cases is also documented in employment law (Davis, Haire, & Songer, 1993; Farhang & Wawro, 2004; Beiner, 2005). Peresie's (2005) study on 556 decisions by

US federal courts of appeals in sexual harassment and sex discrimination cases reveals that plaintiffs were twice as likely to prevail when a female judge was on the bench. This effect was independent of the political persuasion of the female judge. Scholars have also shown that female judges in Florida were more conscious of gender inequality and observed more gender bias in legal settings than their male colleagues (Martin, Reynolds, & Keith, 2002).

(iii) Feminists in State Institutions

While the impact of women in state institutions is contested, the scholarship seems to agree that the presence of feminists (of all genders) in the legislature, the executive, or the judiciary is helpful for feminist activists. Waylen states in the context of South Africa that the presence of 'sympathetic insiders' in the system (first the Constituent Assembly and later the Parliament and the government) was more influential than 'sheer numbers' of women in ensuring positive gender outcomes in the Constitution and new legislation (Waylen, 2007, p 538). Such interaction between feminist activists *outside* the state institutions and those 'state feminists' or 'femocrats' *within* has been documented in other contexts, too (McBride Stetson, 2001c; Lovenduski, 2005b; Nazneen & Hickey, 2019a).

In Canada, the presence of feminist judges in the Supreme Court has been regarded as crucial for the success of feminist activists approaching the Court (Chappell, 2002, p 174; Manfredi, 2004, p 20). Chappel (2002, p 124) opines:

> It is naive to presume that by simply increasing the number of women judges the law will be any less gender biased. However, if, as has occurred in Canada, judges with a feminist approach to the law and men sympathetic to women's experiences are appointed to the bench, then there is a much greater likelihood that women's experiences in the public and private spheres will be better understood and will be taken into account in legal judgments.

C. Women's Policy Agencies

Women's policy agencies are state-based structures at the government level that are assigned to promote the rights and status of women (McBride & Mazur, 2013, p 655). These could be ministries for women's affairs, commissions on gender equality or equality offices. Early examples include the US and the Canadian Women's Bureaus, created in 1920 and 1954, respectively, and the French Study Group on Women's Work, established in 1965 (McBride & Mazur, 2013, p 655). More such agencies were set up worldwide after the first UN World Conference on Women in Mexico City in 1975, which had called for establishing women's policy machineries (McBride & Mazur, 2013, p 655). Later, their focus shifted from focusing on 'women' or 'gender' issues towards a broader focus on diversity and (intersectional) discrimination on the grounds of race, ethnicity, age, sexual orientation, disability, and other aspects (McBride & Mazur, 2013, p 656).

Scholars have argued that the existence of women's policy agencies enhances the chances of women's movements' success on issues such as abortion (McBride Stetson, 2001c), sexual harassment (Baker, 2008), or violence against women (Weldon, 2002). Women's policy agencies thereby function as intermediaries between the women's movements and the Parliament or the government, translating feminist goals into state policies (Haussman & Sauer, 2007, p 22). In principle, they offer the possibility to 'further feminist goals through public policies from inside the state apparatus' and can 'increase women's access to the state by furthering women's participation in political decision-making and by inserting feminist goals into public policy' (Lovenduski, 2005a, p 4).

However, here again, the context is essential. Women's policy agencies need to have adequate resources (staff and budget), be sympathetic to feminist issues and be open towards the demands of women's groups to be helpful intermediaries for feminist activists (Weldon, 2002; McBride & Mazur, 2013, p 671). The agency's placement in the political hierarchy can also be important: when women's policy agencies are headed by or have close connections to 'power brokers', this is a crucial advantage (McBride & Mazur, 2013, p 671). For instance, in trying to explain why Chile performed much better than Argentina concerning policy responses to the problem of domestic violence, Franceschet (2010, p 2) points, among other reasons, to the different 'resources and power of women's policy agencies'. Chile's National Women's Service, the Servicio Nacional de la Mujer, a centralised state agency created in 1991, had a well-resourced legal reform department. As part of the executive branch, it could propose legislation. Consequently, it played an essential role in policy research, legal monitoring, and the evaluation of laws (Franceschet, 2010, pp 2–3). On the other hand, Argentina's National Women's Council, the Consejo Nacional de la Mujer, created in 1992, had few resources, was not involved in the legislative process and had very little influence within the state, which left advocacy groups without influential insider allies (Franceschet, 2010, p 3).

Whether or not the critical figures of such women's policy agencies are committed to feminist ideals also impacts the role of these agencies vis-á-vis the feminist campaign. In this context, the distinction between 'insider' and 'symbolic' women's policy agencies is helpful (Lovenduski et al, 2005, p 272; McBride & Mazur, 2013, pp 668–69). Insider agencies 'agree with movement goals and are successful in gendering or re-gendering the debate in accordance with movement definitions', while symbolic agencies do neither of these things (Lovenduski et al, 2005, p 271). Insider agencies generally 'assist women's movements in reaching goals', while symbolic agencies have little benefits for feminist activists (Lovenduski et al, 2005, p 283). For instance, Valiente (2007, p 220) argues in the Spanish case that the Women's Institute did not represent the women's movement's goals in debates and refrained from framing those debates in gendered terms, presumably because the agency's directors lacked a feminist profile.

D. International Obligations

A state's international obligations, resulting from ratifying international conventions/treaties, such as CEDAW or the state's membership in regional organisations, may also prove helpful for feminist activists. International law gives feminist activists an additional reference point in their argument for gender equality. It allows them to hold their states accountable, potentially even before a regional or international court. Merry et al (2010, p 102) state that '[f]or social movements, human rights are simultaneously a system of law, a set of values, and a vision of good governance'. They offer the movements 'a variety of discursive, political, and strategic benefits' (Merry et al, 2010, p 102).

One possibility for feminist activists and women's groups is to use international or regional bodies, particularly courts, to hold their state accountable and push for legal or political change on the national level. Brazilian feminist activists, for instance, in 1998 presented a petition regarding the *Maria da Penha* case against the Brazilian state in the Inter-American Commission on Human Rights. The Commission's report held that the Brazilian state had violated the American Convention on Human Rights and failed to fulfil its duties under the Convention on the Prevention, Punishment and Eradication of Violence Against Women (Inter-American Commission on Human Rights, 2001). The report prompted the Brazilian state to pass a federal law addressing domestic violence against women in 2006 (De Silva de Alwis, 2012, p 194; De Aquino, 2013). The so-called 'Maria da Penha Law' (Lei No 11.340/2006) defines domestic violence as a human rights violation (Article 6) and cites CEDAW and the Convention on the Prevention, Punishment and Eradication of Violence Against Women.

Beyond that, women's groups also use international human rights conventions and the language of universal human rights to pressure their national governments or parliaments to make or amend national laws (De Silva de Alwis, 2012; Ertürk, 2019), where this has seemed a promising strategy (see above). In Turkey, for instance, feminists skilfully pushed for their agenda to eliminate discriminatory laws, highlighting the contradictions between Turkey's existing laws vis-à-vis its international obligations under CEDAW (Ertürk, 2019, p 22). Their strategy proved to be successful. The reformed Civil Code from 2002 removed the 'head of household' concept and introduced an equal property regime. The new Penal Code from 2005 recognised sexual violence as a crime against women's bodily integrity, as opposed to crimes against public morality (Ertürk, 2019, p 22). Similarly, in Ghana, the passing of a domestic violence act in 2007 followed a campaign of more than six years by women's rights advocates, in which the international law dimension and the fact that Ghana is a signatory to CEDAW played a central role (Manuh & Dwamena-Aboagye, 2013). Likewise, in Bangladesh, the enactment of the Domestic Violence Act of 2010 was impacted by the fact that the state was soon to undergo a CEDAW review by the Commission on the Status of Women meeting in New York in 2011, and the government sought to avoid embarrassment for not meeting its commitment to enact a law tackling domestic violence (Nazneen & Hickey, 2019a, p 15).

Feminists may use international law to pressure their governments even when states are not directly bound by supra-national law. This is because the mere fact that a 'critical mass' of states shares specific gender equality standards already puts pressure on national governments, even if these standards are not legally enforceable (Weldon & Htun, 2013, p 240). In several Member States of the EU, feminist activists successfully pressured their governments to adopt laws against sexual harassment to comply with EU standards, even though the early policies by the European Community of the 1990s were not directly binding on Member States (Zippel, 2006, p 30). There are several motivations for states to adopt gender equality policies. Economically weaker countries, for example, may seek financial capital and legitimacy, while autocracies and emerging democracies may want to improve their democratic and human rights credentials on the international stage (Htun & Weldon, 2010, p 212).

At the same time, it is also true that states find ways to not abide by obligations resulting from international law. Reservations, for instance, provide loopholes for states to circumvent such obligations. Reservations often sacrifice gender equality in the name of religion or local culture. Notably, CEDAW is the convention with more reservations than any other convention. Feminists in several countries have, therefore, launched dual campaigns aimed at removing reservations to international law obligations and at amending discriminatory national laws (Ertürk, 2019, pp 17–18).

E. State Institutions in India

(i) The Indian Judiciary

For feminist activists in India, the Indian judiciary provides several promising qualities. As Chapter two indicated, the Indian Supreme Court and the high courts have granted themselves the power to undertake judicial review over legislative action and to strike down laws that violate fundamental rights. They have also 'invented' an instrument commonly known as public interest litigation or PIL. The invention of PIL was primarily 'a revolution in procedure' (Bhuwania, 2017, p 2). The Supreme Court held that it was no longer necessary for the petitioner of a case to also be the party that had been injured or wronged. Instead, a citizen could bring a case on behalf of a disadvantaged group of injured people, irrespective of whether they were part of this group (Guruswamy & Aspatwar, 2013, pp 245–346). The Court also gave up the formal requirement of filing a petition when, in a series of cases (for instance, *Sheela Barse v State of Maharashtra*, 1983, and *Rural Litigation and Entitlement Kendra v State of Uttar Pradesh*, 1985) it treated letters and postcards as legitimate writ petitions and thus invented what has been termed an 'epistolary jurisdiction' (Baxi, 1985, p 118).

Furthermore, *suo motu* litigation allows the Supreme Court 'to intervene on its own motion whenever it believes a violation of fundamental rights exists, even without being petitioned by an aggrieved claimant or party' (Rosenberg, Krishnaswamy, & Bail, 2019, p 7). Another innovation that might prove valuable for activists is the 'continuing mandamus process', a device that 'allows the Supreme Court to continually oversee the implementation of its orders rather than having to wait for parties to file new cases alleging non-compliance' (Rosenberg et al, 2019, p 7). Other than these procedural reforms, the Court also made far-reaching decisions in its interpretation of the Constitution. Most prominently, it blurred the line between non-enforceable directive principles and enforceable fundamental rights and expanded the meaning of the right to life under Article 21 of the Constitution.

This 'combination of activism and accessibility' (Robinson, 2019, p 24) has been crucial in shaping the Court's image as a people's court protecting the rights of the marginalised. The Court itself has strengthened this image in decisions of the high times of Public Interest Litigation that engage with a self-reflection on the role of the judiciary. Judges who were at the forefront of creating possibilities for PIL based their argument on the understanding that the judiciary should 'become an arm of the socio-economic revolution and perform an active role calculated to bring social justice within the reach of the common man' (*SP Gupta v President of India*, 1982, paragraph 27).

Over the years, however, the Court's approach shifted from protecting the rights of the marginalised towards furthering neo-liberal interests (Ramanathan, 2002; Rajagopal, 2007; Bhuwania, 2017). Later chapters will also show that while the instrument of PIL holds many promises for feminist activists, the Indian higher judiciary has certainly not gone as far as it could have in the advancement of gender equality.

There are also other challenges for strategic litigation. Although Article 141 of the Constitution binds the rest of the judiciary to the decisions of the Supreme Court, in practice, there is no coherent jurisprudence from the Supreme Court, let alone the judiciary, more broadly. The 27 judges of the Supreme Court do not sit *en banc* but usually in benches of two, three or five (depending on the nature of the case). This results in a situation where, on a single day, the Court may have 12–13 parallel benches sitting and hearing cases simultaneously (Thiruvengadam, 2017, p 111). The result is that different benches give different, sometimes even contradictory, judgments on similar matters. In public interest litigation, certain judges tend to intervene aggressively when dealing with lapses in governance, while others rarely intervene (Robinson, 2019, p 33). Robinson (2016, p 338; 2019, p 33) thus calls the Supreme Court a 'poly-vocal' organ.

This has an impact on individuals and groups who seek to approach the Court strategically. As the outcome of a case might depend on which bench decides on the matter, and the individual or group has no (or at least very little) impact on the allotment of its case, the outcome of the case is often not predictable and therefore, strategic planning of litigation is difficult. In cases where a matter is before a judge who presumably will give an unfavourable judgment, lawyers sometimes try to delay the hearing until the case gets transferred to another bench or to have the Chief Justice relist the case as an urgent matter so that different judges are assigned to it (Robinson, 2019, p 34). Yet overall, a significant degree of uncertainty remains.

Furthermore, since the Supreme Court virtually selects its own judges (Chandra, Hubbard, & Kalantry, 2018; Sindhu & Narayan, 2018), the judges may be viewed as 'less partisan than in some other countries, such as the United States' (Robinson, 2019, p 37). This can have advantages or disadvantages from an activists' viewpoint, but may make the outcome of a case less predictable and thus creates challenges for strategising cases.

A problem of the Supreme Court is that it is notoriously backlogged: Cases often take years and sometimes decades to resolve (Robinson, 2016, p 336). This is commonly explained by the shortage of judges, procedural complexity, poor judicial management of cases, the overuse of appeals, and the relatively rare use of plea-bargaining in criminal cases (Robinson, 2016, p 336).

Women judges are heavily under-represented in the Indian higher judiciary (Chandra et al, 2018; De Souza & Srivastava-Kehrer, 2021). In the history of the Supreme Court, only 11 out of 196 judges have been women. From the 1950s' til 1989, the Supreme Court had no women judges at all. Currently 1 out of 33 judges are women. The situation looks only slightly better at the High Court level, where currently 14 per cent of the judges are women (Kashyap, 2024).

(ii) The Indian Parliament

At first glance, the Parliament does not seem to be a particularly promising institution for Indian feminists. Scholarship has bemoaned the fact that the Parliament's legislative output is limited, that parliamentary behaviour often hinders effective law-making and that many MPs are corrupt and have criminal cases registered against them (D Kapur & Mehta, 2006; Pai & Kumar, 2014).

While the Indian Parliament has generally become more representative of women over time, the number of female MPs remains low. In the Lok Sabha, it rose from below 3.5 per cent in 1977 (19 out of 542), when the Indian women's movement emerged, to 13.6 per cent in the 18th *Lok Sabha*, which was elected in 2024 (74 out of 543). This is lower than the world average, which, according to World Bank data, lies at 27 per cent (World Bank Group, 2024). Rai and Spary's analysis of the bio-profile pages of members of the 16th Lok Sabha shows that around half of the women MPs make claims to represent women and work towards women's empowerment (references to 'empowerment' are made much more often than references to women's 'equality') (Rai & Spary, 2019, pp 148–49). A woman MP who self-identifies as a feminist in their profile and challenges patriarchy in their speeches, however, is the absolute exception (Rai & Spary, 2019, p 153). Instead, many women MPs 'seek to distance themselves from feminist labels to avoid being seen as challenging gender norms' (Rai & Spary, 2019, p 153). Rai and Spary also show that women MPs on average ask fewer questions than their male colleagues and that when they speak in Parliament, their performances are often subject to disproportionately critical scrutiny (Rai & Spary, 2019, pp 168–69, 189). Yet, some women participate very actively in the debates, especially on 'explicitly women-related legislation', such as the discussions around the Domestic Violence Act in 2005) (Rai & Spary, 2019, p 175).

(iii) Women's Policy Agencies

Women's policy agencies exist in India but are rather 'symbolic' than 'insider' agencies, to apply Lovenduski's (2005, p 271) terminology. On paper, the National Commission for Women and the Parliamentary Committee for the Empowerment of Women are tasked with monitoring, scrutinising, and influencing state policies and law-making by focusing on women's equality and empowerment (See the National Commission for Women Act, 1990). In theory, they could thus be significant allies for the women's movement. In practice, however (as Chapter two has indicated), feminists have criticised that these organisations do not pursue the feminist agenda many activists wish for and that their engagement with women's groups is in fact limited (Arya, 2010; Rai & Spary, 2019).

(iv) International Law

International human rights norms are not directly enforceable in India but only apply when domestic legislation gives effect to these norms. Article 253 of the Constitution gives the Parliament the power to make laws to implement any 'treaty, agreement or convention … made at any international conference, association or other body'. Article 51(c) directs the state to 'endeavour to … foster respect for international law and treaty obligations in the dealings of organised peoples with one another' (Article 51(c)).

India signed CEDAW on 30 July 1980 but only ratified the Convention 13 years later, on 9 July 1993, shortly after the Vienna Declaration and Programme of Action had been adopted in June 1993. To the regret of women's rights activists, India made significant declarations and reservations to CEDAW (Mehra, 1998), particularly a declaration that curtails its core obligations under Articles 5(a) (which urges State Parties to take measures '[t]o modify the social and cultural patterns of conduct of men and women, with a view to achieving the elimination of prejudices and customary and all other practices which are based on the idea of the inferiority or the superiority of either of the sexes or on stereotyped roles for men and women') and Article 16(1) (which urges the State Parties to take measures 'to eliminate discrimination against women in all matters relating to marriage and family'). India's declaration states that the Indian state abides by these provisions only 'in conformity with its policy of non-interference in the personal affairs of any community without its initiative and consent (United Nations, 2006, p 14). For Indian feminists, these declarations have meant that in their campaigns regarding religion-based family law, they could only draw on international human rights law to a limited extent.

IV. Society

A fourth dimension of factors that impact feminist legal activism is societal factors. These include public opinion about a particular issue area, the degree of counter-mobilisation that challenges the feminist goals, religion's role in a state and (legal) culture.

A. Public Opinion and Media Coverage

Public opinion is a crucial factor that can impact the decisions of legislators and the judiciary and can help or hinder the success of feminist activists and women's movements. While parliamentarians consider public opinion because they aim to be re-elected (Kolb, 2007, p 59), the scholarship shows that judges are influenced by public opinion too, as they do not wish to have their decisions altered, overridden, or not enforced (Collins, 2004). Nancy Stearns (1988, pp 5–6), for instance, states:

> The United States Supreme Court does not decide cases in a political vacuum … Supreme Court justices, like other judges, and for that matter, legislators, read the newspapers, listen to the radio, watch TV, and are aware of burning social issues. Their decisions often reflect what at least appears to be the popular consensus about such issues.

If feminists do not have the wider public on their side to push for a reform project, it is challenging to succeed with it. For instance, in Bangladesh, the feminist endeavour to reform family law through the introduction of a Uniform Family Code is presumed to have failed because the feminist demands were primarily perceived as an 'elite' project with no relevance for the 'common' people (Nazneen, 2013).

In shaping public opinion or altering the salience of an issue, media coverage plays a central role and can influence policy-making directly or indirectly (Kolb, 2007, p 62; Fuchs, 2013, pp 206–7). Media reports about particularly outrageous cases can provide 'windows of opportunity' for feminist activism. For instance, in Ireland, media reports about the tragic case of a 14-year-old girl who had become pregnant as a result of rape and was prohibited by the court from leaving the country and undergo an abortion abroad triggered protests and led to an appeal in the Supreme Court and a referendum that broadened women's reproductive rights (Irving, 2008, pp 202 et seq). Similarly, in Colombia, the media reports about a nine-year old Nicaraguan girl who had become pregnant as a result of rape and other 'real-life stories that captured the public's imagination' made the Colombian public more sympathetic to abortion liberalisation and facilitated the

Constitutional Court's decision in 2006, mentioned above (Reuterswärd et al, 2011, p 814).

Zippel (2006, p 213) shows how media coverage of 'scandals' can impact feminist activism. One example that she mentions is Anita Hill's 1991 allegations against the US Supreme Court nominee, Clarence Thomas,[9] in the emerging discourse around sexual harassment:

> The media played a major role in diffusing the concept of sexual harassment and opening these windows of opportunities to raise awareness. Because of the explosive mixture of sex and power, media coverage of scandals reaches national and international audiences. Even if Anita Hill's allegations did not preclude Clarence Thomas's confirmation, her testimony created public awareness across North America and Europe. Many Americans and most Europeans heard the term sexual harassment for the first time during the Hill–Thomas hearings. In the United States, the scandal rejuvenated the anti-harassment movement; a new wave of activists working within institutions lobbied for legal reforms and revisions of workplace policies in the aftermath of the hearings. The incident created a policy opportunity window for promoting the passage of the Civil Rights Act of 1991, even under a Republican president (Zippel, 2006, p 213).

However, media coverage of 'scandals' is not always helpful to the demands of feminist activists. Zippel (2006, pp 78–79) argues that in media reports about sexual harassment, the gendered dimensions to the case often disappear, while debates about 'morality' and the question of whether or not women who make accusations can be 'trusted' come to the forefront and too often women are presented as 'vengeful creatures who prey on innocent politically powerful men for political or financial goals'.

Both public opinion and mass media are external factors to a movement. Yet, the movement may also try to influence public opinion as a part of its larger strategy. For instance, feminist activists seeking to reform family law in Palestine (Shehada, 2013, pp 39–40) and Morocco (Al-Sharmani, 2013, p 96; Ennaji, 2014, p 146), to legalise abortion in Colombia (Reuterswärd et al, 2011, p 814), and to push for laws against sexual harassment in the US (Zippel, 2006, p 71) strategically used the media to raise public awareness, shift dominant frames of discourse, and influence public opinion.

B. Counter-mobilisation

Another factor potentially influencing success in feminist legal activism is the strength of counter-mobilisation in the form of other social movements or organised interests (Derichs & Fennert, 2014). Strong conservative or religious organisations or men's rights groups, for instance, can significantly hinder feminist

[9] Anita Hill was Thomas's subordinate at the US Department of Education and (somewhat ironically) the Equal Opportunity Commission.

success, either because they have a direct impact on legislators and judges or because they manage to shape public opinion and media coverage on an issue area in a way that is obstructive to the feminist agenda.

For example, the early campaign for the legalisation of abortion in the US, while otherwise largely successful in terms of legal change,[10] suffered one complete failure in the mid-1970s with the enactment of the Hyde Amendment, which restricted federal funding for abortions. This was presumably because counter-movements were particularly strong during the debate around the Hyde Amendment, and anti-abortionists dominated the parliamentary debate (McBride Stetson, 2001b, pp 257 and 264). In Morocco (Evrard, 2014) and Egypt (Zuhur, 2014), feminist reform attempts that sought to bring about changes in family law were weakened by Islamic counter-movements which argued that such reforms would lead to 'Westernisation' and destroy the traditional family. Similarly, in Ghana, women pushing for the passing of a domestic violence Act were faced with a counter-movement that portrayed them as purveying 'foreign ideas' that threatened Ghanaian culture and tradition (Manuh & Dwamena-Aboagye, 2013, p 208). Due to this resistance, the sought after law reforms were ultimately passed in a watered-down version and included compromises to ensure that certain sections of society would not feel threatened (Manuh & Dwamena-Aboagye, 2013, p 213). Yet, not all counter-movements seem to be able to hamper feminist activism. Cross-national studies focusing on several European states found that counter-movements were insignificant for a movement's success or failure (Sauer et al, 2007, p 292).

While anti-feminist mobilisation is often organised by conservative, right-wing or religious groups, counter-mobilisation to feminist goals might come from other angles, too. For example, opposition to female suffrage in the US came largely from the liquor and brewing industries, which feared that female voters would favour prohibition (McCammon et al, 2001, p 55). Winning the vote thus became easier once prohibition laws had been passed and that opposition was no longer there (McCammon et al, 2001, p 55).

Regarding feminist litigation, scholarship provides mixed accounts of whether counter-mobilisation hinders the success of women's movements. Manfredi (2004, p 22) stresses in the Canadian context that one phenomenon from which LEAF benefitted was 'the relative absence of opposing nongovernmental interests in its cases'. In a similar vein, O'Connor and Epstein (1983, p 141) partly link the success of the US women's movement in litigation in the 1970s to the relatively low levels of organised third-party opposition (see also Epstein & Kobylka, 1992, p 202). On the other hand, the fact that in the 1980s, the US women's movement faced more opposition seems not to have hindered feminist success in litigation. Instead, women's groups fared even better than in the 1970s (George & Epstein, 1991, p 321). Similarly, the Colombian women's movement was not put off by

[10] The legal achievements were later overturned with the Supreme Court's decision in *Dobbs v Jackson Women's Health Organization*, 597 US 215 (2022).

conservative counter-mobilisation, but instead developed creative litigation strategies to fight back – efforts that found support from the Colombian Constitutional Court, which rejected the petitions on the part of the counter-movements (Ruibal, 2014, p 48). Counter-movements can thus also have a uniting and strengthening effect on feminist activists.

C. Religion

A strong presence of religious groups and a high degree of religiosity among the population can hinder the success of feminist activism. This is because, firstly, religious groups might act as counter-movements to feminist activism; secondly, spokespersons of religious communities might significantly impact the dominant discourse on a particular issue in a way that disadvantages feminist campaigns; and thirdly, religious values broadly shared among a society affect parliamentary law-making and judges' interpretation of those laws. Legal systems that strongly draw on religion and grant religious law a particularly prominent role are also more likely to pass anti-women reservations regarding international human rights laws.

Looking at feminist campaigns to reform divorce and abortion law in Argentina, Brazil and Chile, Htun (2003, pp 7–8) shows that opposition to feminist campaigns from the Roman Catholic Church posed an 'enormous obstacle' to law reforms, with the result that restrictive laws have endured 'in spite of social changes, international pressures, and widespread acceptance of new ideas about gender and the family'. She elaborates on this point as follows:

> Governments may uphold laws conforming to Church doctrine, not always because they agree with it, but because they need the Church's political support. The Church helps the state maintain social control; it also deploys symbols that help to legitimize state rulers and their policies … More liberal policies run the risk of alienating an important political ally. Regardless of their beliefs, many state leaders have been unwilling to risk the Church's wrath by legalizing divorce and abortion (Htun, 2003, p 174).

However, when the relationship between the church and the state is weakened, a window of opportunity might open up for feminists to push for legal reforms because the government has less to lose in such a situation (Htun, 2003, p 23). For instance, in the 1970s and 1980s, Latin American bishops condemned the human rights abuses of the ruling military governments and supported social movements in their fight to end authoritarian rule – a shift in the church–state relationship that opened opportunities for feminist activists (Htun, 2003, pp 23–24).

In assessing whether religious opposition may create a challenge for feminist activists, Htun and Weldon's (2010) distinction between 'doctrinal' and 'non-doctrinal' policies is helpful. Doctrinal policies contradict the doctrine, tradition or discourse of the dominant religious or cultural group – think about (religion-based) family law, the right to abortion and reproductive freedom, or state funding for abortion and contraceptives (Htun & Weldon, 2010, p 210). Feminist campaigns regarding these areas will often face challenges from strong religious groups. Non-doctrinal policies, on the other hand, do not contradict the doctrine, tradition or discourse of the dominant religious or cultural group in the same manner – think about topics such as violence against women, gender employment quotas, child care, or parental leave (Htun & Weldon, 2010, p 210). Feminist campaigns regarding these areas will typically not be challenged as much by strong religious groups.

D. Legal Culture

Another phenomenon that might impact the outcome of campaigns for legal change is legal culture, especially in the narrower sense referring to 'attitudes about law' (Friedman 1975, p 15) or people's 'way of thinking about law' (Cotterrell, 2008, p 721 drawing on Pierre Legrand). In Alan Watson's (1983, p 1154) words, legal culture determines 'the timing, the extent, and the nature of legal change'. Karl Klare (1998, p 168) states: 'Legal culture has a powerful steering or filtering effect on interpretive practices, therefore on adjudication, and therefore on substantive legal development (at least in societies in which adjudication is a significant source of law making)'. '[L]egal culture and socialization', he continues, 'constrain legal outcomes quite irrespective of the substantive mandates entrenched in constitutions and legislation' (Klare, 1998, p 151).

Two forms of legal culture can be distinguished: the 'internal' legal culture of legal professionals (judges, public prosecutors, practising lawyers, legal academics, etc) and the 'external' legal culture of the wider public (Friedman, 1987 [1975]; Nelken, 2014b; Grødeland & Miller, 2015). Internal legal culture includes, for example, parliamentarians' and judges' beliefs about their roles and competencies. External legal culture is related to public opinion about law and legal institutions, for instance, the public's ideas about the law's performance and its role in society (perceptions of the law as just or unjust and the like) and about the efficiency, accessibility, and fairness of legal institutions, their duties, and the limits of their competencies.

Internal and external legal culture can impact the success of feminist legal activism. For example, when judges regard themselves as agents of social change rather than mere mouthpieces of the law (Aguiar-Aguilar, 2020), this opens up opportunities for litigants seeking a change in legal doctrine. Where the public perceives a particular law as unjust, values the rights of vulnerable groups, or strongly emphasises redressing past injustices or strengthening equality and non-discrimination, this helps the feminist endeavour to bring about legal change. On the other hand, a legal culture (internal or external) that does not place a strong focus on equality, non-discrimination, and the rights of the marginalised will provide challenging terrain for feminist legal activism. Scholars have, for example, elaborated how a 'missing culture of anti-discrimination' in Germany has made the German Parliament reluctant to transpose EU directives on anti-discrimination into German law (Wrase, 2020).

Furthermore, where parliamentarians, judges, and society at large believe that the state may only regulate the 'public' realm and is limited in interfering with the more 'private' areas of life, this creates challenges for feminists who seek to bring about reforms in family law or the laws on domestic violence. For instance, in Bangladesh, it was difficult for feminists to push for a new family code, as society perceived religion-based family law as a private issue (Nazneen, 2013, p 115). Similarly, in Ghana, Members of Parliament and religious leaders often interfered with domestic violence cases pending in court, asking that these be amicably settled at home because domestic violence was understood as a private matter not to be dealt with by the state (Manuh & Dwamena-Aboagye, 2013). In Brazil, on the other hand, feminists successfully brought about a domestic violence statute, partly because domestic violence was no longer understood as a private but rather a public issue (De Aquino, 2013, p 181).

Related to the discourse around legal culture is the topic of legal transplants. Examples from Morocco (Evrard, 2014), Egypt (Zuhur, 2014), and Ghana (Manuh & Dwamena-Aboagye, 2013, p 208) show that parliamentarians may be sceptical about passing laws that, in their opinion, do not 'fit' the local culture and judges may be reluctant to base their reasoning on 'foreign' concepts. This can hinder the success of feminist legal activism pushing for law reforms inspired by international human rights law or legal developments in other countries. Scholarship has also shown that in cases where 'foreign' concepts *do* find a way into the local legal system, they are often changed quickly, ignored or misused by state institutions and society at large (Okoth-Ogendo, 1993; Legrand, 1997; Wenzel, 2010, 2014).

Of course, feminist activists can work – and have worked – towards changing legal culture. Despite its relative stability, legal culture, 'like all culture, is a product of the contingencies of history and is always undergoing change' (Nelken, 2014a, p 314). Attempts to change legal culture are closely connected to the abovementioned attempts at changing public opinion.

E. Societal Context in India

(i) Public Opinion and Counter-mobilisation

To judge public opinion and the degree of counter-mobilisation against feminist goals in India, we need to assess different topics individually. Regarding religion-based family law, scholarship shows that while the issue used to be strongly affiliated with ideas of nation-building, national unity and modernity, the gendered dimension became more present over time (Agnes, 2004; Schneider, 2005; Gangoli, 2007). At the same time, the topic of religious personal laws also polarises opinion, as I will elaborate in Chapter four. Counter-mobilisation opposing reforms in family law is very strong and particularly comes from (self-declared) representatives of religious communities.

The topic of violence against women is less polarised, and there is less counter-mobilisation against feminist reform attempts. Yet, the argument that women 'misuse' pro-women laws is powerfully articulated by men's rights groups (Basu, 2015, p 180 et seq) and by some media, as I will elaborate on in Chapter five. Individual cases of sexual assault have regularly generated strong media attention and brought large parts of the public to the streets to protest along with feminists. Such public attention and agitation have often helped the feminist reform campaigns. Yet, as I will show in Chapter five, the public demands that followed particular incidences of sexual assault were often primarily for harsh punishments of the perpetrators and an increase in the minimum sentences rather than for laws that address systemic violence and discriminatory societal structures.

(ii) Religion

Religion plays a central role in Indian law, politics, and society. Sunil Khilnani (2012 [1997], p 59) terms religion and caste 'the antique social identities of India'. While the Constitution, in its preamble, defines the Indian state as secular, the judiciary tends to interpret the freedom of religion (Article 25 of the Constitution) in a broad manner, often trumping the right to equality. The postcolonial Indian state has maintained a system of 'non-interference', according to which it refrains from changing the personal laws of any religious community unless there is a strong demand for reform *from that community* – a principle that is, however, applied with severe inconsistencies (Williams, 2006).[11] I shall elaborate on these aspects in Chapter four.

(iii) Legal Culture

Apart from the strong role granted to religion and religion-based personal law, three aspects of legal culture in India seem particularly noteworthy. Firstly, the idea of the public–private divide was very strong when the Indian women's movement first emerged and is still present. Not only do religious groups and sections of society articulate the demand that the state refrain from interfering in 'private' matters of religion and the family, but state institutions such as the Indian Law Commission and the Indian higher judiciary reiterate this argument regularly, as I will elaborate in Chapters four and five. The most prominent example here is the

[11] Williams (2006, p 10) states that '[t]he use of noninterference by the Indian government – both colonial and postcolonial – was dictated more by political considerations than by any consistent application of the principles of noninterference'. 'Far from reacting to community initiative, noninterference entailed the government responding to external political imperatives and then justifying their policies using the language of noninterference, community demand, and popular support' (Williams, 2006, p 10).

Delhi High Court's infamous reasoning in *Harvinder Kaur v Harmander Singh Chodhury* from 1983 that the

> [i]ntroduction of constitutional law in the home is most inappropriate. It is like introducing a bull in a china shop. It will prove to be a ruthless destroyer of the marriage institution and all that it stands for. In the privacy of the home and the married life, neither Article 21 nor Article 14 have any place (paragraph 33).

Secondly, a strong focus lies on protecting (heteronormative) marriage as a fundamental pillar of society. Scholarship, for instance, shows that judges in family courts often encourage couples who seek a divorce to give their marriage one more chance and advise women to 'reconcile' with their violent partner (Basu, 2015). The legislature has been sceptical towards broadening divorce rights or criminalising marital rape as it was feared this would lead to an erosion of the institution of marriage (on the argument of an erosion of marriage see Agnes, 2011, p 18; 2012, p 338 et seq; Mirchandani, 2017; Rajan, 2019). State institutions often argue that the protection of marriage is in the interest of the broader society. The Indian Supreme Court has, for instance, held that 'society is generally interested in maintaining the marriage bond and preserving the matrimonial state with a view to protecting societal stability' (*Reynold Rajamani v Union of India*, 1982). According to the Indian Law Commission (2009, p 12), the '[p]ublic interest demands … that the married status should, as long as possible, and whenever possible, be maintained'.

Thirdly, external and internal legal cultures are strongly shaped by India's system of legal pluralism (Griffith, 1986; Eckert, 2004; Eberhard & Gupta, 2005). This means that a large segment of the Indian population 'lives and manages its affairs outside the pale of state laws' and state institutions (Agnes, 2011a, p 2). People instead frequently feel bound by non-state normative systems and approach non-state dispute settlement fora in case of conflict (Vatuk, 2005, 2008a, 2008b, 2013; Narain, 2008; Schneider, 2009; Solanki, 2011; Dusche, 2017; Hong Tschalaer, 2017; Kokal, 2020). State organs tolerate (or even support) this co-existence of dispute settlement systems. Shalini Randeria (2003, 2006), therefore, calls the Indian state a 'cunning state' that deliberately chooses to exercise selective and partial sovereignty over its territory and citizens. Gopika Solanki (2011) speaks of a model of 'shared adjudication' according to which the Indian state willingly splits its adjudicative authority with (informal) societal sites. Chapter six will elaborate on this.

V. Conclusion

This chapter has provided an overview about factors that may impact the outcome of feminist legal activism. The table below summarises them. I suggested dividing the various factors into four dimensions: rights, activism, state institutions, and society. There are overlaps between several factors, and some of them influence each other. The following two chapters will engage with specific campaigns that the Indian women's movement has led in the last 50 years, thereby referring to this chapter's analytical framework in explaining which factors have been particularly influential in the Indian context.

Table 1 Factors impacting the outcome of feminist legal activism

Dimension	Impact Factors
Rights: Provisions in the Constitution and directly applicable international law	• Provisions recognising gender equality and anti-discrimination, and courts' interpretation of these (especially with regard to formal vs substantive equality) • Provisions on human dignity, and courts' interpretation of these • Competing rights claims (for instance, rights to religious freedom, cultural rights, rights to dignity/life of the foetus), and courts' interpretation of these
Activism: Characteristics of the social movement and its actors	• Social movement's strength (membership, resources, visibility, unity of the movement, movement actors' expertise) • Strategies (lobbying vs litigation, combination of strategies, outside vs inside strategies, confrontational vs conciliatory strategies, framing, alliances, timing)
State Institutions: Features of the receptors of change: Most importantly the Parliament and the courts	• Powers of the judiciary and access to justice (standing and judicial review, funding for litigation and access to justice, judicial interpretation) • Composition and partisanship of state institutions (parties in power, women in state institutions, feminists in state institutions) • Women's policy agencies (feminist vs symbolic) • International obligations (state's ratification of international treaties, pressure from the international community, international developments)
Society: Factors in the socio-cultural context in which the social movement operates	• Public opinion and media • Counter-mobilisation (for instance by religious/ conservative/ anti-feminist groups) • Religion (religion's role in society, autonomy of religious communities, doctrinal vs non-doctrinal policies) • Legal culture (for example, ideas about the public–private divide, religious law, marriage and family)

4

Marriage and the Family

Family law in India is highly discriminatory. When the women's movement emerged in the 1970s, the laws in place made it harder for wives than for husbands to obtain a divorce. They granted daughters fewer inheritance rights than sons and gave mothers fewer guardianship rights than fathers. Many of these discriminations are still in place today.

Like in other settings, particularly in the Global South, family and inheritance law in India is not uniform for its citizens. Instead, each religious group is governed by its own religion-based, so-called 'personal' laws. Feminists have mobilised actively and vocally against these discriminations for decades.

Looking at the issue through a constitutional lens only, one would assume that the movement has had a good chance of success with its activism. Many personal law provisions discriminate against women and violate the equality provisions in Articles 14 and 15 of the Constitution. Religious freedom, on the other hand, is made subject to other fundamental rights (Article 25). The Indian higher judiciary, with its power to undertake judicial review, could thus strike the discriminatory provisions down as unconstitutional. In addition, the personal law system clashes with the Constitution's directive principle to introduce a Uniform Civil Code (Article 44) and the preamble's emphasis on secularism.

In reality, however, the success of feminist legal activism in this area has so far remained limited. In Indira Jaising's (2022) words,

> [t]oday, the biggest challenge for any feminist lawyer to further equality through the Constitution is the challenge of personal laws. Patriarchy has found its shelter in 'personal laws' immunized from being challenged on constitutional grounds in the name of the right to religion.

Drawing on the success factors listed in Chapter three, this chapter will explain why feminist attempts to reform family law have been limited. I will show that factors related to feminist activism and the societal context were particularly influential.

I will do so by looking at four feminist campaigns, some of which have lasted for several years, some even decades. After a brief introduction of the personal law system in the context of the Indian Constitution (section I), I begin by engaging with the campaign for a Uniform Civil Code that feminist activists led through the 1980s (section II). Secondly, I deal with feminist attempts to reform Christian divorce and inheritance law in the 1980s and 1990s (section III). My third example is the feminist campaign to reform Hindu guardianship and inheritance law in the 1990s (section IV). Lastly, I deal with the feminist campaign to reform Muslim divorce law (section V) before explaining the findings in the conclusion (section VI).

I. Religion-Based Personal Laws in the Indian Legal System

According to the Indian personal law system, Hindus, Muslims, Christians and Parsis[1] are governed by their respective religion-based laws. Sikhs, Buddhists, and Jains, who respectively make up 1.7, 0.7 and 0.4 per cent of the Indian population (census of 2011), fall under the purview of Hindu personal law (see, for instance, Section 2(1)(b) of the Hindu Marriage Act, 1955). While some of these personal laws are codified, others remain customary. Most codified Acts stem from the colonial period and were introduced by the British. They remained in place after India's independence because the Indian Constitution stipulates the continuation of pre-Constitution laws until they are amended or repealed (Article 372).

Personal laws concern matters relating to marriage, divorce, guardianship, adoption and inheritance – traditionally regarded as 'personal' as they relate to the family or personal sphere (Sunder Rajan, 2003, p 148). Besides these different sets of personal laws, the Special Marriage Act of 1954 (a re-enactment of the Special Marriage Act of 1872) operates as an optional secular code of marriage and divorce.

Personal laws may be seen as violating the constitutional right to equality in two ways: firstly, they make different religious communities subject to different treatment, and secondly, they treat men and women within the same religious community differently. An early engagement with the constitutional validity of personal laws occurred in *State of Bombay v Narasu Appa Mali* (*Narasu Appa Mali*), which the Bombay High Court decided in 1952. The Court tested whether the Bombay Prevention of Hindu Bigamous Marriages Act, 1946, which imposed monogamy on Hindus but not on Muslims, discriminated on the grounds of religion. To answer this question, the Court, in a first step, asked whether Muslim men were actually still allowed to practise polygamy or whether, at the moment of the introduction of the Indian Constitution, the *uncodified* Muslim personal law permitting polygamy had also become void because it violated Articles 14 and 15 for reasons of discrimination on the grounds of sex. In this context, the judgment includes a sentence that later became a key reference point but is often

[1] The Parsi community, a group that numerically is so small that the census report only includes it under the 0.7% 'other' communities group (census of 2011), is governed by Parsi personal law. It was the community's strong political and economic significance during the colonial era that enabled it to negotiate for a separate law (Agnes, 2011a, p 84). For a detailed engagement with the history of Parsi law and legal culture see Sharafi (2014). The Parsi legal system will not be dealt with in this study because there has been relatively little activism by the Indian women's movement towards reform in this area.

taken out of context. In the opinion of the judge, both Hindu and Muslim personal laws were not '"laws in force" within the meaning of Article 13(1) and their provisions permitting polygamy would not be void even if it is assumed that they offend against Article 15(1) of the Constitution' (paragraph 21).[2] Consequently, according to the Court, the uncodified permission of polygamy under Muslim personal law was still valid. However, according to the Court, prohibiting polygamy for Hindus was still not unconstitutional, as the state 'may rightly decide to bring about social reform by stages', dealing with one religious community first and another later (paragraph 10).

The judgment somewhat contradicts itself when, on the one hand, it does test an Act that is part of personal laws, the Bombay Prevention of Hindu Bigamous Marriages Act, 1946, against Articles 14, 15 and 25, while at the same time, it states that 'personal laws' cannot be tested against these provisions. The only way to make sense of this is to understand that the Court meant that *uncodified* personal laws could not be tested against fundamental rights while *codified* personal laws could. However, those opposing the challenge of personal laws often overlook this detail and understand *Narasu Appa Mali* as arguing that personal laws generally could not be tested against the Constitution. This is even after the Supreme Court, in an *obiter dictum* in *C Masilamani Mudaliar v The Idol of Sri Swaminathaswami Thirukoli* (1996), had clarified that: 'Personal laws … must be consistent with the Constitution lest they become void under Article 13 if they violated fundamental rights' (paragraph 15). In practice, as the following sections will show, courts have, on several occasions, tested personal laws against the Constitution. Where they refrained from doing so, this was not because personal laws cannot be tested against the Constitution but because the courts held that the legislator should intervene in the matter instead – an argument that is also questionable and will be dealt with later.

International human rights norms are of limited support when challenging religion-based personal law. Indeed, Articles 5(a) and 16 of the Convention on the Elimination of All Forms of Discrimination Against Women (CEDAW) urge

[2] The Court justified this understanding by stating that the provisions in Article 17, which abolishes untouchability, and Article 25(2)(b), which allows the state to make a law to open 'Hindu religious institutions of a public character to all classes and sections of Hindus', would have been unnecessary, had these practices been unconstitutional and void under Article 13 anyway (paragraph 13). Furthermore, the judgment held that Article 44 itself recognised and therefore acknowledged the existence of personal laws (paragraph 13). Neither argument is convincing. Even if one agreed with the argument that Article 44 recognised the existence of the personal law system, this could not be equated with stating that the Constitution attempts to exclude the personal laws from being tested against the fundamental rights. Nor does the explicit outlawing of some discriminatory religious practices (such as untouchability) necessarily mean that other discriminatory aspects cannot be tested against the fundamental rights. The judgment then went on to say that even if one was of the opinion that (uncodified) personal laws were 'laws in force', 'it would be difficult to say that the institution of polygamy would constitute a discrimination against members of one sex only on the ground of their sex', as '[p]olygamy is justified, if at all, on social, economic and religious grounds and hardly ever on grounds of sex' (paragraph 14). This argumentation, too, is not convincing. The fact that a discrimination is 'justified' by its supporters for cultural reasons cannot exempt it from the test of constitutionality.

the states parties to eliminate discrimination against women. However, India has made far-reaching declarations stressing that the state may refrain from interfering with personal laws.

Feminists and women's rights activists have, therefore, primarily had recourse to the constitutional provisions, particularly Articles 14, 15 and 21, but also to the principle of secularism and Article 51A (fundamental duties of Indian citizens) to make their claims. Opponents of legal change in family law – primarily religious groups – have frequently drawn on the right to freedom of religion and the doctrine of non-interference to argue against any interference in the domain of personal laws. The challenge for the feminists was to argue that the freedom of religion must not override gender equality. Indira Jaising, for instance, states:

> There is a failure to understand that religion is not a right but a freedom, that is, the freedom of conscience. We all have the right to believe what we must; what we don't have is a license to act in a discriminatory manner (Jaising, 2022).

In the following sections, I will show how successful the feminist campaigns were with their struggle around family law.

II. 'Living with a Medieval Concept of Family Law': The Campaign for a Uniform Civil Code

One of the early campaigns that was widely supported by feminist organisations emerging in the 1970s was the call for a Uniform Civil Code that would replace the personal law system. The UCC was a central aim of the women's movement in the 1980s and was upheld as a goal by some organisations until the mid-1990s (when it was largely given up as a feasible goal). In these early decades of feminist activism, women's groups, feminist scholars, and journalists not only called the legislature to action but also drafted model codes themselves. Ultimately, however, feminists were unsuccessful in their goal. As this section will show, this was primarily due to the wrong strategies: The UCC was too big a project; the confrontational strategy that the movement used was counterproductive; and with the right-wing Bharatiya Janata Party (BJP) also arguing for a UCC, the movement had the wrong 'ally' on its side.

A. 'Towards a Uniform Civil Code'

For the nascent women's movement in the late 1970s and early 1980s, the discriminatory aspects of the personal law system were a key concern. Despite demands for a UCC dating back to pre-independence times (Menon, 2012, p 151) and Article 44 calling for a Uniform Civil Code, no UCC had been introduced in the years after independence. Hindu personal law had been reformed in the 1950s but still contained discriminatory provisions. So did Christian and Muslim personal law, which had largely remained unchanged since colonial times.

The media and the public discourse had engaged extensively with the Uniform Civil Code. Still, this discourse revolved mainly around the topics of nationhood, secularism, minority rights and modernity, thereby largely ignoring the gendered dimension that the personal law system had (Agnes, 2004; Baird, 2005; Gangoli, 2007). Furthermore, the critique of personal laws essentially concerned Muslim personal law, but not the other personal law systems (Agnes, 2004; Schneider, 2005). The general impression was that with the reform of Hindu law, Hindu women had already achieved equal treatment, while Muslim personal law was still 'backward' and discriminatory (Agnes, 2004; Schneider, 2005).

The protagonists of the early women's movement of the 1970s and 1980s, for the most part, understood themselves as secular and sought to achieve gender equality through secularising society and the law. The demand for the Uniform Civil Code fitted into this secular agenda. The resolution of the National Conference of Women's Groups that took place in Mumbai in 1985, for instance, stated:

> [P]ersonal laws have meant inequality and subordinate status of all women in relation to men. We, therefore, must strive for a civil code where all women get rights, equal to men in matters of marriage, divorce, maintenance, custody, inheritance, property, adoption and other such matters. Women's organisations should strive to get adequate representation in framing these laws (Conference resolution, reprinted in Saheli, 1986a).

Similar statements were repeated by various feminist activists and women's groups in the following years.[3]

In its approach, the campaign for the UCC was highly confrontational and critical towards not only religion-based personal law but religion per se. Saheli (1986b), for instance, stated that 'most religions are products of a less developed society, and to implement religious codes of conduct which might have been appropriate at some point of time would be to negate all growth and development and would be regressive'. The introduction of a UCC would mean that women would no longer have to 'live with a medieval concept of family' (Saheli, 1986b). To strengthen its point on the outdatedness of religion-based family law, the organisation drew a parallel between religious family law and religious criminal law, which had been in place before the British colonisers introduced the Indian Penal Code in 1860. Just as nobody would demand any longer that a criminal be punished

[3] Madhu Kishwar (1986b, p 13), for instance, wrote in 1986, in *Manushi*: 'We should urgently proceed to draft a uniform secular code available to all in this country'. In the same year, Saheli (1986b) expressed its 'demand for an Equal Family Law which should be the same for all communities'. The Joint Women's Programme (1986) regarded the UCC as 'the only way by which equal rights can be given to the oppressed 50% of the total population of India' and 'an important step towards the removal of communal disharmony'. Likewise, the Forum Against Oppression of Women (1989) found that family and inheritance law 'should be removed from the realm of the "religious" and "personal" and be governed by a uniform, secular and non sexist civil law'.

according to *Sharia* law – '[n]obody promotes chopping off of limbs' – it would be unreasonable to ask for different standards when it came to family law (Saheli, 1986b). Similar lines of argumentation can be found in Dhagamwar's work (1989, pp 53 et seq) and publications of the Working Group on Women's Rights (1996).

The movement pursued its goal of introducing a UCC through different strategies. One strategy included informing, educating, and raising awareness about personal laws' flaws. Several women's groups produced articles or newsletters that pointed to the discriminatory aspects of the personal law system and described the UCC as a solution (Saheli, 1986b, 1995, 1997a; Forum Against Oppression of Women, 1989). Feminists articulated their thoughts in newspapers and magazines (Kishwar, 1993, 1994; Karat, 1995). Women's groups and activists also used poster campaigns to visualise the importance of the topic, depicting women as strangled and burdened by religion and religion-based and other laws.[4]

The aspect of framing that I elaborated on in Chapter three played a vital role. In a context in which the debate around personal laws and the UCC largely revolved around issues of nationalism, secularism and modernity, women's rights activists attempted to re-frame the discourse in a two-fold manner. Firstly, they sought to emphasise the gendered dimension of the personal laws. The organisation Jagori (n.d.), for example, bemoaned the fact that in the 'tug-of war between communal interests, the real issue gets lost. And the real issue is the rights of women'.[5] Secondly, feminists and women's groups attempted to disrupt the notion that only Muslim personal law was archaic and anti-women, and pointed out that all sets of personal laws contained discriminatory provisions. For instance, the Forum against Oppression of Women (1989) held that: '*All* personal laws have a deep sexist bias which comes from very basic patriarchal assumptions and conceptual frameworks' (emphasis added). And the Joint Women's Programme (JWP) (1986) argued: 'Though these laws are different for different communities, they have one common thread running through them and that is giving religious sanction to the subordinate position of women'. Feminists often repeated that despite the improvements that the reforms in the 1950s[6] had brought about, Hindu law was still far from providing equal rights to men and women (Kishwar, 1986b, 1994; Saheli, 1986b; Karat, 1995; Kapur & Cossman, 1996, p 101).

The second strategy that feminist activists used was that of legislative lobbying. Women's organisations, academics, and civil society groups made recommendations and drafted model codes, some of which were also forwarded to the

[4] Many posters are reprinted in the book *Our Pictures, Our Words: A Visual Journey Through the Women's Movement* by Laxmi Murthy and Rajashri Dasgupta (Murthy & Dasgupta, 2011) and on the website of *poster women*, a project by Zubaan to visually map the Indian women's movement through the posters the movement had produced; available at: www.posterwomen.org/.

[5] Similar statements were made by the Working Group on Women's Rights (1996) and by commentators in *Economic and Political Weekly* (Bano, 1995).

[6] The Acts passed were the Hindu Marriage Act, 1955, the Hindu Succession Act, 1956, the Hindu Minority and Guardianship Act, 1956, and the Hindu Adoptions and Maintenance Act, 1956.

government (Forum Against Oppression of Women, 1989; Agnes, 2011, p 177; Jagori, n.d.). The JWP (1986) described this strategy as follows:

> As a women's organisation we have been concerned about a uniform civil code for several years and have sent recommendations to the Law Ministry with signatures demanding it. We have conducted group meetings and discussions with people, specifically women in rural areas, urban slums, colleges and institutions in all parts of the country with the intention of finding out the feelings of the public regarding this matter.

One such model code was developed by the Forum Against Oppression of Women (1989). The code provided, among other aspects, that marriage should be a dissolvable contract between two consenting adults; both parties should jointly own all property acquired after marriage; the wife should have an unconditional right to reside in the matrimonial home; the husband should not be permitted to sell the marital home without the wife's consent; and divorce should be possible through mutual consent or at the initiative of one party in cases of irretrievable breakdown of the marriage. The organisation also suggested provisions on lump-sum settlement and post-divorce maintenance. It stressed that whenever possible, the maintenance to be paid by the husband should be directly deducted from his salary. Furthermore, the state should provide divorced women and their children with housing and other basic amenities and offer crèches to working women's children.

B. Rethinking Strategies: Why the Campaign for the UCC Failed

The 1980s were a period full of optimism when feminist scholars and women's rights activists were confident that a Uniform Civil Code would become a reality soon. A Muslim feminist journalist I interviewed, for instance, remembered:

> There was a lot of excitement because we really thought that this [UCC] was about to come into existence. And there was a lot of pressure from Muslim women, particularly, who had been the victims of the law … By the 80s, we really thought that we would end the decade with reforms (Interview with the author on 5 September 2014).

Yet, the women's movement's campaign for a UCC remained unsuccessful. Several Bills were introduced into Parliament (Agnes, 2011, pp 172 et seq). The Supreme Court called for introducing a UCC in several decisions and reminded the legislator of its responsibility under the directive principle of Article 44 of the Constitution.[7] Still, ultimately, Parliament did not enact a UCC. I see two reasons

[7] For example, in *National Textile Workers v PR Ramkrishnan* (1982), the Court stressed that Article 44, along with other directive principles, should be 'implemented either by the Legislature or by the Executive'. In *Mohamed Ahmed Khan v Shah Bano Begum* (1985), the Court held that it is 'a matter of regret' that Article 44 'has remained a dead letter'. In *Jordan Diengdeh v SS Chopra* (1985), the Court pointed to the 'urgency of infusing life into Art. 44' and described the lack of a Uniform Civil Code as a 'totally unsatisfactory state of affairs'. In *Sarla Mudgal v Union of India* (1995), the Court bemoaned

for the failure of the feminist campaign. The first one lies in the social context of the women's movement, and the second is related to the movement's activism.

(i) Societal Context: The BJP and the 'Communalisation' of the Debate

The socio-political context and the 'communalisation' of the debate around personal laws made it difficult for feminists to be successful in this area. Indeed, the women's movement was not the only actor that called for a UCC. So did the BJP. This put feminists and women's rights activists in a dilemma, as, for the most part, the movement did not want to be affiliated with the BJP and other Hindu nationalist forces. As one activist from the organisation Saheli (interview with the author on 29 September 2014) remembered:

> So, [the] women's movement's position at that point of time [in the early and mid-1980s] was that we want a uniform civil code … But we were clear that when we are saying 'uniform civil code', it meant that it gives equal rights to men and women … That was our understanding, til the terminology was co-opted by rightist forces … Obviously, their agenda and [the] women's movement's agenda were different.

Women's rights activists and groups were, therefore, keen to clarify that the code they envisioned differed significantly from the one the BJP aimed at. They argued that while feminists had a secular, gender-just UCC in mind, the BJP's project would be disguised as secular but infiltrated with Hindu nationalist values. In an attempt to disassociate themselves from the BJP's project, some women's groups changed their terminology, dropping the word 'uniform' and now speaking of a 'common', 'gender-just', or 'egalitarian' civil code (see, for instance, Saheli, 1995, 1997a) or explicitly referring to a 'uniform, secular and non sexist civil code' (Forum Against Oppression of Women, 1989).

Yet, despite pointing to the demarcation lines between the feminist project and the BJP's endeavour, feminists faced opposition from opponents of the BJP and from other feminist groups. Saheli (1986b), for example, stated:

> Our demand for an Equal Family Law which should be the same for all communities has many opponents … We are told that we are encouraging Hindu communalist forces which are also demanding a Uniform Civil Code! We are told that we are fanning

that the '[r]ulers of the day', were apparently 'not in a mood to retrieve Article 44 from the cold storage where it is lying since 1949'. And in *John Vallamattom v Union of India* (2003), the Court called on the Parliament to 'step in for framing a common civil code in the country'. While at first sight, these calls for a UCC would seem to indicate that the Supreme Court took the topic seriously, a deeper analysis shows that they can hardly be seen as an outcome of the feminist campaign. Notably, the judges rarely drew on the aspect of gender equality, but instead frequently seemed to base their pro-UCC agenda on anti-Muslim stereotypes. In addition, comparing these cases with cases in other areas of law also makes the calls for a UCC seem like mere rhetoric that was never met with concerted action. Its reluctance to exhibit more concrete action shows that it did not prioritise the matter. For an in-depth engagement with this matter, see Herklotz (2016).

> communal tensions! That we don't care for the rights of minority communities! That we will cause this country to disintegrate!

This tense political climate was born from the controversy surrounding the case of *Mohamed Ahmed Khan v Shah Bano Begum* in 1985, in which the Supreme Court had applied a secular provision to grant maintenance rights to a Muslim woman after divorce – a decision that met with fierce opposition among the Muslim community, since Muslim personal law does not recognise post-divorce maintenance beyond the three-month *iddat* period. The political tensions in the years after this judgment peaked with the destruction of the Babri Mosque in December 1992 and the riots that followed. According to the Muslim feminist journalist that I interviewed, this moment was the turning point, after which feminists could no longer hold on to their earlier pro-UCC position:

> [T]he real landmark change came with the demolition of the Babri Mosque because that was suddenly a sort of a stop … [T]he women were more bothered about the larger political security than security at home … All the organisations who retreated did a lot of soul searching: What had gone wrong? How do we re-strategise? … And it was at that particular time that a new discourse came out … And from then on, nobody [among the women's movement] has ever picked that [the UCC] up. And it has remained a call only of the Sangh Parivar[8] (Interview with the author on 5 September 2014).

Similarly, a Saheli activist (interview with the author on 29 September 2014) told me:

> As part of Saheli, I can say that all of us were actually addressing the communal situation more than the issue of personal laws per se … In a situation of highly increased communal violence, it really became difficult to raise the issue of personal laws in the manner that we were raising it til [the] mid-1980s … So the last pamphlet that we brought out was in 1996 because after that, surely the issue of personal laws … went into the background. Because we got into some other kinds of issues, or maybe we didn't know how to handle it.

As a consequence of these developments, which coincided with the concept of intersectionality gaining importance, feminist activists and women's groups began to revise their position, and a large number of them gave up the idea of a UCC as a feasible option. The same Saheli activist (interview with the author on 29 September 2014), for example, stated:

> At that point of time [in the 1980s], we were actually not talking so much of religious identities. We were looking at women's rights in a secular framework … But post [the] mid-80s and as the turn happened around [the] 1990s, that secular space started shrinking. And within that shrinkage of space, it became difficult to argue for one code which is based on gender equality.

From the mid-1990s onwards, the feminist demand for gender equality was then de-linked from the demand for a UCC. In 1995, Brinda Karat, the then general secretary of the All India Democratic Women's Association, which had initially

[8] The Sangh Parivar ('family of organisations') is a group of organisations that includes the Rashtriya Swayamsevak Sangh and affiliated organisations which draw on a Hindu nationalist ideology.

supported a UCC, held that '[g]ender justice and the fulfilment of constitutional guarantees of equality need not necessarily be linked to an umbrella legislation' (Karat, 1995). In a similar fashion, the feminist scholar Kumkum Sangari (1995, p 3386) opined in *Economic and Political Weekly* that: 'What can potentially unite women is not a uniform civil code but a common understanding of patriarchies and common aspirations'.

(ii) Activism: Wrong Strategies

Another hindrance to the feminist campaign was that the UCC was simply too big a project. In Chapter two, I mentioned that feminist projects tend to be more successful when they pursue their goals step by step, by seeking small reforms that the system can handle. With the UCC, Indian feminists aimed at a massive legislative intervention, without proposing a central plan on what this legal change would look like. Although several draft codes were developed by different organisations and academics, there was no agreement on one version of the code. On a large scale, it remained unclear whether only issues related to marriage and divorce should be included or whether topics such as violence against women or women's economic rights should also be addressed.

Secondly, the confrontational rhetoric that many women's groups used was counterproductive. As stated above, the movement positioned itself in opposition to religious law and religious communities. They not only called religious personal law regressive ('medieval') but also pushed back against the powers and privileges of religious communities. The resolution passed at the National Conference on Women, Religion and Family Law in 1989, for instance, held: 'We demand that the state stop aid grants and withdraw tax exemptions to religious trusts' (Saheli, 1989). This approach could not win support from the spokespersons of religious communities. There was almost no conversation[9] with representatives of the religious clergy. Consequently, feminist groups had no allies among the religious communities.

Yet, the feminist campaign for a UCC has not been without any effect. The feminist focus on gender (in)equality found its way into the media and the public discourse around the topic. While earlier, the debate revolved primarily around issues of nationalism, identity, and secularism, over time, the issue of gender equality became more prominent. Also, while the media in the 1980s focused mainly on Muslim personal law when it engaged with the discriminatory aspects of the personal law system (depicting Muslim personal law as 'inhumane', 'backward'

[9] The advances by the Joint Women's Programme are an exception here. As Jyotsna Chatterji (n.d.-a) describes, in 1978, the JWP along with the Christian Institute for the Study of Religion and Society organised a national conference on the 'Plea for a Uniform Civil Code' in Bangalore, at which representatives of the Christian and Muslim communities were present. The meeting, however, did not bring about any agreement on the issue of the UCC. In 1982, Chatterji organised another national consultation on the theme of 'Authority of the Religions and the Status of Women' to further discuss the issue of the UCC with representatives from various religions; but her suggestions met with opposition, most importantly from the All India Muslim Personal Law Board (Chatterji, n.d.-a, p 2).

and 'pre-modern'), the media coverage from the early 2000s onwards has been more differentiated and the media have tried to avoid sweeping negative collective attributions of Islam and Muslims (Schneider, 2005).

After giving up the idea of a compulsory Uniform Civil Code, feminist activists made several different suggestions on how to reform the family law system. Some organisations focused on the idea of an optional gender-just civil code. According to this concept, the personal law system was to remain in place, but in addition, a gender-just UCC would be applicable as 'an option for those who wish[ed] to be governed by it' (Jagori, n.d.).[10] Others suggested that the uniform code would be the default option, but people should be able to opt out if they wanted to be governed by personal laws (Working Group on Women's Rights, 1996, p 1182). Yet, this suggestion was criticised by some feminists, who stressed that the 'option' to choose between secular and religious laws would benefit only a limited number of women. 'Given the present imbalance of power and resources', most women would practically be excluded from such an option to choose, and the law would 'remain ineffective' (Saheli, 1997a).

The new position that gained a foothold throughout the 1990s was to keep the personal laws in place but gradually reform the different sets of personal laws (Rahman, 1990; Monteiro, 1992; Bano, 1995). Flavia Agnes and her Mumbai-based organisation, Majlis, were prominent pro-speakers of this position. In Agnes' (2001, p 3973) view, 'small and significant reforms within the personal laws governing minority communities have greater relevance to minority women than the rhetoric of an all-encompassing and overarching Uniform Civil Code (UCC) with its communal undertones'.

III. 'Shedding the Century-Old Shackles': The Campaign for Reforms in Christian Personal Law

A second area where the Indian women's movement pursued legal activism – both legislative lobbying and litigation – was Christian personal law. The movement was partly successful: it achieved some High Court judgments deciding in favour of the feminist position and critical law reform with the passing of the Indian Divorce (Amendment) Act in 2001. These goals were, however, only reached after two decades of legal activism, and only partly reflected feminist thought. This section will focus on two aspects of Christian personal law that the feminist campaign addressed: The regulation of divorce under Section 10 Indian Divorce

[10] While, in some ways, such an optional code had already been introduced with the Special Marriage Act of 1954, the idea here was to broaden the scope of the Act. Ideas for an optional code included the broadening of the concept of the family to include homosexual relationships and couples living together without being married and to ensure women's rights in cases of sexual violence, labour rights and social security benefits (Working Group on Women's Rights, 1996, p 1182; Menon, 1998, p 258).

Act, 1869 (IDA) and inheritance law under the Travancore Christian Succession Act of 1916.

A. Christian Divorce and Inheritance Law

In the early 1980s, when the women's movement's campaign on Christian personal law began, Indian Christians were governed by an array of different laws that had been introduced during the colonial period, primarily to regulate the marital affairs of the British living in India and those Indians that had converted to Christianity. While some of this legislation was applicable throughout most of the Indian state (the Indian Christian Marriage Act, 1872, the Indian Divorce Act, 1869 and the Indian Succession Act, 1925), there also existed several local acts, such as the Travancore Christian Succession Act, 1916 and the Cochin Christian Succession Act, 1921, which applied to Christians living in the former princely states of Travancore and Cochin, which today form part of Kerala and Tamil Nadu.

Divorce was regulated in Section 10 of the Indian Divorce Act. The provision stated that a husband could petition for the dissolution of marriage on the ground, among others, that 'his wife has been guilty of adultery'. However, for a wife seeking a divorce, the husband's adultery would not suffice as a reason. Instead, she had to prove other circumstances besides her husband's adultery, such as cruelty on the husband's side, desertion for a minimum of two years, or marriage with another woman. The law thus granted men wider rights than women and thereby discriminated against women. The law also meant that women who had been 'deserted' by or experienced violence at the hands of their husbands but whose partners had not been adulterous were not eligible for divorce.

Early court decisions nevertheless held that Section 10 IDA was constitutional. The Madras High Court, for instance, in 1953 ruled that the provision did not constitute discrimination based on sex because it was based on the different *consequences* that adultery by men and women had: a wife's adultery may lead to pregnancy and make her husband the legitimate father of the child, obliging him to maintain a child which is biologically not his (*Dr Dwaraka Bai v Professor Nainan Mathews*, paragraph 30). A husband's adultery would not have such consequences for his wife (ibid). For the Court, the 'obvious' consequence followed that the divorce rules in place were not discriminatory (ibid). The courts largely followed this precedent until 1995 (Subramanian, 2014, p 254).

The situation regarding the inheritance rights of Christians in India was slightly more complicated. Matters of succession were governed either by the provisions of the Indian Succession Act of 1865 (re-enacted in 1925) or by other local laws. One such local Act was the Travancore Christian Succession Act of 1916. Sections 24, 28 and 29 of the Act declared that when a man died intestate (ie without leaving a will), his daughter was not entitled to the same share of his property as her brother(s) but would receive a quarter of the allocation of a son or 5,000 Rupees, whichever was less. The provisions thus granted daughters lesser rights than sons and thereby discriminated against women.

The Indian Law Commission suggested reforms to Christian personal law twice: in its 15th report, from 1960, and its 90th, report from 1983 (Law Commission of India, 1960, 1983a). Yet, no immediate action was taken by the government or the legislature. The Supreme Court, too, refrained from interfering in this area, holding that it was 'the business of the legislature and not of the courts' to regulate the matter (the Supreme Court in *Reynold Rajamani v Union of India*, 1982). At the same time, the Court stated that maintaining marriages (even through rigid divorce laws) was in the interest of society at large. It held: 'It cannot be denied that society is generally interested in maintaining the marriage bond and preserving the matrimonial state with a view to protecting societal stability' (ibid.).

From the early 1980s onwards, feminists and women's rights activists began to critique Christian personal law's discriminatory aspects and to demand change. The Joint Women's Programme, headed by Jyotsna Chatterji, played a vital role in this campaign, which began in 1983 (Subramanian, 2014, p 226; Chatterji, n.d.-a). Chatterji's (1984a, p 11) opinion was that 'Christian Personal Law in its various aspects is outdated, irrelevant and inhuman. It does not meet the needs of the present century' and therefore needed reform.

Regarding divorce, Chatterji (1984a, pp 10–11) suggested that Section 10 IDA 'should be struck down', the fault theory should no longer be applied, and divorce grounds should be made the same for women and men. Regarding inheritance law, she recommended replacing the various Acts and customary laws with a common gender-just Succession Act for all Christians (Chatterji, 1984a). She propagated the idea that the Travancore Christian Succession Act 'should be struck down as inhuman and discriminatory. A daughter should have as much right to the property of her parents as the son' (Chatterji, 1984a, p 11). To Chatterjee, the reform of the Christian personal law was not in conflict with the goal of the UCC, which at this time was still widely shared, but would instead provide 'the first prerequisite towards a Uniform Civil Code' (Chatterji, 1984a, p 12).

B. Legislative Lobbying

As with the call for the UCC, the first strategy in the campaign for a reform of Christian personal laws was to inform, educate, and raise awareness about the discriminatory aspects of the law and the need for reform. In 1984, the JWP brought out a booklet entitled 'Changes in Christian Personal Law' with a collection of short papers by activists, academics and members of the Indian Law Commission that demanded specific changes (Chatterji, 1984b). Closely linked to information dissemination was the actual act of lobbying for legal change. Chatterji (n.d.-b) elaborates that, from the early 1980s onwards, 'JWP has been continuously lobbying for change in the [Christian personal] Law by holding meeting[s] of Christian women, lobbying with several Prime Ministers and Law Ministers'. This lobbying process involved drafting new Bills, directly contacting politicians, and a public campaign for law reform. Later, part of the lobbying campaign was 'to telephone the Law Ministry once every month ever since February 1994 and request the Joint Secretary to place the matter before the Law Minister' (Chatterji, n.d.-a).

In contrast with the campaign for a UCC, the Joint Women's Programme ensured it involved the Christian clergy in its campaigns. The JWP initiated a process of lobbying and consultations with the churches, out of which, by the mid-1990s, three draft Bills emerged: the Christian Marriage Bill, 1994; the Indian Succession Amendment Bill, 1994; and the Christian Adoption and Maintenance Bill, 1994. Section 31(1) of the Christian Marriage Bill suggested the introduction of equal divorce grounds for men and women. Section 33 provided for the 'dissolution of broken marriages' when the couple had lived separately for two years or more and mutually agreed that the marriage should be dissolved. Chatterji sent the three draft Bills to the Prime Minister on 12 December 1995. In the letter that accompanied the Bills, she stated:

> The Christian community in India has been very anxious to amend their existing Christian Personal Laws and [has] therefore prepared a fresh set of legislations ... These new legislations are supported by churches of all denominations ... We will be much obliged if this consensus is considered and the Christians in India get new legislations on the basis of the proposed bills (Chatterji, 1995).

Notably, the letter presents the Christian churches as allies in the reform project. It also speaks about '[t]he Christian community in India' as the demander of change, rather than JWP, the women's movement, or Christian women. Chatterji attached to her letter several statements by church officials supporting the reform project.

Other than in the campaign for the UCC, Chatterji and her organisation, as well as other groups calling for a reform in Christian personal law, mostly refrained from criticising Christianity or religion as such. Instead, their central argument was that the Christian personal law was a foreign product imposed on Indian society by the British colonisers and that the mores and norms had changed significantly since the making of the law. Flavia Agnes (1986, p 11), for instance, stated:

> The Christian Personal Laws, which were framed exclusively for the benefit of our colonial rulers, reflect a rigid Victorian code of morality. What is baffling about them is that they have remained unchanged in our statute books for over a century and what is more significant – 40 years after independence!

Similarly, Chatterji (1984a, p 10) said:

> [T]he *Indian Christian Marriage Act* 1872 should be brought up to date. This Act was made by the British to suit their policies ... The Indian Church must not be governed by the rules laid down by the English law.

At times, spokespersons also used Articles 14 and 15 of the Indian Constitution (Chatterji, 1984a, p 7) as well as international human rights law, such as CEDAW (*Kali's Yug*, 2000, p 49), as reference points to call for reforms.

Despite the movement's campaign and the Law Commission's report demanding changes in Christian personal law, there was no response from either the government or the Parliament to the movement's demands throughout the 1980s and 1990s. Instead, it was the courts that stepped in first, albeit reluctantly.

C. Litigating for Inheritance Rights

Besides lobbying for better laws, individual women and women's groups used litigation at the High Courts and the Supreme Court to push for legal change. One of the women whose case became famous was Mary Roy.

Mary Roy was a member of the Syrian Christian community in Kerala. After her father died in 1959 without leaving a will, Mary Roy, as per the Travancore Christian Succession Act, was denied an equal share of the familial property and thus decided to challenge the constitutionality of the Act. Later, she recalled how she made this decision:

> My mother and brother arrived in Ooty with several *goondas* (goons) and ordered me to vacate my father's cottage in which I had been living with my children ... It was then that I first heard about the Travancore Christian Succession Act which denied daughters any share in intestate property. I refused to leave the cottage. There was nowhere to go. On a salary of Rs. 350 there was no question of renting rooms in Ooty. So it would have to be a court action. The court would have to be the Supreme Court. The action would have to be a plea for my constitutional right to equality. I was confident of securing justice from the government of Kerala and the Union of India. I knew I had a good case (Roy, 1999, pp 210–11).

Due to a lack of support, limited financial means, and her reluctance to affront her community, Roy's court action was only realised much later.

> When I needed help everyone laughed at me. No lawyer would accept my brief. So, 25 years later, when I was economically independent, and therefore unconcerned about 'what people would say', I travelled to Delhi and found a lawyer who filed a public interest litigation suit in the Supreme Court. And so in 1984, I challenged the Travancore Christian Succession Act as violative of my constitutional right to equality (Roy, 1999, p 211).

The lawyer Roy found in Delhi was Indira Jaising, the feminist lawyer and activist who would later found the Lawyers Collective Women's Rights Initiative. Jaising (2011, p 356) later stated about her client:

> Mary Roy refused to succumb to an unfair legal regime ... Armed only with an unshakeable belief in equality, she approached the Supreme Court for justice ... [T]ogether we worked for making the right to equality a reality for her.

Roy used a writ petition under Article 32 of the Constitution to challenge the constitutional validity of the Travancore Christian Succession Act in front of the

Supreme Court. In court, Roy argued that the respective sections granting daughters lesser inheritance rights than sons discriminated against women and violated Articles 14 and 15 of the Constitution. Feminist journals reported about the case, holding that it was 'of great importance' and that '[m]ore such cases need to be filed challenging the various discriminatory laws' (*Manushi*, 1984).

Mary Roy's case was a fight for a broader cause. According to newspaper reports from the time, Roy was not primarily interested in the money she would be granted if she won, but brought the case to the court 'because she couldn't stomach the injustice meted out to her' and sought to better the situation for other women (Pillai, 1986, p 149). Roy is quoted as saying: 'It is the common Christian girl exploited by her family while she works as a nurse in the Gulf or as a teacher in north-eastern states or becomes a nun, who will benefit from the judgment' (Pillai, 1986, p 149). Later, Roy stated: 'I took the matter to court to establish a principle' (Roy, 1999, p 211).

In its judgment, the Indian Supreme Court struck down the Travancore Christian Succession Act (*Mary Roy v State of Kerala*, 1986). However, contrary to what Roy had expected, the Court did not declare the Act unconstitutional because it violated Articles 14 and 15 of the Constitution. Instead of engaging with the gender dimension of the Act, the Court decided that with the coming into force of the Part B States (Laws) Act, 1951,[11] the Travancore Christian Succession Act, 1916 stood repealed. Intestate successions of the members of the Indian Christian community were now governed by the Indian Succession Act of 1925 (ibid). With this observation, it became 'unnecessary to consider' whether the sections that had been challenged were unconstitutional (ibid). Thus, while *Mary Roy* clarified a legal situation and benefitted those Christian women who were in similar situations to that of the petitioner, women's rights activists articulated some dissatisfaction with the fact that the Court had not dealt with the gender dimension at all (Jaising, 2005b, p 6; Agnes, 2011, pp 146–47).

D. Litigating for Divorce Rights

Around the same time as Mary Roy's court challenge to Christian inheritance law, several other women approached the courts to broaden Christian women's divorce rights by having Section 10 IDA struck down as unconstitutional. Their first attempts were, however, unsuccessful. While benches of the Kerala, Bombay and Andhra Pradesh High Courts, as well as the Supreme Court, engaged critically with the Christian personal laws and held that legal amendments to the Indian

[11] Section 6 of the Part-B State (Laws) Act provided that if immediately before 1 April 1951 there was in force 'in any Part B State any law corresponding to any of the Acts or Ordinances now extended to that state, that law shall … stand repealed'. The Court held that the Travancore Christian Succession Act was such a law 'corresponding' to the Indian Succession Act.

Divorce Act were constitutionally imperative (Subramanian, 2014, p 255), they refrained from declaring the law unconstitutional.

For instance, in *Jordan Diengdeh v SS Chopra* (1985), the Supreme Court held that:

> We suggest that the time has come for the intervention of the legislature in these matters to provide for a uniform code of marriage and divorce and to provide by law for a way out of the unhappy situations in which couples like the present have found themselves.

Yet, it did not hold that Section 10 as it then stood violated the constitutional equality provision. In *Swapna Ghosh v Sadananda Ghosh* (1988), the Calcutta High Court even held concerning Section 10 IDA that: 'it is difficult to understand as to why this provision shall not be held to be discriminatory on the ground of sex alone and thus to be ultra vires Article 15 of the Constitution'. Still the Court limited itself to stating: 'We are inclined to think that our Parliament, or the State Legislatures … should very seriously consider the question of introducing … amendments' (paragraph 2).

The cases of Mary Sonia Zachariah and EJ Ammini (in the Kerala High Court) and Pragati Varghese (in the Bombay High Court) brought about some new developments. In their fight against Section 10 IDA, the plaintiffs got the support of different Christian organisations and women's groups, including the Indian Federation of Women Lawyers and Majlis. The plaintiffs argued that Section 10 IDA, by providing lesser rights to women than to men, violated Articles 14 and 15 of the Constitution. They further contended that since the provision compelled a woman to live as the wife of a man who treated her cruelly or who had deserted her and thus to live a 'sub-human life', the provision violated the right to live a life in dignity, guaranteed by Article 21 of the Constitution (see, for instance, *Pragati Varghese v Cyril George Varghese*, paragraph 5).

In *Mary Sonia Zachariah v Union of India*, the Kerala High Court in 1989 issued an interim order directing the government to decide within six months on whether and how it would act on the recommendations of the Law Commission's 90th report for making amendments to Section 10 IDA. When the government did not act accordingly, a full bench of the Kerala High Court in 1995 decided again on the matter, combining the cases of Mary Sonia Zachariah and EJ Ammini. Here, the Court held that to deny a Christian woman the right to divorce in a case where her marriage has broken down irretrievably due to her husband's desertion or cruelty would be wrong, since compelling her to live

> as the wife of a person whom she hates and considers as the wrecker of her married life can only be treated as highly unjust, unfair and oppressive and as such arbitrary and violative of the rights guaranteed under Articles 14 and 21 of the Constitution of India (*Mary Sonia Zachariah*, paragraph 26).

In addition, the Court also held that by making divorce harder for Christian women as compared to women of other religious communities, the law would differentiate solely on the grounds of religion and would, therefore, violate Article 15 (*Mary Sonia Zachariah*, paragraph 36). Concluding, the Court stated:

> We would accordingly sever and quash the words 'incestuous' and 'adultery coupled with' from the provision in Section 10 of the Act and would declare that Section 10 will remain hereafter operative without the above words' (*Mary Sonia Zachariah*, paragraph 47).

Without these words, the Act stipulated that the wife may petition for the dissolution of marriage on the ground that her husband had been guilty of adultery, cruelty, or desertion.

While the decision to strike down parts of the Act because they violated Articles 14, 15, and 21 of the Constitution was a much more significant step than previous judgments had made, it is interesting here that the Court did not regard the law as discriminatory because it treated Christian men and women differently, but because it treated Christian wives differently from wives governed by other personal laws. On this basis, the Court saw the law as conflicting with Article 15. The Court mentioned Article 14, but its reasoning about a violation of the right to equality between men and women remained imprecise: it simply described the Act as 'highly unjust, unfair and oppressive'.

After *Mary Sonia Zachariah*, other High Courts, including the High Courts of Bombay, Delhi, and Karnataka, issued similar judgments. In 1997, in *Pragati Varghese v Cyril George Varghese*, the Bombay High Court struck down parts of Section 10 IDA as violative of Articles 14, 15 and 21 of the Constitution. It further held that 'the legislature should intervene and carry out suitable amendments to "the Act" at the earliest' (*Pragati Varghese*, paragraph 56). In its reasoning, the Court explicitly referred to the reform process initiated by the Joint Women's Programme and Jyotsna Chatterji:

> In 1983, Mrs. Jyotsna Chatterjee [*sic*], Director of [the] Joint Women's Programme ..., mobilised community support and a memorandum signed by around ten thousand members was sent to the Law Ministry demanding changes in the personal law ... After arriving at a consensus [a] draft Bill on Christian Personal Laws was submitted to the Prime Minister and the President along with supportive letters from different churches and organisation[s]. But despite this systematic and organised community initiative the government did not introduce the Bill in Parliament. The fact that [the] government has not bothered to take any steps in the mailer [*sic*] clearly indicates the lack of concern on the part of the government to reform Christian Personal Law (*Pragati Varghese*, paragraph 30).

The legislator only reacted in April 2000, when the then Law Minister, Ram Jethmalani, invited church leaders, Christian Members of Parliament, feminist activists, and others to discuss the Minister's proposed Christian Marriage Bill. The Parliament passed the Bill in August 2001. The Indian Divorce (Amendment) Act, among other significant changes, made adultery and desertion independent grounds for divorce and introduced the remedy of mutual consent divorce (Section 10A). It also amended the title of the Indian Divorce Act, 1869 to the Divorce Act, 1869.

E. Evaluation

The impact of the feminist campaign vis-à-vis Christian personal law can be described as partly successful. Courts have (albeit reluctantly) stuck down the most discriminatory aspects of Section 10 IDA, and with the passing of the Indian Divorce (Amendment) Act in 2001, the Parliament removed the most discriminatory provisions and introduced an option for divorce on mutual consent. Agnes (2011, p 73), therefore, considers the story of the reform of Christian personal law as an example of successful women's rights activism: 'Christian women finally succeeded both in legal battles within courts as well as in their negotiations with the church and the State, to shed the century-old shackles under which they had been burdened for well over a century'.

The factors that seem particularly influential here are related to feminist activism, particularly the strategies chosen by the movement and its cultural-political environment.

Firstly, compared with the UCC, the reform of Christian personal law was a much more modest goal. Christian personal law affected a much smaller percentage of the population. The campaign did not suggest abandoning Christian personal law altogether but simply reforming specific aspects of it. This aligns with Gelb and Palley's (1982, pp 10–11) finding that single-issue reform attempts that do not challenge the status quo are often easier to achieve than broad reform attempts that challenge existing power configurations.

Secondly, it was a wise strategy of the feminist groups to bring the Christian clergy on board the reform attempts. Unlike in the campaign for the Uniform Civil Code, feminists did not work in opposition to the religious leaders but in collaboration with them. The Christian churches also supported some of the litigation. For instance, in *Mary Sonia Zachariah*, two of Kerala's important reformed orthodox churches and Christian reform organisations were involved in the case and requested that the Court strike down parts of Section 10 IDA (Subramanian, 2014, pp 255–56).

Thirdly, in contrast to the campaigns for a UCC, feminists used a different framing in this campaign. Activists and women's organisations did not pit religion against gender equality but spoke about a joint reform project supported by the Christian community. They frequently stressed that Christian personal law had been made by and for the British colonisers in India and that Indian Christians were now ready to give themselves a new set of rules. They could thereby portray the reform of Christian personal law as an act of shaking off the colonial baggage that India was still carrying.

Fourthly, feminist activists presumably also benefitted from what Waylen (2007) calls 'sympathetic insiders' in the system. Ram Jethmalani, the then Law Minister who proposed the Christian Marriage Bill of 2000, which Parliament passed in 2001, was the father of Rani Jethmalani, an activist lawyer who had passionately engaged in the struggle to broaden women's rights. Rani Jethmalani, the founder of WARLAW and the magazine *Kali's Yug* ('the age of Kali', Kali is the Hindu goddess of time, death and destruction), had been critical of personal laws. This connection might have impacted her father's decision to take up the issue as a Law Minister.

We must, however, also see the failures and shortcomings in the movement's campaign in this area. The legislation process took almost two decades – a fact that Chatterji (n.d.-a) strongly bemoans. Until the mid-1990s, the High Courts were reluctant to declare discriminatory provisions unconstitutional. When they finally did, they based their decisions on comparing the situation of *Christian* women with *non-Christian* women, not on comparing the rights of Christian *women* with those of Christian *men*. In the *Mary Roy* case, the Court did not have to engage with the gender dimension of the case, as it struck down the problematic norm because the laws enacted by the erstwhile princely states had been repealed. Legislature and judiciary have used arguments of 'non-interference' and separation of powers to justify their inactivity. Both seem to be fig leaves to cover their failure to fulfil their constitutional duty and declare discriminatory laws unconstitutional, rather than consistently applied concepts.

IV. 'Family Stability Rests on Gender Inequity': The Campaign for Reforms in Hindu Personal Law

Despite the reforms of Hindu personal law in the 1950s, several discriminatory aspects remained. Feminists in the 1980s and 1990s were active in pointing out that while Hindu law was 'commonly considered to be progressive', in reality, it contained an 'inbuilt prejudice against women' (Forum Against Oppression of Women, 1989).[12] They thereby attempted to broaden the view from a focus on the personal laws of the religious minorities to including the laws of the majority community. This section focuses on two aspects of Hindu personal law in which feminists suggested reforms: guardianship law and inheritance law.

A. Hindu Guardianship Law

Section 6 of the Hindu Minority and Guardianship Act, 1956 (HMGA) provided that:

> The natural guardians of a Hindu minor … are—
>
> (a) in the case of a boy or an unmarried girl – the father, and after him, the mother: provided that the custody of a minor who has not completed the age of five years shall ordinarily be with the mother;

[12] See also Madhu Kishwar (1994), who stated that the reforms of Hindu law in the 1950s had created 'the false notion that Hindu women now have equal legal rights, which is far from being the case'. Similarly Saheli (1997c) opined that: 'Though Hindu personal laws have been extensively reformed … inequalities persist in certain key areas'.

(b) in the case of an illegitimate boy or an illegitimate unmarried girl – the mother, and after her, the father;
(c) in the case of a married girl – the husband.

The word 'after' in Sections 6(a) and (b) HMGA was generally understood as meaning after the father's or mother's death. In *Jijabai Vithalrao Gajre v Pathankhan* (1970), for instance, the Supreme Court held that 'normally when the father is alive he is the natural guardian and it is only after him that the mother becomes the natural guardian'. Section 6 HMGA thus treated fathers differently from mothers, married minor girls differently from married minor boys, and children of parents who were married differently from those whose parents were not. This violated the right to equality.

Like the campaign for reforms in Christian personal law, feminists called for law reforms and used the courts as vehicles for reform. A resolution passed at the National Conference on Women, Religion and Family Law in 1989, for instance, held:

> We feel that there is an inherent sexist bias in all the existing laws that make the father the natural guardian of the child. This bias must be removed and both the father and the mother should be recognised as the natural guardians of the child (resolution reproduced in Saheli, 1989).

The first prominent court action was initiated by Neela Deshmukh and the organisation *Manushi* in 1986, who filed public interest litigation before the Supreme Court challenging the constitutionality of the HMGA. The petition (reproduced in *Manushi*, 1986) argued that Section 6(a) HMGA violated Articles 14 and 15 of the Constitution as it granted the father broader rights than the mother and thus discriminated on the grounds of sex. It further held that the distinction between 'legitimate' and 'illegitimate' children in Section 6(a) and (b) HMGA violated Articles 14 and 15, as it discriminated on the grounds of birth and reinforced the 'prevalent social injustice by assigning primary responsibility for an illegitimate child to a woman' (*Manushi*, 1986, p 35). The petition also argued that Section 6(c) HMGA, which made husbands the natural guardians of their minor wives without making wives the guardians of their minor husbands, discriminated against women on the grounds of sex and, therefore, again, violated Articles 14 and 15 (*Manushi*, 1986, p 35). The petition requested 'that the said provisions be declared null and void' and that the Court declare both parents of a minor child, whether they were married or unmarried, to have 'equal rights to be considered natural guardians of the minor, in preference to any other person, including the spouse of the said minor' (*Manushi*, 1986, pp 34–35).

The case of Neela Deshmukh and Manushi, however, remained unsuccessful. Although in 1998, the Indian Law Commission, in its 133rd report, had recommended that changes be made to the Hindu guardianship law (Law Commission of India, 1989), the Court was not impressed by the petition. According to Madhu Kishwar's discussion of the unreported judgment, the case developed as follows:

> After nearly eight years of being buried in oblivion, this writ petition came up in the Supreme Court on January 12, 1994 before a bench consisting of Justice Kuldip Singh

> and Justice Yogeshwar Dayal. Apart from summarily dismissing the writ petition, the judges made some derogatory comments as well. Justice Kuldip Singh repeated several times that this was 'luxury litigation' as it was filed by a women's organisation and by the woman who had the custody of the children at the time of filing the petition, and hence the petitioners could have no grievance … [The judges] insisted that articles 14 and 15 promising gender equality were inapplicable as there was no gender discrimination involved in this case … The judges declared that in practice they were sympathetic to women but if they persisted in coming to the court and asking for too many amendments, sympathy for women would go away (Kishwar, 1994, p 20).

Yet, a few years later, another claimant succeeded with a court case against Section 6 HMGA. In January 1995, the novelist Githa Hariharan filed a petition to challenge the constitutionality of Section 6 HMGA. Hariharan had applied to a bank for a bond in her minor son's name. The bank had denied her application because only the father, as the natural guardian, was entitled to make such an application. Hariharan (1999)

> discovered that though I am an adult citizen of India, a working, tax-paying citizen, a wife and a mother – all things acceptable and respectable – I am still not considered the 'natural guardian' of my child … [I]f I wanted to sign as my child's guardian, I would have to produce a certificate from a competent authority to prove that my husband was 'unfit'; or that he was dead; or that he had taken to vanaprastha.[13]

As in Mary Roy's case, here, too, it was Indira Jaising who appeared in support of the petitioner to argue that Section 6 HMGA discriminated against women and therefore violated the Constitution's equality provision.

In 1999, in *Githa Hariharan v Reserve Bank of India*, the Supreme Court decided that Section 6 of the HMGA must be reinterpreted. The Court made references to the gender equality provisions in the Indian Constitution as well as to international human rights law like the Universal Declaration of Human Rights (UDHR) and CEDAW (*Githa Hariharan*, paragraph 1). It acknowledged that 'the cry for equality and equal status' was present worldwide (ibid, paragraph 1). The Court further stressed that '[w]e, the people of this country gave ourselves a written Constitution, the basic structure of which permeates equality of status and thus negates gender bias' (ibid, paragraph 2). The judgment then posed the question of whether, against the backdrop of the Constitution's equality provision, it was 'justifiable to decry the rights of the mother to be declared a natural guardian' (ibid, paragraph 16).

Ultimately, however, the Court refrained from declaring Section 6 HMGA unconstitutional and limited itself to reinterpreting the provision. It held that Section 6 HMGA 'on a plain reading … depicts that the mother's right to act as a natural guardian stands suspended during the lifetime of the father' (ibid,

[13] *Vanaprastha* literally means 'to give up the worldly life' and refers to a concept in Hindu tradition, according to which a person withdraws from worldly responsibilities to focus on his or her spiritual development.

paragraph 18). Yet, by looking at the legislative intent ('[t]he whole tenor of the Act of 1956 is to protect the welfare of the child') and interpreting the provision in the light of the Constitution ('gender equality is one of the basic principles of our Constitution'), the Court opined that 'the word "after" would not necessarily mean after the death of the father' but rather 'in the absence of', be it a temporary or a permanent absence or a 'total apathy of the father towards the child or even inability of the father by reason of ailment or otherwise' (ibid, paragraphs 14–25).

While the interpretation that 'after' means 'in the absence of' benefitted women, it did not grant them equal rights to men. Even after *Githa Hariharan*, in cases where the husband was present, he and not the mother was the child's 'natural guardian'. The Court could indeed have gone further and, for instance, struck down the words 'unmarried' and 'after him' altogether so that the norm would have stated that the natural guardians of a Hindu minor are the father and the mother. Feminist scholars have criticised it for not taking this route (Jaising, 2005b; Agnes, 2011, p 147). Discriminations in Section 6(b) and (c) HMGA also remained, as the Court did not engage with these provisions. In addition, the judgment also made remarks about gender relations that heavily draw on gender stereotypes. It was, for example, the understanding of the Court that 'nobility and self-denial coupled with tolerance mark the greatest features of Indian womanhood' (*Githa Hariharan*, paragraph 1).

In conclusion, one may say that Githa Hariharan was an important decision, as it altered Hindu women's rights, but it remained limited in its scope.

B. Hindu Inheritance Law

A second area of Hindu law that feminist activists criticised as discriminatory was inheritance law. This was mainly for two reasons. Firstly, Section 4(2) of the Hindu Succession Act (HSA)[14] exempted from its purview significant interests in agricultural land, which was governed by different tenurial laws of the states, many of which denied women equal rights (Agarwal, 2002, p 8). Such discrimination in the states' tenurial laws was possible because the Indian Constitution provided under Article 31B that none of the Acts mentioned in the Ninth Schedule of the Constitution could be declared void on the ground that they violated fundamental rights and all the major tenurial laws had been placed on the Ninth Schedule (Agarwal, 2002, p 8).

Secondly, Hindu succession law drew on a concept of 'coparcenaries', according to which specific property was owned by a 'joint family', ie an extended family or household. Under patrilineal systems like the *mitakshara* system, only men were

[14] Section 4(2) HSA stated that 'nothing contained in this Act shall be deemed to affect the provisions of any law for the time being in force providing for the prevention of fragmentation of agricultural holdings or for the fixation of ceilings or for the devolution of tenancy rights in respect to such holdings'.

given full rights in this joint family. This meant that coparcenary property was shared between a father, his sons, and his son's sons, etc, not his daughters or their sons and daughters. When a son was born, he acquired a right to the coparcenary property equal to that of his father. The father remained entitled to act as manager or *karta* and had power over income and expenditure. Section 6 HSA acknowledged this system when it stipulated that when a male Hindu died having an interest in a *mitakshara* coparcenary property, 'his interest in the property shall devolve by survivorship upon the surviving members of the coparcenary and not in accordance with this Act'. Conversely, women had a right to *stridhan* (or *stidhana*), female-owned and inherited property. In contrast to coparcenary property, which usually consisted of land property, *stridhan* included gifts made to a woman by her natal family or others.

Feminist scholars and activists campaigned actively to reform these provisions, demanding for Hindu women 'an equal share in the family property' (Anklesaria, n.d., p 13) and 'women's ownership and control of land' (Agarwal, 1994, p 468). In short, activists called for three significant changes in the law: firstly, they demanded equal rights of daughters in tenurial laws – a goal that could be achieved by way of deleting Section 4(2) HSA (Kishwar, 1988; Agarwal, 1994, 2002; Saheli, 2005a).

Secondly, activists demanded that men's advantages resulting from the *mitakshara* coparcenary system be abolished (Agarwal, 1994; Sivaramayya, 1997; Agarwal, 2002; Saheli, 2005a; Kishwar, n.d.). Here, feminists often referred to positive examples from state-level legislation that had abolished the concept of joint family holdings or had granted women the right to coparcenary (Agarwal, 1994, p 478; 2002, p 29) and referred to the 'Towards Equality Report', which had already demanded abolition of the *mitakshara* coparcenary in 1974 (Committee on the Status of Women in India, 1974, p 136).

Thirdly, feminists demanded that the law make it impossible to exclude daughters from an equal share in inheritance (Kishwar, 1986a, 1988; Forum Against Oppression of Women, 1989; Sivaramayya, 1997; Saheli, 2005a). They suggested that wills that exclude daughters from inheritance rights and documents in which daughters waive their right to property in favour of their brothers or other relatives should be considered void (Kishwar, 1986a; 1988; Forum Against Oppression of Women, 1989). In Kishwar's view, strengthening inheritance rights for daughters was also a means to diminish the dowry problem. 'If women's inheritance rights were to become real', she stated, 'dowry in its present form would almost certainly disappear' (Kishwar, 1988, p 13).

Feminists fought a long and cumbersome struggle. Resistance to the reform suggestions was often based on the fear that broader inheritance and property rights would break up the family. Bina Agarwal (2003, p 201), one of the protagonists in this campaign, for example, recalled that in 1989, after she had given a presentation on Hindu inheritance law, 'the then Minister of Agriculture exclaimed: "Are you suggesting that women should be given rights in land? What do women want? To break up the family?"'. She explains: 'What this statement effectively implied was that family stability rests on gender inequity which women, once they have property, may be unwilling to tolerate' (Agarwal, 2003, p 201).[15]

Yet, ultimately, the feminist campaign was successful. Hindu succession law was amended quite significantly. In 1997, the Ministry of Rural Areas and Employment set up a Committee for Gender Equality in Land Devolution in Tenurial Laws under the chairpersonship of Bina Agarwal to work out reform suggestions for the rules governing the inheritance of agricultural land (Agarwal, 2002, pp 28–29). The Committee's report recommended full gender equality in the devolution rules and detailed which changes were needed in the existing tenurial laws (Agarwal, Sivaramayya, & Sarkar, 1998).

In 1999, the Indian Law Commission conducted research to suggest reforms to the national legislation regarding succession (Agarwal, 2002, p 29; Subramanian, 2014, p 188). The Commission sent out questionnaires to NGOs and individuals in which they asked the respondents' opinions on a wide range of issues, including the possibility of bringing agricultural land under the purview of the HSA and either doing away with joint family property altogether or making daughters coparceners on the same basis as sons (Agarwal, 2002, p 29). The majority of respondents favoured the dissolution of *mitakshara* coparcenaries, the limitation of testamentary rights, the invalidation of land tenure laws that discriminated against women, and the extension of equal rights to daughters in the ancestral home (Subramanian, 2014, p 189).

Yet, the Law Commission's (2000b) report ignored the public preferences, and its recommendations remained 'limited and conservative' (Agarwal, 2002, p 29). For instance, although 81 per cent of the respondents had favoured the abolition of discriminatory tenurial laws, the report made no recommendations in this direction (Agarwal, 2002, p 29). Similarly, instead of recommending the complete abolition of joint family property, which many respondents had supported, the Commission recommended that daughters be included as coparceners (Agarwal, 2002, p 29).

Based on the Law Commission's recommendations, the Law Ministry developed a Bill presented to the *Rajya Sabha* in December 2004 (Subramanian, 2014, p 190). The Bill met with opposition from feminists, who demanded further reforms. In January 2005, 47 women's groups and other rights organisations sent all parliamentarians a memorandum with reform suggestions (Subramanian, 2014, pp 190–91). The memorandum demanded that agricultural land be brought on a par with other property by deleting Section 4(2) HSA, that *mitakshara* coparcenary property be abolished, and that the right to will away one's property be restricted so that daughters could not be excluded from inheriting (Saheli, 2005a).

[15] We see this understanding that inequality should be tolerated to keep marriages intact also in other cases. In *Madhu Kishwar v State of Bihar*, the Supreme Court, in deciding about discriminatory tribal laws, held that it 'would rather … refrain from striking down the provisions' to not 'bring about a chaos in the existing state of law'. And the Delhi High Court in *Harvinder Kaur v Harmander Singh Chodhury* (1984), which I cited in Chapter 3, stated that the 'leading idea' of the provision on the restitution of conjugal rights (Section 9 of the Hindu Marriage Act) is 'to preserve the marriage', a goal that according to the Court was central to the 'well-being of the nation' (ibid, paragraph 1).

The Bill was further amended in response to the memorandum (Saheli, 2005a). In September 2005, the Parliament passed the Hindu Succession (Amendment) Act. The women's organisations had been successful with most of their demands. The Act abolished Section 4(2) HSA and thus brought all agricultural land on par with other property (Section 2). This meant that Hindu women's inheritance rights were equal to men's across Indian states. Furthermore, the Act allowed daughters to become coparceners and made them subject to the same rights and liabilities as sons (Section 3). Feminist groups and activists found that the Act opens 'immense opportunities' for women (Saheli, 2005b) and that '[b]oth economically and symbolically, the Act has the potentiality of enhancing the woman's status within her natal family' (Agnes, 2011, p 40).

Yet, a few flaws remained. For instance, the Act did not abolish *mitakshara* coparcenary property altogether. Nor did it provide a limit to bequeathing one's property. The organisation Saheli thus worried that

> given the Indian social context of the prevalence of gender biases towards son[s] and against daughters, there remains the possibility of families/men actively disinheriting women through their will, and thus negating all the achievement[s] of this amendment process (Saheli, 2005b).

C. Evaluation

Overall, we can say that the feminist campaigns for reforms in Hindu guardianship and inheritance law achieved some critical success. Significant achievements were made with *Githa Hariharan* and the Hindu Succession (Amendment) Act of 2005, although some flaws remain, and in both areas of law, the reforms were achieved relatively late.

As in the case of Christian personal law, feminists made small and specific demands rather than challenging the system as a whole. This strategy was successful. Feminist campaigns regarding Hindu personal law had some advantages compared to the campaigns regarding Christian and Muslim personal law. For the Hindus as the majority religious community, the personal law system was less tied to religious identity. Therefore, law changes were not perceived as threatening the community's autonomy. With Bina Agarwal, the campaign for reforms in Hindu inheritance law had a prominent spokesperson with much expertise on the issue, which impacted the legislative debates in a significant way. A strategy that turned out to be successful was the collaboration of different groups. When the Bill to reform Hindu succession law was introduced into Parliament, the memorandum that 47 organisations had signed made it possible for the legislative process to be postponed, and the groups were successful in impacting the law-makers so that ultimately, some of their demands were taken up in the law that Parliament passed in 2005.

V. 'A System that Favours Men, will not be Changed by Men': The Campaign for Reforms in Muslim Personal Law

Like Christian and Hindu personal law, Muslim personal law also contained discriminatory provisions. The husband's right to polygamy and unilateral divorce and the concept of *nikah halala* (in-between marriage) are key examples of where the women's movement has been actively campaigning for change. This section will focus on the husband's right to divorce by triple *talaq*.

A. 'Three Seconds' Divorce

One particularly discriminatory aspect within Muslim personal law was the Muslim legal tradition of the husband's right to divorce by triple *talaq*. *Talaq* is divorce at the husband's initiative, and three different modes of this form of divorce are usually distinguished: *talaq-e-ahsan, talaq-e-hasan*, and that discussed here, *talaq-e-biddat* or triple *talaq*. All three divorce forms require the husband's pronouncement of the word 'talaq' towards his wife. However, while in the former two forms of *talaq*, there is a defined period between the first pronouncement and the point at which the divorce becomes effective, in triple *talaq*, the three pronouncements of *talaq* are effected in one go, and the divorce is effective immediately.[16] Triple *talaq* is, therefore, also referred to as instant divorce or oral divorce – although *talaq* can also be pronounced in writing.

While from a gendered point of view, all forms of *talaq* were problematic, as the right to divorce through *talaq* was only granted to the husband and not to the wife,[17] the feminist movement in its campaign focused particularly on triple *talaq*, which often went hand in hand with the wife being thrown out of the house from one moment to the next without a place to go. According to a survey that the Muslim women's organisation Bharatiya Muslim Mahila Andolan (BMMA, 'Indian Muslim women's movement') conducted in the mid-2000s, 78 per cent of the divorced Muslim women that BMMA spoke to had been divorced through

[16] For a detailed engagement with the practice of *talaq* see, for instance, Vatuk (2005). Notably, triple *talaq* is not legally accepted among all but only some Muslim communities; in particular it is perceived as legally valid by *Sunni* Muslims of the *Hanafi* school.

[17] While the Muslim wife cannot dissolve her marriage with the same ease as her husband, she can initiate an extrajudicial divorce by *khul*. In this procedure, she asks her husband to release her from the marriage in return for a consideration; typically she offers to forfeit her *mehr* (a form of dower) along with her right to maintenance during the *iddat* period (roughly three months from the day of the divorce). Furthermore, the Dissolution of Muslim Marriages Act, 1939, granted a Muslim woman a right to obtain a decree for the dissolution of her marriage on the grounds of her husband's polygamy, adultery, imprisonment, impotency, cruelty or failure to maintain her for two years, or when the husband has been missing for four years (Section 2).

instant triple *talaq* (BBC, 2017a). While this survey is not necessarily representative, it is true that triple *talaq* divorces were widespread.

Triple *talaq* is not explicitly regulated in the codified law. The only provision that mentions *talaq* is Section 2 of the Muslim Personal Law (Shariat) Application Act of 1937, which states: 'Notwithstanding any custom or usage to the contrary, in all questions … regarding … dissolution of marriage, including talaq … the rule of decision in cases where the parties are Muslims shall be the Muslim Personal Law (Shariat)'.

During the colonial era, courts that dealt with *talaq* generally held that the practice was 'good in law, though bad in theology' (Bombay High Court, *Sarabai v Rabiabai*, 1905, paragraph 7). This meant that although it was 'condemned in the Koran and in the reported sayings of the Prophet', this would 'in no way, affect the legal validity of a divorce duly effected by the husband' (Madras High Court, *Asha Bibi v Kadir Ibrahim Rowther*, 1909, paragraph 4). The courts in colonial times generally allowed *talaq* divorces in a vast array of circumstances (Serajuddin, 2015; Dequen, 2016). They held that even a *talaq* pronounced under compulsion or in jest was valid (Bombay High Court, *Saiyid Rashid Ahmad v Mussammat Anisa Khatun*, 1931); that the husband, to pronounce a valid *talaq*, did not have to show any reasonable cause for the divorce, but could pronounce it at his mere whim and caprice (Calcutta High Court, *Ahmad Kasim Molla v Khatun Bibi*, 1931); and that *talaq* was valid even if it was pronounced in the absence of the wife (ibid). This route was followed in Indian courts after independence. In 1968, for instance, in *Pathayi v Moideen*, the High Court of Kerala held that:

> The only condition necessary for the valid exercise of the right of divorce by a husband is that he must be a major and of sound mind at that time. He can effect divorce whenever he desires. Even if he divorces his wife under compulsion, or in jest, or in anger that is considered perfectly valid. No special form is necessary for effecting divorce under Hanafi law …; the husband can effect it conveying to the wife that he is repudiating the alliance. It need not even be addressed to her (paragraph 2).

From the early 1980s onwards, courts slowly gave up this understanding. In 1981, the Gauhati High Court argued that *talaq* was only valid if there was a reasonable cause for the divorce and if it was preceded by unsuccessful attempts at reconciliation between the husband and wife (*Jiauddin Ahmed v Anwara Begum* and *Mustafa Rukia Khatun v Abdul Khalique Laskar*). The courts, however, refrained from declaring triple *talaq* (or other provisions of Muslim personal law) unconstitutional.

B. Quran and Constitution

While Muslim women's activism against *talaq* dates back to pre-independence times (Subramanian, 2014, p 212), systematic campaigns for reforming Muslim personal law and abolishing triple *talaq* as a vital part of these started in the 1980s. Street campaigns and *talaq mukti morchas* ('movements for the liberation from *talaq*') were launched in various cities (see for instance Shikhare, 1986). The campaigns gained impetus with the founding of Muslim women's rights organisations in the 1990s and 2000s, which I described in Chapter two. These campaigns aimed to abolish triple *talaq* either through the intervention of the judiciary declaring triple *talaq* unconstitutional, or through law reform explicitly outlawing the practice.

In these early feminist campaigns, demands for reforms within Muslim personal law were closely linked to the call for a Uniform Civil Code – much as in the campaign for reforms to Christian personal law. As several interviewees told me, the curtailment of some of the rights of Muslim men via a reform of Muslim personal law was seen as a first step towards a UCC. This changed in the 1990s when feminists essentially gave up the idea of a Uniform Civil Code as a feasible option. The focus of Muslim feminists was then on keeping Muslim personal law in place but making it more gender-just.

The legislator, however, was reluctant to act according to the feminist demands. Muslim personal law has undergone remarkably little legislative change until 2017. The only significant reform in Muslim personal law was the introduction of the Muslim Women (Protection of Rights on Divorce) Act, 1986, which, however, was not a reaction to feminist reform campaigns but an attempt by the Indian government to undo the Supreme Court's judgment in *Shah Bano* and to maintain the status quo of Muslim personal law.

One of the central organisations in the struggle against triple *talaq* was BMMA. The organisation, along with several other groups,[18] has led a vocal campaign against the practice of triple *talaq* (BBC, 2017a) and has been involved in drafting a Muslim family law code. BMMA's project to draft a 'Quran-based Muslim personal law upholding the principles of gender justice enshrined in the Holy Quran' began in 2007, after a national consultation held in Mumbai in December 2006 had shown that a large number of Muslim women were in favour of a codification of Muslim personal law (Niaz & Soman, 2015, p 52). A member of BMMA in Mumbai described to me the drafting process as follows:

> We had 300 to 400 consultations, … largely with women, because we felt that women are victims of discriminatory law, and it is important that the victim has a say in what the law should be. Then we had consultations … with different kinds of groups: with judges, with lawyers, with village people and with women. It took us seven years – 2007 to 2014 – and multiple consultations. We came up with this [draft law]. It really reflects the aspirations of Muslim women … So that's a unique aspect of the law. We made it

[18] Among the other groups who campaigned for changes in Muslim personal law were the All India Muslim Women's Rights Network, Awaaz-e-Niswaan, the Muslim Women's Forum, the Committee for the Protection of the Rights of Muslim Women, STEPS, the Progressive Muslim Association and the Hindustani Muslim Forum (Subramanian, 2014, p 222). Besides the demands to abolish triple *talaq*, the organisations called for reforms in several other areas of law, including maintenance rights, polygamy and inheritance rights in agricultural land. The groups also requested the inclusion of women in prayer groups and mosque councils, and the establishment of separate mosques for women. For an elaborate discussion see Subramanian (2014, pp 222–23).

> into a public document last year, in 2014. … [I]t's a document we want people to accept … as a law. Because in the absence of a codified law, what do people follow? People follow *sharia* laws written by … jurists of the 19th century … How is our law different from that law? In fact, our law is better because it's come out of a wider consultation. It is based on the values of equality and justice, which are, heart of hearts, the Indian constitution as well as part of the Islamic value system (Interview with the author on 29 December 2015).

According to BMMA, women had to take their destiny into their own hands here because the 'men are not victims of retrograde practices and hence don't understand the need to change a system that is so tilted in their favour. A system that favours men will not be changed by men' (Niaz & Soman, 2016).

The draft code strengthened the rights of Muslim women in multiple ways.[19] It made oral triple *talaq* illegal and stipulated that *talaq-e-ahsan* was the preferred form of divorce. It required a mandatory arbitration during a 90-day period and made the *qazi* (the judge in a Sharia court) accountable for violations of the provisions on *talaq*. The statement of objects and reasons of BMMA's Draft Muslim Family Act held that:

> [I]n the absence of a codified law, customary practices which are divergent from the values and principles of the Quran have emerged. New codes have been introduced globally with the hope that they will introduce the rule of law in family matters and end arbitrariness and variances in judicial decisions. In India there is a need to have a comprehensive codified family law to ensure justice within the family. This Act, based on the values and principles of the Quran as prescribed in the Quranic verses, is to consolidate, clarify and codify the provisions of Muslim law (Niaz & Soman, 2015, p 136).

BMMA sent its draft code to the Prime Minister of India, several ministries, the National Commission for Women, and the National Commission for Minorities. In its letter to the Prime Minister from November 2015, the organisation advertised its code, stating that 'just as Hindus, Christians and Parsis have their own personal laws, Muslims too must have their own codified Muslim personal law which ensures equality and dignity to Muslim women' (Bharatiya Muslim Mahila Andolan, 2015). The organisation maintained that the discrimination that Muslim women faced was in 'clear violation' of Articles 14, 15 and 21 of the Indian Constitution (Bharatiya Muslim Mahila Andolan, 2015). It further argued that

[19] The draft code stipulated a minimum age of marriage (18 for women and 21 for men) and made the registration of marriages compulsory. It held that the consent of both parties to the marriage was to be obtained without force or fraud. It further stipulated a minimum *mehr* equivalent of one year's salary of the groom to be paid at the time of the wedding. The draft code made polygamy illegal. According to the code, both the mother and father were the natural guardians of their children. The draft code held the husband responsible for paying his wife's maintenance during the marriage, even if the wife had an independent source of income. After divorce, maintenance was to be granted as per the Muslim Women's (Protection of Rights on Divorce) Act of 1986. The draft code also granted daughters an equal share in inheritance.

since '[a]lmost all Muslim countries' had codified their personal laws, India was not to drag behind (Bharatiya Muslim Mahila Andolan, 2015).

Similarly, as in the campaign for reforms in Christian personal law, the Muslim activists here also argued that an outdated personal law system needed reforms to benefit the Muslim community. They referred to 'justice within the family' rather than to women's rights or 'gender justice' and based their call for law reform on both the Indian Constitution and Quranic principles. They also compared the situation in India to that in other countries, where Muslim personal law had already undergone reforms, making personal law reform a question of modernity and part of an international reform process. They also pointed out that gender equality would ultimately benefit not only Muslim women but also Muslim men. Two members of BMMA, for instance, stated that '[t]he routine discrimination of women affects everyone' (Niaz & Soman, 2016). Personal laws only appear 'on the surface' to be in favour of men but are actually 'detrimental to them' (Niaz & Soman, 2016).

To support its call for codifying Muslim personal law, BMMA also held public hearings and collected about 50,000 signatures calling for a ban on triple *talaq* (BBC, 2017a). The organisation also conducted and published several studies, among them a survey that showed that 92 per cent of the Muslim women who had participated were in favour of a ban on triple *talaq*, and 83 per cent were in favour of a codification of Muslim personal law (Niaz & Soman, 2015). In addition, BMMA, the All India Muslim Women's Personal Law Board, and the Women's Research and Action Group in Mumbai developed model *nikahnamas*, ie binding Islamic marriage contracts that outline the rights and responsibilities of the groom and bride (Subramanian, 2014, p 223).[20] Some of these model contracts also declared triple *talaq* invalid (Hong Tschalaer, 2017, p 128).

The campaign has had no impact on legislation as of today. The Muslim Family Act has remained a draft.

In their campaign to reform Muslim personal law, Muslim feminist activists had to deal with one prominent opponent: the All India Muslim Personal Law Board (AIMPLB). Founded in 1973, the AIMPLB presents itself as the

[20] In doing so, the organisation drew on the experiences of pre-independence activists. For instance, in the 1930s, the then President of the AIWC, Begum Sharifa Hamid Ali, had already worked out a model *nikahnama*. More recent proposals have used this model (Subramanian, 2014, pp 212, 223). The model *nikahnamas* of the different organisations varied in their approaches. The All India Muslim Women Personal Law Board's *nikahnama*, for instance, clung on to rather conservative understandings of marriage but differed from standard contracts in so far as it shifted away from a focus on the woman's duty to obey her husband and towards a focus on mutual respect. It 'advised' against polygamy and 'reminded' the husband that he should only take a second wife if he were financially able to afford her and if the first wife agreed (Hong Tschalaer, 2017, p 125). This model contract also declared the registration of marriage as mandatory and thus challenged the clergy's stance of strict separation between the state and the Muslim community. BMMA's model-*nikahnama* went much further than that: it prohibited polygamy, fixed an age of consent, and made divorce valid only with the agreement of both parties. This contract also focused on the financial rights of the wife (property and maintenance) and declared that the *nikahnama* was subject to the exclusive jurisdiction of state courts.

representative body of Indian Muslims.[21] The Board strongly resists all state intervention in Muslim personal law, be it via legislation or judicial interpretation (Hong Tschalaer, 2017, pp 53–54). Its 'Aims and Objectives' are: '[t]o take effective steps to protect the Muslim Personal Law in India' and '[t]o strive for the annulment of all such Laws … and such judgments by courts of Law which may directly or indirectly amount to interference in or run parallel to the Muslim Personal Law' (All India Muslim Personal Law Board, n.d.-a).

The board bases this rejection of state interference mainly on two arguments, that are widely shared among the Muslim community: firstly, the notion that Muslim personal law is 'sacrosanct' and thus immune to change because personal laws 'are derived from religious texts or scriptures' (All India Muslim Personal Law Board, n.d.-b). Personal laws, according to this notion, are 'divinely-ordained' (Hasan, 2018 [1994], p xiv) and therefore are not subject to the state's scrutiny in the same way as other laws. Secondly, there is an understanding that the personal laws are of 'unique relevance' for 'cultural identity' and consequently 'any kind of interference … is not only a violation of religious freedom in the constitution but will put an end to [the community's] unique cultural identity' (All India Muslim Personal Law Board, n.d.-b).

The AIMPLB favours a situation where the Muslim population is governed by Muslim institutions that are independent of the state. One project fostered by the Board was to set up *darul qazas* (*Shariat* courts) in different Indian cities. These are alternative dispute-resolution mechanisms for Indian Muslims that resolve family issues in accordance with the *Shariat* and the Quran.[22]

The vocal counter-mobilisation by the AIMPLB and the narrative of personal laws as a pillar of Muslim identity created significant hurdles for feminist campaigns seeking a reform of Muslim personal law, as I will elaborate below.

C. Shayara Bano

Feminist groups and individual Muslim women also drew on litigation as part of their campaign against triple *talaq*. An early attempt to use the courts to have triple

[21] The AIMPLB's authority was challenged both by Shia Muslims and Muslim women, who, in 2005, each formed their own organisation – the All India Shia Personal Law Board and the All India Muslim Women Personal Law Board – because they did not see their respective interests being represented adequately by the AIMPLB (for an elaborate discussion see Hong Tschalaer, 2017, pp 61–63).

[22] The setting up of these institutions benefitted from Article 26 of the Indian Constitution, which stipulates freedom for religious groups to maintain and establish institutions for religious and charitable purposes, and to manage their own affairs in matters of religion. The *darul quazas* have become an integral part of India's plurilegal landscape, especially in the northern part of the country, where Islam is more prevalent (Hong Tschalaer, 2017, p 53). Although the *darul qazas* are located outside of the state legal system (the verdicts of *darul qazas* are not enforceable by state authorities and dissatisfied parties cannot approach the state courts to enforce or appeal the verdicts), the Indian state acknowledges these institutions as cheap, community-based alternative dispute settlement bodies (Hong Tschalaer, 2017, p 53). In response to a Public Interest Litigation claim, the Supreme Court ruled that *darul qazas* were not unconstitutional, but that 'no Dar-ul-Qazas … shall give verdict or issue Fatwa touching upon the rights, status and obligation, of an individual unless such an individual has asked for it' (*Vishwa Lochan Madan v Union of India and Others*, Supreme Court of India, 2014).

talaq and other discriminatory practices in Muslim personal law declared unconstitutional was pursued in 1983 by Shahnaz Sheikh, the founder of Awaaz-e-Niswaan ('voice of women'). Sheikh's petition to the Supreme Court attracted considerable media attention (Balasubrahmanyam, 1985, p 1260; Kumar, 1993, p 169). Sheikh remembers this moment as follows:

> In 1983, I filed a writ petition in the Supreme Court challenging Muslim Personal Law as being discriminatory to Muslim women. I was divorced by the utterance of triple talaq and thrown out at midnight by my ex-husband … I consulted five qazis, each of whom gave me a different version of my divorce. I did not know what my legal marital status was. Was I married or divorced? That was when I decided to hire a lawyer and challenge this form of divorce and Muslim Personal Law in the SC [Supreme Court] on grounds of equality guaranteed by the Constitution. This was the first case of its kind in the Court (Sheikh, 2016).

While Sheikh's case never resulted in a judgment,[23] her name is nevertheless often mentioned in line with *Shah Bano* and *Shayara Bano* in the story of Muslim women's litigation (Niaz & Soman, 2016; Saheli, 2018).

In the 1990s, a women's group started a new attempt to challenge Muslim personal law in the courts. The Ahmedabad Women's Action Group initiated a PIL case. The petition challenged the constitutionality of various discriminatory aspects of Muslim and Hindu personal law, among them divorce through *talaq*, on the basis of Articles 13, 14 and 15. The case, however, was unsuccessful. The Supreme Court held that the arguments by the women's group were 'to be dealt with by the legislature' and dismissed the petition (*Ahmedabad Women's Action Group v Union of India*, 1997). Although, as I elaborated in Chapters two and three, the Indian judicial system allows for such abstract petitions in the name of the public interest, Agnes (2011, p 148) assumes that the case was unsuccessful because there was no aggrieved woman directly affected by the discriminatory provisions.

In the early 2000s, the courts made a few tentative approaches towards reinterpreting the prerequisites for a successful divorce through *talaq*. Following the Gauhati High Court (*Jiauddin Ahmed v Anwara Begum* and *Mustafa Rukia Khatun v Abdul Khalique Laskar*), in 2002, in *Shamim Ara v State of Uttar Pradesh* the Supreme Court held that triple *talaq* without a reasonable cause or a previous attempt at reconciliation was invalid.

The key case, however, and the culmination of the campaigns against triple *talaq* was the case that Shayara Bano filed in 2015.[24] The claimant, Shayara Bano, had been married to her husband, Rizwan Ahmad, since 2002. By her account, she faced acts of violence and persistent demands for more dowry from her husband and his family. In October 2015, Rizwan Ahmad divorced Shayara Bano by way of triple *talaq*. Bano thereafter filed a petition in the Supreme Court, where she

[23] The descriptions of this case remain cryptic. Kumar (1993, p 170) states that after the *Shah Bano* judgment Sheikh's case 'lapsed into obscurity'. Niaz and Soman (2016) state that 'Shahnaz was forced to withdraw from the very struggle she initiated'.

[24] For a detailed engagement with this case see Dequen (2016) and two discussions of the judgment that I published elsewhere (Herklotz, 2017a, 2017b).

challenged the constitutionality of triple *talaq* and other aspects of Muslim personal law. Her case was supported by several women's groups who filed intervention petitions, including BMMA and Bebaak Collective ('collective of the fearless'). The critical question of the case was whether Section 2 of the Muslim Personal Law (Shariat) Application Act of 1937, in so far as it referred to (triple) *talaq*, was unconstitutional.

The petitioner and the intervening women's groups based their contention on the argument that triple *talaq* violated Articles 14 and 15 of the Constitution.[25] They held that triple *talaq* was not protected by Article 25 of the Constitution because it formed no 'essential practice' of religion. The argumentation also relied on international treaties and covenants to which India was a party, such as the UDHR, the International Covenant on Economic, Social and Cultural Rights and CEDAW. Beyond that, the petitioners also argued that triple *talaq* was not in tune with the prevailing social conditions, as Muslim women were vociferously protesting the practice. Consequently, triple *talaq* should be abolished in the same manner as the state had done away with practices once prevalent in the Hindu community, such as *sati* or polygamy. That other countries with Muslim majorities had prohibited triple *talaq*, according to the petitioners, not only showed that state institutions were indeed capable of interfering with personal law but also led to the paradoxical situation that Muslim women in secular India had lesser rights than Muslim women in Islamic states.

The rebuttal of the petitioners' contentions, prominently formulated by the AIMPLB, drew on the doctrine of non-interference and opined that triple *talaq* – a mode of divorce that had been practised for 1,400 years – was an essential practice of the faith of at least some Indian Muslims, protected under Article 25. The organisation also stated that individual Muslim couples were free to declare triple *talaq* invalid in their marriage contract (*nikahnama*) or to opt to be governed under the secular Special Marriage Act and could thus decide for themselves whether triple *talaq* would be a valid form of divorce in their case.

In August 2017, the Supreme Court delivered a 'landmark decision' (BBC, 2017b) in *Shayara Bano v Union of India*, declaring Muslim divorce through triple *talaq* invalid. The judgment was a tight 3:2 decision, in which, interestingly, the three judges in the majority regarded triple *talaq* as invalid but used different reasoning to arrive at their conclusion. Two judges held that the Muslim Personal Law (Shariat) Application Act, so far as it referred to triple *talaq*, violated Article 14. They stated that triple *talaq* 'is manifestly arbitrary in the sense that the marital tie can be broken capriciously and whimsically by a Muslim man without any attempt at reconciliation so as to save it' and must, therefore, 'be held to be violative of the fundamental right contained under Article 14 of the Constitution' (*Shayara Bano*, judgment by Justices Nariman and Lalit, paragraph 57). They further reasoned

[25] This and the following arguments can be found in the written submission by Bebaak Collective and the Centre for the Study of Society and Secularism (2017). They are also restated in the judgment by the Indian Supreme Court in *Shayara Bano v Union of India* (2017).

that triple *talaq*, which was perceived as sinful in theology, did not constitute an 'essential religious practice' and was therefore not protected under Article 25(1) of the Constitution (ibid, paragraph 25). They stressed that the earlier decision by the Supreme Court in *Ahmedabad Women's Action Group* had 'no ratio' and contradicted itself (ibid, paragraph 30).

The third judge agreed with the conclusion of his fellow judges that triple *talaq* was invalid but based this understanding on a different reasoning. He held that triple *talaq*, per the Quran, was not a valid practice in Islam and, therefore, illegal. Notably, he stated: 'Merely because a practice has continued for long, that by itself cannot make it valid if it has been expressly declared to be impermissible' (*Shayara Bano*, judgment by Justice Joseph, paragraph 24).

Indian women's groups, activists, and feminist scholars termed the judgment a 'milestone intervention' (Khan, 2017), 'a signpost moment of the women's movement in India' (Sen, 2017) and 'a step in the right direction' (Indira Jaising, cited in Sharma, 2017). But feminist commentators also criticised the judgment. For example, Ratna Kapur (2017) points out that the majority judgment was ultimately not concerned with women's rights but rather with the preservation of marriage when the judges bemoaned that by way of triple *talaq* 'the marital tie can be broken … without any attempt at reconciliation so as to save it' (*Shayara Bano*, judgment by Justices Nariman and Lalit, paragraph 57). The judges refrained from taking a clear position on the relationship between gender equality and religious freedom. The judgment was also limited in scope, as it only concerned triple *talaq* and not the other forms of *talaq*. Overall, while the judgment was a turning point, in so far as the Court positioned itself on Muslim personal law, flaws remained.

In 2019, the Indian Parliament passed the Muslim Women (Protection of Rights on Marriage) Act, 2019. The Act not only declares triple *talaq* void and illegal (Section 3), which would not have been necessary after the Supreme Court's judgment on the issue. It also punishes the pronouncement of *talaq* with imprisonment of up to three years and a fine (Section 4).[26] The justification for the Act was that cases of triple *talaq* persisted despite the Supreme Court outlawing it. Not only people in the Muslim community but also feminist scholars and women's rights activists have been concerned about these developments and have opposed the criminalisation of *talaq*. They have argued that women's rights have been used as a fig leaf to cover the pursuit of anti-minority politics: The legislation's purpose was not to safeguard women's rights but to 'criminalise Muslim men' (Valiramani, 2017). This is an example of 'femo-nationalism', which I mentioned in Chapter two.

On the other hand, some Muslim women's rights organisations have welcomed the attempt to make the practice of triple *talaq* a punishable offence. For example, when the Muslim Women (Protection of Rights on Marriage) Ordinance, 2018,

[26] In January 2025, the Supreme Court began hearing challenges to the constitutionality of the Muslim Women (Protection of Rights on Marriage) Act, 2019. The argument in these cases is that by singling out *talaq* pronouncements by Muslim men for criminal punishment, the Act violates Article 14's mandate of formal equality.

which preceded the Act of 2019, was promulgated, Zakia Soman, the founder of BMMA, was quoted in *Al Jazeera* as saying:

> We welcome this. The Muslim woman is happy today because she wants legal protection. Despite the Supreme Court order, instant triple talaq has been taking place, so we needed this to be criminalised (Saberin, 2018).

D. Evaluation

Like the feminist campaigns regarding Christian and Hindu law, feminist activism around Muslim personal law can be described as partly successful. While several attempts to have the Supreme Court intervene with Muslim personal law have failed, in *Shayara Bano*, Muslim women brought about a landmark judgment.

Several factors helped to win this case and to overcome the obstacles that the movement faced in the area of Muslim personal law. Regarding activism strategies, it was undoubtedly helpful that several different (Muslim and non-Muslim) women's groups united in this case and made the petition seem like a project by and for Muslim women. As in Christian personal law, it probably helped the campaign to draw on a framing that linked religion and gender equality and did not treat them as mutually exclusive. The *Shayara Bano* case was also embedded in a more extensive campaign that demanded a broadening of rights for women. This involved drafting a gender-just Muslim family code, setting up women's *sharia* courts, building mosques for women, and conducting studies showing that large numbers of Muslim women were in favour of banning triple *talaq*. Activists also used the media strategically to make their point. Sharaya Bano gave several interviews explaining her motivation for pursuing the case. Other activists and women's groups regularly updated about the case via *Twitter*, newsletters and other (social) media. This certainly put the Court under pressure: it could no longer pursue its previous avoidance strategy and had to act.

Yet, the success remains limited. The Court in *Shayara Bano* refrains from positioning itself clearly on the gendered discrimination of triple *talaq*. Other discriminatory aspects in Muslim personal law have not been declared unconstitutional by the Supreme Court. BMMA has not succeeded with its law reform attempts despite its attempts to involve the Muslim community and to use a careful and non-confrontational framing.

In explaining why it was so challenging to change Muslim personal law, societal factors play a central role. Muslim personal law is probably the most sensitive of all the personal laws. This is not only because Muslims are a minority community – so are Christians and Parsis, and there is less controversy around the respective personal laws of these communities. However, the Muslim personal law is particularly politicised and is linked much more to community identity than other personal laws – a narrative that the AIMPLB constantly revives. Any interference bears the risk of a backlash, as seen in the aftermath of the *Shah Bano* case. This scenario has made it particularly challenging for feminists to lead a successful campaign in this area. This is coupled with another factor that hindered the feminist campaign in this area: the strong counter-mobilisation from the AIMPLB, which has actively opposed any interference in Muslim personal law.

VI. Conclusion

Indian feminists have led several strong and vocal campaigns regarding the laws on marriage and the family. Activists and women's groups have used legislative lobbying and litigation. Achieving success in the area of personal law, however, has been far from easy. Out of the four campaigns depicted in this chapter, one – the campaign for a Uniform Civil Code – was unsuccessful and three – the campaigns for reforms in Christian, Hindu, and Muslim personal law – were only partly successful.

While feminists were able to strengthen women's divorce, inheritance, and guardianship rights in each of the three sets of personal laws, they also experienced significant setbacks. Law reform regarding marriage and the family has remained scarce and occurred only several decades after the beginning of the feminist campaigns. Out of the many cases that individual women or women's groups brought to the courts, several were lost or never decided. Even though the higher judiciary has the power to undertake judicial review in India, courts have frequently drawn on the argument of separation of powers, holding that it was the legislator and not the courts who should decide on the issue. Even in those cases that are regarded as landmark decisions – like *Mary Roy*, *Mary Sonia Zachariah*, *Githa Hariharan* and *Shayara Bano* – the judgments refrained from striking down unconstitutional laws as violating the Constitution's right to equality. Indira Jaising (2022) thus draws a disillusioned conclusion:

> Over the years, the Supreme Court was presented with various obvious opportunities to strike down personal laws which were blatantly discriminatory, but it failed to do [so]. The courts chose to cop out of actually deciding the issue of equality and bringing down a wall of discrimination. Handy tools of 'reading down' were used or reliefs were provided to the immediate petitioner without dismantling the codified patriarchy of Indian laws.

Returning to the success factors developed in Chapter three, this concluding section will briefly explain why it was so difficult to bring about change in the ambit of family law.

A. Rights

In theory, personal law provisions that discriminate against women by granting women lesser rights than men could have been struck down easily based on (formal) equality. Yet, the courts mostly refrained from doing so. Instead, they focused on the freedom of religion (and discrimination on the grounds of religion) rather than on the gender aspect. The rights factor can thus not explain the feminists' limited success in this area. Instead, other factors impacted the outcomes of their campaigns.

B. Activism

The forms of activism were of crucial importance in impacting feminist success. We see this when we compare the campaign for the UCC to the three other campaigns. The UCC campaign failed because feminists used confrontational rather than conciliatory tactics; they sought no alliances with religious groups; and they aimed for changes that the system could not handle. Timing also played a role. The campaign became almost impossible after the destruction of the Babri mosque and in a socio-political climate in which tension between religious communities was extreme. In later campaigns, feminists learned from this experience and acted differently, which proved successful – at least in part. With their step-by-step approach, in which they called for individual reforms within the different sets of personal laws, they brought about some legal change.

(i) Lobbying and Litigation

Feminists used both lobbying and litigation and achieved some success with both strategies. The combination of both legal tactics was often a good choice. In Christian personal law, for instance, the legislator would probably not have stepped in if several High Court judgments had not struck down parts of Section 10 IDA. The Supreme Court in the *Shayara Bano* case might not have struck down triple *talaq* if Muslim women had not simultaneously campaigned for reforms in Muslim personal law. At the time that Shayara Bano's petition was debated in the Court, Muslim women's groups like BMMA were advocating their draft for a reformed gender-just Muslim family law, conducting studies on Muslim women's opinions on personal law reforms and making their positions and demands public in newspapers, blog posts and social media. This backing up of the litigation with broader legal campaigns made it possible to show that Muslim women widely shared and supported the claimant's demand in court.

(ii) Framing

Another factor that has played a vital role in the campaigns is framing. After the failed campaign for a UCC, feminists realised that the sweeping rejection of religion and the framing of religious personal law as 'products of a less developed society' (Saheli, 1986b) was not helpful to their goals. In the campaigns for reforms in Christian and Muslim personal law, feminists used a different framing: they presented legal change as a demand of the women from the respective religious communities and in the interest of the communities at large, including men. In their argumentation, feminist scholars and women's rights activists drew on various sources, including the Constitution, religious texts and (to a lesser extent) international human rights law. They also stressed that personal laws were products of colonialism and were ill-suited to governing family affairs in India today. This framing found some resonance with the legislature and the judiciary.

Activists and women's groups have also been willing to compromise with feminist ideals in order to achieve at least some legal change, even though this led to reforms that do not 100 per cent reflect feminist goals. The reform suggestions on Christian personal law that the JWP worked out in collaboration with Christian churches, and the Muslim family code which BMMA drafted, can be described as balancing acts or the result of a 'bargaining' process (Kandiyoti, 1988; Hong Tschalaer, 2017) that attempted to accommodate gender equality as well as religious perceptions on gender roles.

(iii) Building Alliances and Learning from Others

Building alliances with other women's groups and collaborating with religious community leaders was helpful for feminist legal activism. The *Shayara Bano* case, for instance, had the support of several women's groups calling for an end to triple *talaq*. Chatterji's attempt to convince several churches to support her endeavour to reform Christian divorce and inheritance law provides a positive example of the involvement of religious communities.

C. State Institutions

While one would assume that feminist activists benefitted from the institution of PIL, particularly the broad rules on standing, surprisingly, the courts were highly reluctant to decide in favour of women in the area of family law. In several decisions, the courts refrained from deciding the matter and instead called on the legislator to take action, often drawing on an argument of separation of powers. This is not convincing in cases where a legal norm violates women's constitutional right to equality. Cases seem to have been more successful when the claimants were directly affected by the specific law under question. Although Public Interest Litigation allows for cases to be filed in the broader interest and does *not* require that the claimant is directly concerned, cases such as *Ahmedabad Women's Action Group* show that feminists faced challenges when they brought forward an abstract claim. When Neela Deshmukh and Manushi petitioned against the discrimination in Hindu guardianship law, the judge termed this 'luxury litigation' (Kishwar, 1994, p 20). In contrast, cases where the claimant was directly affected by the law in question – like *Mary Roy*, *Githa Hariharan* and *Shayara Bano* – had better chances of success.

D. Society

Societal factors, too, impacted the outcome of feminist activism, mainly in a way that hindered the feminist campaigns.

(i) Religion

The central role that religion plays in Indian society and the fact that the Indian state grants religious communities a great deal of autonomy provided significant challenges to the feminist campaign. Two related understandings about religion-based personal laws play a role in this context. First is the notion that 'sacrosanct' or 'eternal' personal law is immune to change or may only be changed by religious experts. This notion draws on an idea of separate spheres – a secular and a religious one – and allows the state to interfere only in the former and not in the latter. Speaking about 'religious' laws in the first place is part of this understanding, which somewhat obscures the fact that personal laws, like other laws, at least when codified, are state-made. Yet, state organs have, in some cases, adhered to this argument.[27]

Secondly, there exists a widely shared idea that religion-based personal laws define religious identity and that any legal change in this area is an existential threat to the religious communities (critically Parashar, 2013, p 17). In particular, 'for some Indian Muslims, the personal laws have become associated with group identity in such a way that calls for abolition are perceived as an attack on their identity group, and as forced assimilation' (Ahmed, 2019, p 238). The All India Muslim Personal Law Board (n.d.-b) firmly adheres to this position. The Indian government, too, has shared the 'assumption … that there exists a clear equation between [personal] law and community identity' (Hasan, 2018 [1994], p xiv).

(ii) Counter-mobilisation

Religious groups and spokespersons of religious communities use these arguments to make a case against reforms in personal laws. The campaigns this chapter has engaged with show how counter-mobilisation from religious groups, particularly the AIMPLB, against reforms of the personal laws hindered feminist success. Where feminists could 'bargain' with religious communities to work out a joint position, they succeeded in curtailing the opposition and achieved limited successes.

[27] In *Sri Krishna Singh v Mathura Ahir* (1979), for example, the Supreme Court overruled a High Court judgment, holding that personal laws were not to be tested against the Constitution's fundamental rights and that the High Court judge instead of applying 'his own concept of modern times … should have enforced the law as derived from recognised and authoritative sources of Hindu law'.

(iii) Legal Culture

The ideas about religion and religious law mentioned above are closely linked to other aspects of legal culture that hinder feminist campaigns. Apart from the divide between the religious and the secular, there also exists a widely shared understanding of a division between a 'public' and a 'private' sphere, whereby the latter should be excluded from state interference. The notion of the public–private divide 'has been an important dimension of the legal reinforcement of women's subordination' (Kapur & Cossman, 2013, p 255). Family law, in this dichotomy, belongs to the private realm and is to be excluded from state interference.

Another, related, impactful notion is the idea that (heteronormative) marriage is a fundamental pillar of society and that any destabilisation of this pillar, for instance, though the granting of broader divorce rights, would constitute a threat to the stability of society (on this argument see Agnes, 2011, p 18; 2012, p 338 et seq; Mirchandani, 2017; Rajan, 2019). While unlike other constitutions, the Indian Constitution does not explicitly protect marriage, we find several examples where Indian law-makers and judges have invoked the preservation of marriage as a crucial aspect for the wellbeing of the Indian nation. This includes the Supreme Court's observations in *Reynold Rajamani* on society's interest in 'maintaining the marriage bond' or in the Indian Law Commission's (2009, p 12) opinion that the '[p]ublic interest demands … that the married status should, as long as possible, and whenever possible, be maintained'. Scholars have spoken about 'familism' to describe this understanding of the unity of family and society (Notz, 2015).

These factors have made it difficult for feminist activists to push for law reforms and explain why their campaigns were only partly successful. The next chapter will juxtapose the feminist campaigns regarding personal laws with those in the area of violence against women.

5

Violence against Women

'Brides are not for burning' is what it said on the placards of women's rights activists who, in the 1980s, campaigned against dowry-related killings. It was feminists who first pointed out that many of the so-called 'kitchen accidents' were, in reality, cases of murder, where members of the husband's family had poured kerosene over their daughter-in-law and set her on fire because she had not brought enough dowry into the groom's family. The anti-dowry campaign, which led to significant law reforms, is one of several feminist legal interventions that focused on acts of gender-based violence.

Unlike in family law, in the area of violence against women, there were few norms that directly and explicitly discriminated against women. Criminal law provisions that dealt with acts of violence rarely made a distinction between men and women. If they did, they tended to treat women more favourably than men. This 'preferential' treatment, however, was often based on gendered stereotypes, drawing on ideas that gave women no sexual agency and saw them as property of their husbands (R Kapur, 2005a; Guruswamy & Katju, 2020). For instance, Indian rape law was (and still is) gender-specific: it held that only a woman could be a rape victim and only a man could be a rapist (Section 375 of the Indian Penal Code; since 1 July 2024, Section 63 of the Bharatiya Nyaya Sanhita, 2023[1]).

The reasons why feminists campaigned in this area were thus more subtle. Some norms indirectly discriminated against women, while others drew on or fostered gendered stereotypes. In other cases, it was not the laws themselves that feminists found fault with, but the practices around them, for instance, the fact that (predominantly male) lawyers, judges, police officers, and other personnel of the judiciary or law enforcement were biased against women. In yet other cases, the existing laws – the Indian Penal Code (IPC) of 1860 (which remained in place until 1 July 2024, when it was replaced by the Bharatiya Nyaya Sanhita, 2023, BNS) and the Dowry Prohibition Act of 1961 – were deemed insufficient to deal adequately with discriminatory societal phenomena, such as sexual harassment in the workplace and dowry-related and domestic violence.

[1] The Bharatiya Nyaya Sanhita, 2023 (Indian Justice Code, BNS) replaced the Indian Penal Code of 1860. It was passed by the Indian Parliament in December 2023 and came into effect on 1 July 2024. The BNS maintains the provisions of the Indian Penal Code on rape and other sexual offences against women, such as insulting the modesty of a woman. It increases the threshold for the victim to be classified as an adult, in the case of gang rape, from 16 to 18 years of age (Section 70).

Feminist demands concerning violence against women have thus differed from those concerning personal laws. Rather than fighting for formal equality via law reforms or judicial review, they have sought to bring about new legislation that adequately addresses the violence that women routinely face, to prevent gendered stereotypes from impacting the application of the laws and to make it easier for women to access the law.

From a purely legalistic viewpoint, these reform attempts have faced challenges. Feminists and women's rights activists have had to go beyond demanding formal equality and instead had to argue that the Constitution provided for substantive equality – a position that (as Chapter three has shown) was not dominant among scholarship and the judiciary (especially in the early decades of feminist activism in the 1970s, 1980s, and 1990s) and even today is not shared by all scholars and judges. Judicial review was thus of limited help. In demanding law reforms, feminists were challenged by the fact that while Article 15(3) of the Constitution *allows* the state to enact special legislation for women, it does not *compel* the state to do so. On the positive side, however, feminists attempting reform in this area of law could draw on the Convention on the Elimination of All Forms of Discrimination Against Women (CEDAW) to a greater extent than when seeking reforms of personal laws – at least from 1993 onwards, when India ratified the treaty.

This chapter will show that despite these challenges, women's groups and activists have been very successful with their campaigns concerning violence against women. They have brought about several legislative changes and some critical judgments. This chapter tells this success story by looking at four feminist campaigns concerning laws on sexual violence (section I), dowry-related violence (section II), domestic violence (section III), and sexual harassment in the workplace (section IV). The conclusion will provide reasons for the successes and failures of the campaigns (section V). There are, indeed, overlaps between the different forms of violence that I distinguish here. For instance, both rape and dowry-related violence might take place in the realm of the home and may thus constitute forms of domestic violence. Yet, the distinction made in this chapter reflects the distinct campaigns that differed from each other and aimed at different legal reforms.

I. 'Millions of Mathuras': The Campaign for Reforms in the Laws on Rape

The anti-rape campaign has been one of the central campaigns of the Indian women's movement right from the movement's inception in the 1970s. This section deals with the legal mobilisation concerning the laws on sexual assault, covering a period from the late 1970s until 2013. It begins with the infamous *Mathura* case that the Supreme Court decided in 1978 and covers other essential moments of protest and waves of reforms. It shows how feminist activists and women's groups managed to bring about a series of law reforms in the laws on rape in 1983, 2002 and 2013.

A. The Image of the Liar Woman

When the anti-rape campaign began in the late 1970s, Section 375 IPC read as follows:

> A man is said to commit 'rape' who, except in the case hereinafter excepted, has sexual intercourse with a woman under circumstances falling under any of the five following descriptions:
>
> First: Against her will.
>
> Secondly: Without her consent.
>
> Thirdly: With her consent, when her consent has been obtained by putting her in fear of death, or of hurt.
>
> Fourthly: With her consent, when the man knows that he is not her husband, and that her consent is given because she believes that he is another man to whom she is or believes herself to be lawfully married.
>
> Fifthly: With or without her consent, when she is under sixteen years of age.
>
> Explanation: Penetration is sufficient to constitute the sexual intercourse necessary to the offence of rape.
>
> Exception: Sexual intercourse by a man with his own wife, the wife not being under fifteen years of age, is not rape.

Section 376 IPC provided that the maximum punishment for rape was imprisonment for life.

A number of aspects are important here. First, the provision was gender-specific: according to the law, only men could commit rape, and only women could be victims of rape. Second, although the norm stated that penetration was 'sufficient' to constitute sexual intercourse, the courts' general interpretation was that penile-vaginal penetration was necessary to constitute the offence. Cases of sexual assault not including penile-vaginal penetration could only be tried under Sections 354 and 509 IPC, which addressed conduct that could 'outrage a woman's modesty'[2] or Section 377 IPC, which criminalised 'carnal intercourse against the order of nature'. Third, the fifth case in Section 375 IPC – a man having sexual intercourse with a woman under 16 – was termed 'statutory rape' and constituted an offence even if the woman consented to the act. And fourth, as per the exception to Section 375 IPC, *marital* rape was not a crime when the wife was above 15 years of age. Unmarried women under 16 were thus, as per the law, incapable of giving consent to sexual intercourse. Married women (over 15), on the other hand, were unable to refuse to have sexual intercourse with their husbands. In Ratna Kapur's words, the underlying concept of the marital rape exception was that 'a woman surrenders her right to consent to sexual relations at the time of entering into a marriage, and the husband is given an unconditional, unqualified right to sexual access to her' (R Kapur, 2005a, p 34). According to Kapur, this understanding sustained the idea of 'the wife as exclusive property of the husband' (R Kapur, 2005a, p 35).

[2] Today regulated under Sections 74 and 79 of the BNS.

While rape was defined as sexual intercourse without the woman's consent (and in practice, whether the woman had consented was often the crux of the case), the IPC did not provide a positive definition of consent. Courts understood consent as requiring voluntary participation by the woman 'after having freely exercised a choice between resistance and assent' (High Court of Punjab in *Rao Harnarain Singh Sheoji Singh v The State*, 1957). In determining whether a woman had consented, courts frequently based their opinions on what they deemed 'objective' criteria, including reports of the women's medical examination and assessments of the women's character. Section 155(4) of the Indian Evidence Act (IEA) of 1872 – which Pratiksha Baxi (2014, p 8) calls 'one of the most degrading and discriminatory evidentiary provisions in legal history' – stated that when a man was prosecuted for rape or an attempt to rape, the 'credit of a witness may be impeached' by showing 'that the prosecutrix was of generally immoral character'.

The legal system thus not only worked with a relatively narrow definition of rape, excluding marital rape and all forms of rape other than penile-vaginal intercourse, but also drew on misogynist gender stereotypes.

In addition, it was the practice around rape trials that was particularly dehumanising for victims. In particular, the cross-examinations were often traumatic for rape survivors, who were expected to narrate in detail what happened, turning rape trials into 'pornographic spectacles' (P Baxi, 2014). Furthermore, judges frequently based their decisions on questionable medical 'evidence' and the past sexual history of the rape victim/survivor. Case law is filled with examples where judges from the lower courts, the High Courts, and the Supreme Court have based their decisions on 'rape myths' (Satish, 2016) that led them to acquit the accused ultimately. Rape myths include ideas about how a rape victim should behave in the situation of the assault and after that. Where rape survivors deviate from this 'normal' behaviour, the courts tend to grant them less credibility (Satish, 2016). I shall mention two early cases to illustrate this. Both cases were essential triggers for feminist demands to reform the legal system.

In *Pratap Misra v State of Orissa*, three men were accused of having raped Pramila Kumari Rout, a midwife, who at the time of the incident was five months pregnant. As per Rout's account, she and her husband were on holiday when three men came to their hotel room, two of whom forcefully dragged the husband away while the third one raped her in her hotel room, and subsequently, the two other men also raped her. Later that night, the couple filed a first information report[3] (FIR). A few days later, Rout miscarried, presumably because of the rape.

The sessions court declared the three accused guilty and sentenced them to five years of rigorous imprisonment for rape.[4] The High Court upheld these sentences. The Supreme Court, however, overturned the judgments in its verdict

[3] A first information report that informs the police about the commission of an offence usually initiates the criminal process (Section 154 CrPC). It is not necessarily the victim who has to file such an FIR: any person can file it (Satish, 2016, p 17).

[4] Sessions courts are hierarchically above the magistrates' courts (see Sections 6, 9 and 15 CrPC) and below the High Courts and the Supreme Court, which function as courts of appeal (see Sections 374(2) and 374(1) CrPC respectively).

of 23 February 1977. While the Court held that sexual intercourse between Pramila Kumari Rout and the three accused had been established, it assumed that the intercourse had taken place with the woman's consent.

The Court based this finding on the following arguments. It stressed that before marrying Pramila Kumari Rout, the husband had already been married to another woman and had not obtained a divorce. The later marriage was, therefore, void, which led the Supreme Court to hold that Rout lived 'in a state of concubinage' and was, therefore, of 'immoral character' (*Pratap Misra*, paragraph 2). It further stated that '[t]he opinions of medical experts show that it is very difficult for any person to rape single-handed a grown up and an experienced woman' because, in such case, the person should be 'able to resist a sex assault' (paragraph 8). The Court also held against Pramila Kumari Rout that after the first man had raped her, she did not get up immediately to shut the door of her hotel room (paragraph 11). Lastly, the Court stated that if Rout had been forced to have sexual intercourse against her will, the medical examination of the accused would have found injuries over their bodies 'caused by the nails of the prosecutrix' (paragraph 8). As this was not the case, the Court found that 'the only irresistible inference can be that the prosecutrix was a consenting party' (paragraph 8).

In the second case, *Tuka Ram v State of Maharashtra*, better known as the *Mathura* case, the facts, as provided by the Supreme Court judgment, are as follows: Mathura, who at the time of the incident was between 14 and 16, had lived with her brother Gama, ever since the parents of the siblings had died. She began a relationship with Ashok, which her brother opposed. Gama lodged a report at the police station against Ashok on the charge of abduction.[5] On the same day, Mathura and Ashok were brought to the police station at about 9 pm to record their statements. In the police station, one policeman took Mathura to a latrine and had sexual intercourse with her, and another police officer attempted to have sexual intercourse with her, which failed due to his level of intoxication. Mathura later informed Ashok and others about the incident and registered a rape complaint. About 20 hours after the incident, Mathura and the accused police officers were sent for medical examinations.

The sessions court acquitted the policemen, stating that Mathura was 'a shocking liar' whose testimony was 'riddled with falsehood and improbabilities' (cited by the Supreme Court in *Tuka Ram*, paragraph 3). He assumed that Mathura had 'surrendered her body to a Police Constable' and later 'invented the story' of rape to 'sound virtuous' before her boyfriend (cited by the Supreme Court in *Tuka Ram*, paragraph 3). The Bombay High Court reversed the order of acquittal. It convicted one officer under Section 375 IPC and the other one under Section 354 IPC ('outraging a woman's modesty') (P Baxi, 2014, p 13).

[5] Baxi (2014, p 236) argues that it is a common practice for parents or other relatives to file criminal complaints against the partners of the women when they disapprove of the relationship, charging them with statutory rape, abduction or kidnapping in order to 'recover' the woman who has entered into an 'improper' alliance.

Upon appeal against the conviction, the Supreme Court, in September 1978, acquitted the two police officers. In its decision, the Court drew on the fact that the medical examination conducted on Mathura had revealed that her 'hymen revealed old ruptures' and her 'vagina admitted two fingers easily', from which the Supreme Court concluded that Mathura was 'habituated to sexual intercourse' (*Tuka Ram*, paragraph 2). Furthermore, as per the medical examination, 'no marks of injury were found on the person of the girl after the incident', which led the Court to hold that 'the alleged intercourse was a peaceful affair' (*Tuka Ram*, paragraph 5).

In both cases summarised here, the Supreme Court perceived the women who claimed to have been raped as liars. The Court based this perception on the woman's behaviour in the situation of the assault, on her previous sexual history and questionable medical 'evidence'. This was typical for judgments at this time and still occurs today. Medical evidence in the form of medical examination reports was admitted into the trial under Section 45 IEA. The presence or absence of visible injuries on the body of the prosecutrix or the accused was supposed to determine whether the woman had consented or not. Medical 'evidence' based on the 'two fingers test' that led doctors to conclude that the woman was 'habituated to sexual intercourse' regularly led lawyers and judges to argue that the woman was of immoral character and had lied about being raped (P Baxi, 2014). Pratiksha Baxi (2014, p 63), in this context, speaks of a 'medicalization of consent'.

In addition, gender stereotypes are often linked to prejudices against lower caste, lower class, or Muslim women.[6] That Pramila Kumari Rout was a midwife (a profession with a low social standing), that her marriage was not legally valid, and that Mathura was a tribal woman who had entered a non-marital relationship is likely to have played a role in the argumentation and outcome of the judgments.

B. The Emergence of the Anti-Rape Campaign

While time and again rape cases and the courts' responses to them had called the attention of the nascent feminist movement of the 1970s, the *Mathura* case was undoubtedly the trigger for the widespread anti-rape campaign by the women's movement (Gangoli, 1996; Butalia, 2005, p 329; Datta, 2007, p 137; Murthy & Dasgupta, 2011, pp 33–34). As a response to the Supreme Court's acquittal of the two police officers, four law professors – Upendra Baxi, Vasudha Dhagamwar, Raghunath Kelkar and Lotika Sarkar – on 16 September 1979[7] published an open letter to the Chief Justice of India demanding a re-trial of the *Mathura* case. The

[6] A case that spelled out these stereotypical ideas of 'good' and 'bad' rape survivors was the Supreme Court's decision in *Bharwada Bhoginbhai Hirjubhai v State of Gujarat* (1983). On rape myths and this case in particular see Satish (2016).

[7] Although the Supreme Court had already decided the *Mathura* case on 15 September 1978, the judgment was only reported about a year later, soon after which the letter was publicised.

letter called the *Mathura* judgment 'an extraordinary decision sacrificing human rights of women' (U Baxi, Dhagamwar, Kelkar, & Sarkar, 1979). The letter's authors exposed the absurdity of the arguments in the *Mathura* judgment. They sarcastically asked whether the Supreme Court judges believed

> that Mathura was so flirtatious that even when her brother, her employer and her lover were waiting outside the police station, she could not let go the opportunity of having fun with two policemen and that too in the area adjoining a police station latrine? (U Baxi et al, 1979).

The letter bemoaned the fact that the Court had not adequately considered the context of the case, especially Mathura's low socio-economic status, age, and lack of knowledge of legal rights (U Baxi et al, 1979). It further bemoaned the general situation that economically weaker people face when they claim their rights against the state. That Mathura's case even reached the courts was against all odds. There were 'millions of Mathuras' in similar situations, stated the authors, 'who have no access to legal services at any level' (U Baxi et al, 1979).

The open letter was circulated amongst women's organisations and activists and received an 'overwhelming' response (P Baxi, 2014, p 17). By referring to the 'millions of Mathuras' in India, the letter had gone beyond criticising a specific judgment and had pointed to the widespread phenomenon of (custodial) rape and the structural deficits of the Indian legal system in addressing this phenomenon. This structural violence became the focal point of the feminist campaigns. Many activists strongly identified with Mathura. Nandita Haksar (1999, p 73), for instance, recalled: 'We were outraged. In fact our predominant feeling was that we were asking for justice for ourselves, not for an unknown girl in a village in Maharashtra'.

On 8 March 1980, international women's day, women organised a nationwide demonstration against rape, demanding changes in rape law and a re-trial of the *Mathura* case (Kumar, 1993, p 129; Gangoli, 1996; Murthy & Dasgupta, 2011, p 46). On 17 March 1980, women's groups organised another demonstration outside the Supreme Court to reinforce their demand for a re-opening of the *Mathura* case (Kumar, 1993, p 131; P Baxi, 2014, p 17). In response, Chief Justice Chandrachud advised the organisations to file a review petition, which the Bharatiya Mahila Federation ('Indian Women's Organisation') and the Women Lawyers' Council did (P Baxi, 2014, p 17). The Supreme Court, however, held that the women's organisations had no standing to file a review petition and upheld the Court's earlier decision (P Baxi, 2014, p 18). This was in April 1980 – before the high times of public interest litigation in India.

The women's movement, however, remained active. And other tragic rape cases[8] fuelled its activism. The anti-rape campaign that began in the late 1970s continued

[8] These included the case of Rameeza Bee and Maya Tyagi. Rameeza Bee, a Muslim woman, had been raped in 1978 by police officers who accused her of being a prostitute. When her husband tried to protest, the police officers beat him to death. Maya Tyagi was assaulted by the police, stripped naked

through the 1980s and 1990s and would later see a revival after the fatal gang rape of Jyoti Singh in 2012. The campaigns involved street protests and, where incidents of rape had become manifest, the public shaming of the perpetrators. Calls for law reform were a vital component of the anti-rape campaign. Notably, activists and women's rights groups focused mainly on legislative lobbying and only resorted to litigation to a small extent, as the following section will show.

C. Feminist Demands for Reform

A central goal of women's groups and feminist activists was to make rape survivors' sexual history irrelevant in rape trials by abolishing Section 155(4) IEA (*Manushi*, 1980; Lawyers Collective, 1996; Saheli, 1999). For example, the journal *Manushi* (1980, p 46) criticised the 'categorization of women into the "good" and the "bad", the chaste, and the non-chaste', which underpinned the section. Similarly, the Lawyers Collective (1996, p 6) argued that the state must do away with a culture in which judges protect 'only the chaste and the virgin while any woman used to sexual intercourse is disbelieved when she alleges rape'. And Saheli (1999) stated that it was unjust that 'the character of the rapist does not come under scrutiny while that of the rape survivor is open to questioning and examination'. Related to this issue, women's groups also demanded the abolition of the two-fingers test, which helped the defence and the judges to establish a case against women by branding them as promiscuous (see, for instance, Saheli, 1999).

Many organisations also called for a shift in the burden of proof in rape trials when it came to determining whether an established act of sexual intercourse was consensual or not (*Manushi*, 1981b; Saheli, 1999; Jagori, 2009; Joint Action Committee Against Rape and Sexual Harassment, n.d.). They criticised the fact that 'only the woman has to prove that she did not consent. In the absence of injuries, this becomes almost impossible' (*Manushi*, 1981b, p 41). And they suggested that 'the onus of proving innocence should be on the man, not on the woman' (Joint Action Committee Against Rape and Sexual Harassment, n.d.). Indeed, this demand to shift the burden of proof clashed with concerns about the rights of the accused, articulated by human rights groups (Agnes, 2002, p 844).

As courts commonly perceived the definition of rape in Section 375 IPC to include only penile-vaginal penetration, another demand by feminists was to broaden the definition of rape to include other forms of sexual assault, which could be 'equally, or more traumatic' (Saheli, 1999), including forced oral intercourse or the penetration of a woman's vagina with other body parts or an object (Kumar, 1993, p 137; Gangoli, 1996; Saheli, 1999).

and paraded through the marketplace, before being raped in a police station in 1980. Her husband was also killed. For a detailed engagement with these cases see Butalia (2005, pp 327–29).

Feminists also pointed to the fact that rape often had little to do with sexual lust and a lot to do with power dynamics and the intersection of different forms of discrimination. They stressed that it was too simple to view rape as a crime committed by men against women and demanded that the complex circumstances that surrounded rape cases – including questions of caste, class, religion, and hierarchies more broadly – be reflected in the law and at rape trials (Kumar, 1993, p 128). Saheli (1999), for example, stressed that rape was frequently 'used as a weapon of revenge or assertion of power of one community or caste over another'. Another phenomenon that women's groups addressed was cases of custodial rape, where police officers or other officials in a situation of power raped women in their custody. Some feminists therefore demanded the introduction of an offence called 'power rape' into the Indian Penal Code (for an engagement with this demand see Gangoli, 1996, p 336; P Baxi, 2014, p 34). 'Power rape' thereby referred to incidents of rape where the perpetrator was in a situation of power, control or domination and was supposed to include cases of rape committed by landlords, officials, management personnel, employers, or moneylenders.

Another central demand by feminist scholars and women's rights activists was to criminalise marital rape (Manushi, 1980, p 46; Bohra, 1992; Saheli, 1999; Agnes, 2002, p 846; R Kapur, 2005a) so that the law would no longer be based on the understanding that '[a]fter marriage the woman becomes the property of the husband' (Agnes, 1984, p 5).

In their demands for reforms, women's groups and feminist activists often used the argument that the Indian rape laws were more than a century old and thus 'outdated' (Saheli, 1999). One activist from the organisation Vimochana ('liberation'), for instance, remembers:

> Of course, we all fought … for a change in the rape law because the rape law was passed sometime in the 1860s or 1870s by the British. The British have changed their laws, but in our own country, the laws still were not changed. And so we campaigned for a change (Interview with the author on 9 July 2019).

Though the various women's groups and activists agreed on most of the positions regarding rape law reforms, specific issues also divided the women's movement, for instance, the question of whether Section 375 IPC should be made gender-neutral. While some sections of the women's movement wanted to make the rape laws gender-neutral to acknowledge that people of all genders could be both victims and perpetrators, others argued that only a gender-specific law would reflect the reality that rape was primarily committed by men against women (Agnes, 2002, p 846).

D. Rape Law Reforms

The anti-rape campaign achieved several successes over several decades. Reforms came in three waves, culminating in legislation passed in 1983, 2002, and 2013.

(i) The 1983 Law Reforms

Feminists obtained their first success relatively quickly. As a reaction to the protests that followed the *Mathura* case in 1980, the Ministry of Law, Justice and Company Affairs asked the Law Commission of India to undertake a detailed examination of the rape laws. The Commission not only invited submissions from women's organisations but also held discussions with the representatives of women's organisations when it produced its 84th report (Law Commission of India, 1980). The Commission's report, among other aspects, suggested raising the age for statutory rape to 18 years and making marital rape punishable in cases where the wife was below the age of 18 (Law Commission of India, 1980, p 10). It did not suggest broadening the definition of rape. It proposed more severe punishment in cases of gang rape (Law Commission of India, 1980, p 10). It further suggested including a new Section 354A in the Indian Penal Code to deal with cases of 'indecent assault on a minor', ie acts of sexual assault not amounting to rape committed against children below the age of 16, even if the respective act was conducted with the minor's consent (Law Commission of India, 1980, p 11).

In 1983 Parliament passed the Criminal Law (Amendment) Act 1983 – the first amendment of the Indian rape laws since Independence. The Act introduced some changes that feminists had demanded to the Indian Penal Code and the Indian Evidence Act, but not all of them. The Act substituted the heading 'rape' before Section 375 IPC with 'sexual offences'. It introduced a new element in Section 375 IPC by which sexual intercourse with the woman's consent in cases where she was 'unable to understand the nature and consequences of that to which she gives consent' (for instance, due to intoxication) would constitute rape. The law further stipulated a minimum sentence of seven years' imprisonment for rape cases, under Section 376(1) IPC.[9] In addition, a new Section 376(2) IPC held that in cases of aggravated rape, the minimum sentence was rigorous imprisonment for 10 years. These cases included situations where the perpetrator was a police officer (a), a public servant (b), the manager or a member of staff of a jail (c) or of a hospital (d), when the raped woman was pregnant and the rapist knew about her pregnancy (e), when the raped woman was under 12 years of age (f) or in cases of gang rape (g). The law thus acknowledged some of the aspects of abuse of power relations and the intersectional dimensions that feminists had articulated in their campaigns.

Cases of aggravated rape under Section 376(2) IPC now also triggered a shift in the burden of proof, as feminist activists had demanded. According to a newly inserted Section 114A IEA, in cases where the prosecution was able to prove that

[9] Mrinal Satish (2016, p 3) notes that by setting minimum and maximum punishments, the legislature had provided a statutory range within which courts could sentence, in practice; however, the minimum punishments were not actual minimums as they were not mandatory. Courts had the discretion to impose punishments lower than the prescribed minimum when they provided 'adequate and special reasons' for doing so (Satish, 2016, p 3). This discretion of the courts to impose sentences below the statutory prescribed minimum sentence was removed by the Criminal Law (Amendment) Act 2013.

sexual intercourse had taken place, the court would presume that the intercourse was non-consensual if the woman so testified. This presumption applied in all cases of aggravated rape, regrettably except for the rape of a girl below the age of 12.

The reform also introduced a new Section 376A IPC that dealt with sexual intercourse by a man with his wife during separation and new Sections 376B to 376D IPC that dealt with sexual intercourse not amounting to rape by public servants with women in their custody, in jail or a hospital. The amendments further inserted a new Section 228A into the IPC, which stipulated that the identity of the rape survivor and the offender must not be disclosed, and provided a punishment of imprisonment of up to two years and a fine for breaches of this norm.

Despite the insistent demands by feminist activists, however, the 1983 law reforms did not repeal the provision that allowed rape trials to take the prosecutrix's 'immoral character' into account in determining her credibility (Section 155(4) IEA) and left *marital* rape unpunished when the wife was over 15 years of age. In cases of marital rape where the wife was below 15 but over 12 years of age, the new law provided for a reduced punishment, a maximum of two years' imprisonment (Section 376(1) IPC).

While feminist activists and women's rights groups welcomed the changes as an essential step in the right direction, the anti-rape campaign was far from over with the 1983 amendment. In the years that followed, rape and rape law reforms remained a central topic – articulated in writing rather than through street protests, however. Feminists stressed the shortcomings that remained after the reforms of 1983: that marital rape had not been made a criminal offence (Kumar, 1993, p 133; Lawyers Collective, n.d.-c, p 5); that the law continued to distinguish between the age of consent for married and unmarried women (Kumar, 1993, p 133); and that courts continued to be able to use the prosecutrix's moral character in their reasoning (Agnes, 2002, p 844). In 1993, 10 years after the first reform, the National Commission for Women (NCW) drafted the Sexual Violence Against Women and Children Bill, which provided for further changes in the rape laws (Agnes, 2002, p 845). However, while the Bill provoked some debate, Parliament never passed it (Agnes, 2002, p 845).

(ii) The 2002 Law Reforms

The second wave of reforms began in the late 1990s. In the meantime, the courts had given several important judgments. The Supreme Court in several decisions had confirmed that the presence of injuries was not essential to prove a charge of rape (*Balwant Singh v State of Punjab*, 1987; *Karnel Singh v State of Madhya Pradesh*, 1995). Furthermore, it condemned drawing on the sexual history of the victim in rape trials. In 1996, in *State of Punjab v Gurmit Singh* the Supreme Court stated that '[e]ven if the prosecutrix ... has been promiscuous in her sexual behavior earlier, she has a right to refuse to submit herself to sexual intercourse to anyone and everyone'. It further held that '[n]o stigma … should be cast against such a witness by the Courts, for after all it is the accused and not the victim of [the] sex crime who is on trial in the Court' (ibid).

In 1997, the organisation Sakshi ('Witness'), a Delhi-based group that dealt with violence against women, filed a writ petition demanding a broadening of the definition of rape.[10] Several NGOs, including the All India Democratic Women's Association (AIDWA) and the NCW, joined Sakshi as co-petitioners (P Baxi, 2014, p 26). The groups contended that the narrow understanding of rape as including only penile-vaginal penetration ran 'contrary to the existing contemporary understanding of rape as an intent to humiliate, violate and degrade a woman or child sexually' and thus violated Article 21 of the Constitution (*Sakshi v Union of India*, 2004, paragraph 3). The petition demanded that the Court redefine the term 'sexual intercourse' in Section 375 IPC to broaden the purview of the norm (ibid, paragraph 4).

On 9 August 1999, the Supreme Court in *Sakshi v Union of India* responded to the writ petition by directing the Law Commission of India to examine whether the definition of rape in Section 375 IPC was inadequate and, if so, how it could be amended. The Supreme Court stressed that the Law Commission might 'call upon the petitioners to assist' it in producing its report (*Sakshi v Union of India*, 1999, paragraph 7).

The Law Commission submitted its 172nd report on the review of rape laws to the Supreme Court in March 2000 (Law Commission of India, 2000a). In its preparation for the report, the Commission had consulted the petitioning women's groups and the NCW. The Commission's suggestions included making rape a gender-neutral offence and broadening the definition of rape to include forced oral intercourse as well as vaginal and anal penetration with either the penis or any other body part or object without the person's consent, except where such an act was carried out for medical purposes (Law Commission of India, 2000a, pp 83–85).

The Commission also recommended the deletion of Section 155(4) IEA, stating that there was 'no relevance or reasonable connection between [an] offence of sexual assault … and the general immoral character of the victim' (Law Commission of India, 2000a, p 73). It further suggested the insertion of a new Section 164A in the Code of Criminal Procedure (CrPC), which would provide that medical examinations 'shall be conducted by a registered medical practitioner, with the consent of the victim', that they should be conducted 'without any delay', and that in cases of female victims, a female doctor should conduct the

[10] The writ petition was filed in response to the *Jhaku* case (*Sudesh Jhaku v KCJ and Others*, decided by the Delhi High Court in 1996), which had dealt with the case of a six-year-old child who had been sexually abused by her father, a high-ranking government official. As the acts did not include penile-vaginal penetration, but finger penetration and oral sex, the police refused to charge the father with the offence of rape. The girl's mother filed a writ petition in the Delhi High Court to bring the offence within the scope of Sections 375 and 376 IPC. The Court, however, dismissed the petition, holding that the said acts would amount only to a 'violation of modesty'. For a detailed engagement with this case, see Agnes (2002, p 846) and P Baxi (2014, pp 23–26).

examination (Law Commission of India, 2000, p 98). The report, however, recommended maintaining the exception of marital rape in Section 375 IPC in cases where the wife was above 16 years. Criminalising marital rape would, according to the Commission, 'amount to excessive interference with the marital relationship' (Law Commission of India, 2000a, p 23).

In December 2002, the Indian Parliament passed the Indian Evidence (Amendment) Act, 2002, which removed Section 155(4) IEA. No longer were courts entitled to draw on the 'immoral character' of the rape survivor in assessing her credibility.[11]

In the parliamentary debates preceding the passing of the Act, several speakers gave credit to the women's organisations who had pushed for this amendment.[12] Reference to equality was made only indirectly; instead, the debate revolved primarily around women's dignity and humiliation. The opening statement of the Union Law Minister, Jana Krishnamurthy, who moved the Bill, illustrates this:

> Under the Evidence Act, it is prohibited to question whether he [the perpetrator] was a man of a dubious character or what was his conduct prior to committing a particular crime. On the other hand, the very same Evidence Act says that when a woman is raped and she stands as a prosecutrix, her character prior to the act of rape is questionable. So, we are moving an amendment to see that the victim of the rape is saved from this humiliation (Minister Jana Krishnamurthy, Lok Sabha debate, 9 December 2002).

Female MPs, too, focused on dignity and their attempt to save women from humiliation.[13] One supporter of the Bill invoked the argument that the IEA reflected patriarchal notions and that the colonial laws were not suitable any more.[14] Another commentator linked rape law reforms to the 'civilisation' of

[11] Ethnographic studies show, however, that even after the deletion of the immoral character clause, the sexual history of the rape survivor continued to inform courts' decisions in rape cases and the 'two-fingers' test continued to be used as medical 'evidence' (P Baxi, 2014). For instance, in *Musauddin Ahmed v State of Assam* (2009), where a young woman had accompanied an acquaintance to a hotel room where he allegedly raped her, the Supreme Court acquitted the accused, arguing that the medical examination of the prosecutrix had found 'that she was used to sexual intercourse and that there was no injury of any kind on her body or private parts' (ibid, paragraph 10) and that the prosecutrix 'appeared to be a woman of easy virtues' (ibid, paragraph 17). In 2017, in the so-called *Jindal Law School* case (*Vikas Garg v State of Haryana*), the Punjab and Haryana High Court cited the victim's 'experimentation in sexual encounters' and her 'promiscuous attitude and voyeuristic mind' as part of its legal reasoning for granting bail to the three men convicted. These cases were no rare exceptions. Scholarship has also statistically shown that in cases where the rape survivor was sexually active outside of marriage, trial courts and High Courts imposed lower sentences on the defendants (Satish, 2016, pp 73–74) and that 'the presence of injuries resulted in a marked increase in sentence' (Satish, 2016, p 76).

[12] See, for instance, the statements by AK Premajam, Beatrix D'Souza and Sunder Lal Tiwari, Lok Sabha Debates, 9 December 2002 13th series, volume XXIX No 14.

[13] Margaret Alva, for instance, stressed that 'women's honour' after rape could not be 'restored with a financial compensation', Lok Sabha Debate, 9 December 2002.

[14] 'Sir, pardon my saying it, these were the laws drafted by men for [the] protection of men. Women were never in drafting committees and they were never consulted. These are old laws which have outlived their utility' (Margaret Alva, Lok Sabha Debate, 9 December 2002).

Indian society.[15] The misogynist stereotypes that inform Section 155(4) IEA, however, were not addressed in the debate. Instead, several male commentators reinforced such stereotypes in their comments: for instance, when they pointed to the danger of the rape law being misused and innocent men becoming the 'victims' of the law reform,[16] when they indicated that women invite rapes if they dress in a certain way,[17] or when they opined that for a victim, rape is worse than death.[18]

While several MPs stressed that the Bill would not go far enough and that more reform was needed,[19] the other recommendations by the Law Commission were not realised at this point. In particular, the definition of 'sexual intercourse' in Section 375 IPC remained narrow.

In May 2004, the Supreme Court articulated itself again on the *Sakshi* case (*Sakshi v Union of India*, 2004). Referring to the reports of the Law Commission and the legal systems of other countries and citing the feminist author and activist Susan Brownmiller, the Court agreed with the opinion that sexual assault beyond penile-vaginal intercourse could equally violate the 'the personal, private inner space' and harm the victim's 'mind, spirit and sense of self' (Susan Brownmiller, cited in *Sakshi v Union of India*, 2004, paragraph 6). Ultimately, however, the Court concluded that 'it will not be in the larger interest of the State or the people to alter the definition of 'rape' as contained in Section 375 IPC by a process of judicial interpretation' (*Sakshi v Union of India*, 2004, paragraph 26).

Yet, while not broadening the definition of rape, as feminists had hoped for, the Court, in this case, gave a precedent on another critical issue: making rape trials less traumatic for rape survivors. To avoid victims of sexual assault having to be confronted with meeting the accused in court, the Court suggested that pictures or videos of the accused be screened during a trial (*Sakshi v Union of India*, 2004). It also recognised that questions posed in cross-examination were often 'purposely designed to embarrass or confuse the victims' so that they would not

[15] The high number of rape cases in India would 'stigmatise the whole society', stated Raghuvansh Prasad Sigh. No country in which 'such societal evils and moral degradation' prevail could call itself a 'civilized' nation (Raghuvansh Prasad Sigh, Lok Sabha Debate, 9 December 2002).

[16] Sunder Lal Tiwari stressed that innocent men could be accused of rape 'in the wake of … emotions'. Prabunath Singh opined that '[m]any [rape] cases are fake and fabricated ones'. These commentators see medical examinations and the punishments of victims who lie about rape as the solution here. Consequently, argued Prabunath Singh, 'persons making false allegations should also be awarded at least half of the punishment as it would have been awarded in case of the rapist' (Lok Sabha Debate, 9 December 2002).

[17] Chandra Bhushan stated: 'I can say with authority that the customs prevalent in Metro-cities under the impact of western culture has also affected such rape cases … Government can't impose dress code but one thing is sure that it certainly ignites such incidents' (Lok Sabha Debate, 9 December 2002).

[18] 'Rape is [a] more heinous crime than murder. In murder, one dies then and there whereas a rape victim suffers life-long', stated Raghuwansh Prasad Singh (Lok Sabha Debate, 9 December 2002).

[19] See, for instance, the statements by Margaret Alva, Beatrix D'Souza and AK Premajam (Lok Sabha Debate, 9 December 2002).

narrate details of the abuse (ibid). Therefore, the Court suggested that questions in cross-examination should be given in writing to the Court so that the judge could rephrase these in more neutral language (ibid).

With regard to the two-fingers test, the Delhi District Court gave a 'historic judgment' (P Baxi, 2014, p 102) that rendered the two-fingers test unconstitutional. In *State v Umesh Singh* (2010), the Court held that the two-fingers test, if performed without the woman's consent, violated her right to privacy and life. In 2013, the Supreme Court conformed this position, holding that 'undoubtedly, the two finger test and its interpretation violates the right of rape survivors to privacy, physical and mental integrity and dignity' and could thus not be used to prove consent (*Lillu @ Rajesh and Another v State of Haryana*, paragraph 13).

(iii) The 2013 Law Reforms

The so-called Delhi rape case, also referred to as the *Nirbhaya* ('the brave one') case, sparked a third wave of law reforms. The case dealt with the rape of Jyoti Singh by a group of men on a bus in Delhi on 16 December 2012. Jyoti Singh was brought to a hospital after the assault and later succumbed to her injuries. The incident provoked large-scale street protests and received much media attention nationally and internationally (Schneider, 2015). The media focused mainly on the brutality of the rape, during which the perpetrators used an iron rod to assault the victim.[20] This brutality and the subsequent protests essentially informed the judgments on the case.

The sessions court charged four of the six accused with rape and murder and sentenced them to death.[21] The Delhi High Court confirmed the judgment,[22] holding that the rape of the young woman 'would have gone [as] unnoticed as scores of other violations of infants, girls and women' if the outraged protestors hadn't taken 'to the streets in their quest for justice' (*State Through Reference v Ram Singh and Others*). The Supreme Court in *Mukesh and Another v State for NCT of Delhi*, 2017, upheld the High Court's judgment. Like the Delhi High Court, it also referred to the public protests that the incident sparked (*Mukesh and Another v State for NCT of Delhi*, paragraph 147). The judgment refers to the shocked 'collective conscience' to explain why this case was one of the 'rarest of rare' cases, which

[20] Allegedly, the perpetrators pushed an iron rod into the woman's vagina and pulled the entrails out of her body. The use of the iron rod was later questioned, and the court's uncritical acceptance of the story about the iron rod was critiqued by some commentators (Teltumbde, 2017, p 10). Teltumbde (2017, p 11) states that the 'Jyoti Singh case is a classic example of the media pandering to the instincts of people to serve their commercial interests, and the government (and judiciary) falling in line, eventually letting the country regress into a dark abyss of medievalism'.

[21] One of the accused died in police custody, possibly from suicide, and another one, the only minor among the perpetrators, was tried in a juvenile court and given the maximum sentence of three years' imprisonment in a reform facility.

[22] Death sentences imposed by sessions courts must be confirmed by their jurisdictional High Courts (Section 28(1) and (2) CrPC).

justified the death penalty. The Court articulated its hope that the incident would 'pave the way' for a 'battle for gender justice' and 'for combating violence against women and ensuring widespread attitudinal changes' (ibid, paragraph 149).

Yet, the judgment does not deserve only praise. Some commentators have held that the case was an act of revenge rather than an establishment of justice (Teltumbde, 2017).[23] Also, the judges seemed less concerned about the fact that sexual assault was a structural problem related to power dimensions and instead seemed to draw on an understanding of rape as a crime of passion. According to the Court, 'unchained carnal desire' and 'passion' had 'ruled the mindset of the appellants to commit a crime' (*Mukesh and Another v State for NCT of Delhi*, paragraphs 147, 356).

Soon after the incident and as a result of the protests, on 23 December 2012, the Indian government set up a committee under the chairmanship of Justice JS Verma, the former Chief Justice of the Supreme Court, to suggest possible amendments to the criminal law relating to sexual assault. Within 30 days, the Justice Verma Committee, as it came to be known, delivered its report of more than 600 pages. The report not only engaged with rape but also tackled sexual harassment in the workplace, trafficking of women and children, child sexual abuse, *khap panchayats*[24] and honour killings. It critically assessed criminal law procedures, including the role of the police and doctors. The Commission militated against the two-fingers test and against the drawing of conclusions on the woman's past sexual history from such tests, which still occurred regularly despite the deletion of Section 155(4) IEA (Verma, Seth, & Subramanium, 2013, p 275). The Committee suggested, among other things, broadening the definition of rape, making the victim/survivor of sexual assault gender-neutral while maintaining the gender-specificity with regard to the perpetrator, criminalising marital rape, replacing the offence of outraging the modesty of a woman with sexual harassment, and including stalking as an offence (Verma et al, 2013).

The legislature responded to these recommendations by enacting the Criminal Law (Amendment) Act, 2013, which came into force on 3 April 2013 and provided for amendments to the Indian Penal Code, the Indian Evidence Act, and the Code of Criminal Procedure. The Act took up some, but not all, of the recommendations made by the Justice Verma Committee. Significantly, it modified the definition of rape in Section 375 IPC to include oral sexual intercourse as well as vaginal and anal penetration with either the penis or any object or body part. Explanation 2

[23] Arvind Narrain (2014, p 38) notes that the death penalty imposed in the Delhi rape case stood in stark contrast to the *Naroda Patiya* judgment of August 2012, which dealt with incidents that involved the murder of 96 Muslims and the rape of Muslim women during the 2002 Gujarat pogrom and where the court refrained from imposing the death penalty and sentenced the perpetrators to prison terms ranging from 14 years to life.

[24] *Khap panchayats* are assemblies of community/ village elders functioning as informal (ie not part of the state system) dispute-resolution bodies, frequently with only male members. *Khap panchayats* have been criticised for deciding disputes in ways that discriminate against women and individuals who do not abide by conservative gender roles.

to Section 375 IPC now defined consent as an 'unequivocal voluntary agreement' by words or gestures to participate in the specific sexual act and stressed that the lack of physical resistance on the part of the woman shall not be regarded as consent. The Act added to the list of cases of aggravated rape in Section 376(2) IPC by including cases where the offender was a member of the armed forces (c), where the rapist was the woman's relative, guardian or teacher (f), where rape was committed during communal violence (g), where the offender was in a position of control or dominance over the woman (k), where the woman suffered from physical or mental disability (l), where the rape caused grievous bodily harm (m) or where the offender repeatedly committed rape against the same woman (n). A newly introduced Section 166A IPC also penalised police for failing to register first information reports in cases of rape. Rape, however, remained gender-specific, and the marital rape exception also remained in place.

Thus, in many aspects, the amendment reflected the demands of the women's movement: it broadened the definition of rape; it clearly stipulated that the woman's lack of physical resistance could not be interpreted as consent; and it recognised the intersectional dimension that the offence of rape often has.

In some respects, however, the law reform went beyond what women's rights activists had demanded and instead fed conservative and paternalistic ideas about sexuality, thereby drawing on an understanding of women's protection rather than gender equality. The new Section 375 IPC, for instance, increased the age of consent to 18 years, which meant that any sexual activity, irrespective of consent, with a woman below the age of 18 constituted statutory rape. The law furthermore allowed for the death penalty in cases of sexual assault that led to the death or a 'persistent vegetative state' of the victim (Section 376A). The death penalty, however, had been explicitly rejected by women's organisations (see, for instance, Saheli, 1999).

E. The Marital Rape Exception

The 2013 reforms did not include criminalising marital rape. When the issue arose in the Parliament, the Standing Committee on Home Affairs rejected the recommendations of the Verma Committee. Instead, the report of the Standing Committee holds that 'several Members felt that … marital rape has the potential of destroying the institution of marriage' (Department-related Parliamentary Standing Committee on Home Affairs, 2013, p 47). And further:

> In India, for ages, the family system has evolved and it is moving forward. Family is able to resolve the problems and there is also a provision under the law for cruelty against women. It was, therefore, felt that if … marital rape is brought under the law, the entire family system will be under great stress and the Committee may perhaps be doing more injustice (Department-related Parliamentary Standing Committee on Home Affairs, 2013, p 47).

Several individuals, women's groups and activist lawyers thereafter challenged the marital rape exception in the courts. Independent Thought, an organisation focusing on child rights, for instance, filed public interest litigation in the Supreme Court arguing that the marital rape exception violated the rights of married girls between the ages of 15 and 18 years. The petitioner saw a conflict in laws, considering that the age of consent per the reformed Article 375 IPC was 18 years. In 2017, the Supreme Court issued a decision reading down the marital rape exception and declaring that the act of a husband having sex with his minor wife (with or without her consent) would qualify as rape under Section 375 IPC (*Independent Thought v Union of India*, 2017). This meant the marital rape exemption would only apply to cases where the woman was aged 18 years or older.

In 2018, the Gujarat High Court held in *Nimeshbhai Bharatbhai Desai v State of Gujarat* that non-consensual sexual intercourse between spouses can be punished under Section 354 as 'outraging the modesty of a woman' and under Section 377 IPC as 'sodomy'. While the Court did not declare the marital rape exception unconstitutional, it *did* engage with the common argument that removing the exception would destabilise the institution of marriage. The Court found that the contrary was the case: marital rape was 'a disgraceful offence that has scarred the trust and confidence in the institution of marriage' (*Nimeshbhai Bharatbhai Desai v State of Gujarat*, paragraph 97).

'The institution of marriage should not include the license to rape', stated Advocate Karuna Nundy, who represented AIDWA and several individuals, including a rape survivor, in a case challenging the marital rape exception (cited in Rajvanshi, 2022). In May 2022, a two-judge Division Bench of the Delhi High Court delivered a split judgment, in which one judge struck down the marital rape exception as unconstitutional as it was 'founded on a stereotypical understanding of ascribed gender roles in marriage' and would deny the wives' 'agency' and 'bodily autonomy' and therefore violate Article 15 (*Farhan v State and Another*, paragraph 57). The other judge, however, upheld the provision. Referring to the standing committee mentioned above, he argued:

> If … the legislature, after interaction with stakeholders and after conscious deliberation and debate, forms the opinion that [the] introduction of the concept of 'rape' into the marital sphere may imperil the institution of marriage, this Court … would, in my opinion, be thoroughly ill-equipped to hold otherwise.

With the replacement of the Indian Penal Code by the Bharatiya Nyaya Sanhita, 2023 the marital rape exception – in cases where the wife was 18 years or older – was maintained (see Exception 2 of Section 63 BNS). A challenge to the marital rape exception is pending in the Supreme Court.[25]

[25] *Hrishikesh Sahoo v The State of Karnataka* (Case Number: SLP(Cr.) 4063-4064 of 2022).

F. Evaluation

Looking at the legal changes that were brought about during the past decades and comparing the legal situation today with the situation in the 1970s, it is fair to say that feminist activism was successful with most of its central goals regarding India's rape laws. Feminists succeeded with their demand to delete Section 155(4) IEA, to shift the burden of proof (at least regarding some forms of aggravated rape) and to broaden the definition of rape. The reformed law also clarified that the lack of a woman's physical resistance could not be interpreted as consent; and it recognised the intersectional discrimination and power dimensions that crimes of sexual assault often have. It further penalised the police for failing to register first information reports, thereby recognising some of the practical hurdles for women who have experienced sexual assault.

Yet, the one area that the legislator has not dared to invade, despite much pressure from feminist activists, is the marital rape exception. Courts have slowly started to shake the foundations of this provision. It remains to be seen whether feminists will ultimately be successful with their attempts to criminalise marital rape.

Several factors seem to have been influential in determining the outcome of the feminist campaign: the movement's strength and its strategies, the relative absence of counter-mobilisation, and the aspect of legal culture.

The anti-rape campaign was strong and vocal. Rape law reform was a prominent topic in the women's movement, especially in the late 1970s and early 1980s, and it had a high priority on the feminist agenda. Except for a few points on which feminists disagreed, the movement was united in its demands for legal change.

In addition, the strategies and timing of the feminist actions played a role. Activists and groups brought the violence that women had suffered to the attention of the broader public and used this attention as a 'window of opportunity' to push for legislative change.

At the same time, it is important to point out that the reforms to India's rape laws were not realised all in one go. They came about in three reform waves culminating in legal changes in 1983, 2002 and 2013. Each reform was limited in some way from a feminist viewpoint. With each reform, however, feminists could build upon their achievements and articulate further demands for change.

Feminists also benefitted from the lack of counter-mobilisation and opposition to their reforms in the media. In the aftermath of the Delhi bus rape case, attention from international media also pushed the government to act quickly. Urvashi Butalia explains this in an interview:

> That the case got so much international media attention pushed our government to take some action. Because they were embarrassed by this attention, because they did not

> want to be seen as a country that is violent towards its women. It destroys the image of India as the rising super power, as the country that is doing well economically, the shining India story is marred by something like this (Goel, 2015, p 133).[26]

Legal culture may explain why the state has been so reluctant to change the marital rape exception in India's laws on sexual assault. The understanding of the public–private divide and the idea that criminalising marital rape would lead to an erosion of marriage impacts the position of the Law Commission, the Parliament and the courts. It remains to be seen whether feminist activists will be able to replace this understanding with a counter-narrative.

II. The 'Death Trap' of the In-Laws' House: The Campaign against Dowry Violence

Other than focusing on the issue of rape, the early women's movement also campaigned very vocally on dowry-related violence. Dowry refers to a custom prevalent primarily, but not exclusively, among Hindus, according to which before the marriage, at the event of a wedding and after that, the bride's family gives money or gifts to the groom or his family or pays for the wedding expenses.

The cases of dowry violence that concerned the early women's movement related to instances where the bride's family could not meet the dowry demands, and the husband's family maltreated the wife psychologically or physically so much that the assaults resulted in the wife's death, either by way of suicide after longstanding physical and/or psychological violence, or by way of murder. 'Dowry deaths', as they were often referred to, frequently occurred in the form of burning: in-laws poured kerosine over the woman's body and set her afire alive, or the woman committed suicide by burning herself. On many occasions, such deaths were covered up as kitchen accidents and were also filed as such by the police – a phenomenon that the women's movement has exposed and publicly denounced.

This section deals with the anti-dowry campaign that began in the late 1970s and in which feminists demanded stricter laws to tackle dowry giving, a better implementation of the existing laws, and the inclusion of dowry murder as a separate offence in the Indian Penal Code. I will show that they achieved significant successes at the level of legislation in the 1980s.

[26] At the same time, Butalia bemoaned the fact that Western media and Western feminists had little knowledge about India's long history of an active women's movement and seemed unaware that the topic of sexual assault had been prominent in their campaigns for several decades. In her words: 'What disturbed me was not only the media's reaction, but also the reaction of a lot of Western feminists, who assumed that there is no women's movement in India and who started to jump up and down saying: we will go in there and help. There was a group of Harvard feminists, who created a project, which says: "We must assist the Indian government and the justice Verma committee"' (Goel, 2015, p 134).

A. Women Burned to Death

When the Indian women's movement emerged in the 1970s, dowry and dowry-related violence was one of its focus areas. Dowry, according to the Towards Equality report by the Committee on the Status of Women (1974, pp 71–74), was 'what is given to the son-in-law or to his parents on demand either in cash or in kind', usually including jewellery, gold or silver, but also cash, furniture and household objects, status symbols, residential accommodation in the cities, financial support for the groom's (foreign) education or his setting up of a business (Committee on the Status of Women in India, 1974, pp 72–74). While the more significant part of dowry was typically transferred at the time of marriage and often settled beforehand, the practice of gift-giving from the bride's to the groom's family frequently did not end with marriage but continued for years after that (Committee on the Status of Women in India, 1974, p 71).

Society largely viewed dowry as a kind of 'premortem inheritance' (Committee on the Status of Women in India, 1974, p 71) for the daughter who traditionally left her natal home after marriage and moved to the house of the husband's family. This concept also justified her partial exclusion from inheritance rights, which I described in Chapter four. However, unlike the property that was typically given to sons as inheritance (real estate, (farm)land, businesses), goods given to daughters as dowry were often not income-generating but depreciated over time (Kishwar, 1986, p 9). In addition, in practice, the woman usually had no, or limited, access to the objects that were part of her dowry, as these were frequently kept by the in-laws (Committee on the Status of Women in India, 1974, p 73).[27]

The Dowry Prohibition Act of 1961 had made the giving and taking of dowry illegal. The Act, however, not only had a limited definition of dowry, as it included only cash or gifts given at the marriage or before,[28] but in practice, also remained 'totally ineffective' (Committee on the Status of Women in India, 1974, p 76) and was 'hardly … invoked' in the first two decades after its enactment (Sarkar et al, 1994). The culture of dowry giving was normalised, even by courts. For instance, in the case of *Shobha Rani v Madhukar Reddi*, which later came before the Supreme Court, the trial court held that: 'The respondent is a young upcoming doctor. There is nothing strange in his asking his wife to give him money when he is in need of it' (cited by the Supreme Court in *Shobha Rani v Madhukar Reddi*, 1987, paragraph 13).

The dowry culture, however, not only frequently put young women and their families under significant financial constraints, but also often affected women's

[27] In this sense, dowry differed from *stridhan*, which meant 'the property of a woman which is hers to do with as she will' (Sarkar, Ramanathan, & Mehra, 1994, p 7).

[28] Section 2 spoke of gifts given 'as consideration for marriage'. The Delhi High Court elaborated that 'property that may pass hands subsequent to marriage … is not dowry', see *Madan Lal and Others v Amar Nath*, 1985.

psychological and bodily integrity. Women's harassment by their partners or in-laws because they had not brought enough dowry was a frequent phenomenon and often culminated in mental and physical violence against the wife, sometimes causing her death. An activist from Vimochana recalls:

> If [the women] didn't give the dowry, they were ill-treated, they were thrown out of the house, they were not given food to eat, they were beaten, slapped, and even set on fire. Setting them on fire seemed to be the easiest thing because they [the in-laws] would say it was a stove bust, or her clothes caught fire when she was cooking. So, when you say that, they all think it's an accidental death. So, burning seemed to be the easiest way out because it burnt away the woman and burnt away all the evidence that was there (Interview with the author on 9 July 2019).

The Law Commission of India (1983b), in its 91st Report on Dowry Deaths and Law Reform, produced a list of 'the factual components of a typical "dowry death"'. According to the Commission, 'The person who dies in a dowry death is always a woman', the victim is 'totally dependent on her husband', '[i]n the vast majority of cases, the death occurs as a result of burns sustained by the woman in a fire', '[t]he death mostly takes place within the house; the victim of the "accident" is always behind closed doors, when she dies' and

> [t]he death, where reported to the police by the husband or his relatives, is reported as caused by suicide [or an accident], but where it is reported by the woman's own parents or relatives, the suspicion of homicide is out forth (Law Commission of India, 1983b, p 3).

Cases of suicide and murder were related to the fact that women frequently had no independent financial means to make a living on their own and often found it impossible to return to their parents' house (Kumar, 1993, p 121). Women were thus frequently forced by the circumstances to stay in violent situations. The organisation Saheli (1984a) stated:

> In almost every case in which a dowry death has occurred, we find that the woman, harassed by her husband and in-laws, fled for shelter to her parental home, only to be returned to her 'rightful place', her 'Sasuraal' [the in-laws' house], which proved to be her death trap.

Cases of murder could be tried under Section 302 IPC, or – when several persons were involved in the murder – Section 302 in combination with Section 34 IPC. However, in practice, many cases of dowry deaths were reported as either accidents or suicides (Das, 1979; Saheli, 1984a). Anecdotal evidence also shows that police officers, when informed about the burning of a woman, regularly refused to file a first information report (Kaur, 1982), often with the argument that they could not interfere in 'family affairs' or 'private' matters (Das, 1979, p 16; Kumar, 1993, p 119). Cases of abetment of suicide could be tried under Section 306 IPC. Proving abetment, however, was difficult in practice.

B. Street Protests and Dowry Boycott

Feminist campaigns against dowry and dowry-related violence began in the late 1970s, with much of the action concentrated in Delhi (Butalia, 2005, p 331). Two groups were particularly active in the early days: Mahila Dakshata Samiti ('Committee for Women's Protection') and Stree Sangharsh ('Women's Struggle') (Butalia, 2005, p 331). The journal *Manushi* and its editor, Madhu Kishwar, also played a central role in the fight against dowry and dowry violence. The movement's slogan was 'Women are not for burning' (Das, 1979).

As in the anti-rape campaign, here too, activists worked on different levels. Meera Mohanty (2001, p 32) stated in *Kali's Yug*: 'Dowry is an evil that needs to be combated at two levels: at the level of the macro structure through legislation and social engineering and also at the level of micro structure, by creating awareness and changing belief systems'. Awareness raising occurred by making the phenomenon of dowry deaths public, by exposing the so-called 'accidents' as murders and by problematising the dowry culture and its consequences (Das, 1979; Manushi, 1981a, 1981c; Kaur, 1982; Krishnakumari & Geetha, 1983; Kishwar, 1986; Mohanty, 2001; Butalia, 2005, p 332). For instance, Saheli (1984b) wrote: 'Each morning we open our newspapers to find one or two women, "burnt while cooking food" or "heating milk"'. In reality, however, stated the organisation, these deaths were the results of 'an extreme form of violence women are subjected to in our society' (Saheli, 1984b). In a similar vein, Flavia Agnes (1984, p 2) pointed out:

> The term 'dowry deaths' is an oversimplification of a far more complex social phenomenon of power relationships within the family. We prefer to call them plain 'wife-murders'. And most of these women are harassed for a long time before [they are] … murdered or driven to suicide and for every woman who dies in her home, there must be a million more who are beaten and harassed, economically deprived and mentally humiliated.

Besides campaigns for awareness raising, activists also demanded law reforms and commented on Bills pending in Parliament (Vanita, 1983). Groups and activists, for instance, passed resolutions urging the government to make dowry giving a cognisable[29] offence and to make a post-mortem obligatory if a woman died within seven years after getting married (Das, 1979, p 15). Feminists criticised '[t]ardy investigations by the police' (Mohanty, 2001, p 32) and 'major lapses in [the] collection of evidence' in court cases (Mehra, 1993, p 6).

[29] The CrPC distinguished between 'cognisable' and 'non-cognisable' offences and in its First Schedule designated offences as belonging to one of these two categories. In the case of cognisable offences (generally the more serious offences) the police are authorised to conduct investigations without the permission of a magistrate and may arrest suspects without obtaining a warrant (Section 2(c) CrPC). In the case of 'non-cognisable' offences (generally the less serious offences), the police must obtain the magistrate's permission to conduct an investigation and have no authority to arrest without a warrant (Section 2(l) and 155(2) CrPC).

At the same time, feminists were clear about the fact that the law itself, 'however well designed, is unlikely to effect concrete changes in the situation unless accompanied by far reaching political, social and economic changes in the status of women both within and outside the family' (Vanita, 1984). Feminists, therefore, focused on implementing the laws through state organs and linked the problem of the dowry culture to the lack of inheritance rights for daughters and women's economic dependence on their husbands (Kishwar, 1986; Mehra, 1993; Mohanty, 2001). Activists, for example, pointed to the fact that dowry in practice would not, as was sometimes argued, strengthen the bride's economic position; nor was it a form of pre-mortem inheritance for daughters. Instead, as Madhu Kishwar (1986, p 6) wrote, dowry was 'essentially a transfer of wealth from men of one family to those of another', with brides functioning as 'vehicles' for the wealth transfer. To challenge this practice, people's mindsets had to change: families needed to start seeing their daughters as 'their own' rather than as '*paraya dhan*' ('someone else's wealth'), and women needed to no longer 'feel compelled to get married and stay married at all costs' (Kishwar, 1986, p 13).

Women's groups often organised spontaneous protest marches when they heard about a dowry death. After the murder of Tarvinder Kaur in 1978, for example, Stree Sangharsh gathered hundreds of protestors to march through the streets of the residential area where Tarvinder Kaur had lived and died (Kumar, 1993, p 118; Butalia, 2005, p 332). Over the years, many such spontaneous feminist protests followed, often attracting media attention (Das, 1979, p 16; Butalia, 2005, p 332; Vimochana, n.d., p 17). Madhu Kishwar (2005, p 3) later recalled this kind of protest as follows:

> [O]ur engagement spontaneously took the form of holding protest demonstrations outside the house of the murdered or dead woman calling for a social boycott of the family, which had tortured the woman to death or drove her to suicide. Each such demonstration would then move on to the local police station, either protesting against their complicity or demand[ing] that they take appropriate and swift action in booking the culprits.

Similarly, one activist from Vimochana remembered that

> [t]here was a lot of campaigning. We used to do protests out[side] of the house where the woman [had] died … [We were] making the whole issue public, carrying posters, doing placards, wall writings, doing street plays and all these kinds of things (Interview with the author on 9 July 2019).

Protests and publications also directly called upon women to 'say NO to dowry – for yourself, your daughters and your sons' (Saheli, 1997d) or to boycott dowry by not attending weddings where dowry had been given. In the late 1970s and early 1980s, *Manushi* organised a campaign in which women vowed that they would not give or take a dowry and that they would stay unmarried if they could not find a partner who would marry them without receiving a dowry (*Manushi*, 1981a, 1981c).[30]

C. The *Sudha Goel* Judgment

One case that provoked a significant amount of attention and fuelled the feminist activism was the *Sudha Goel* case. Sudha Goel had died of burns in December 1980, 10 months after her marriage and a week before she was supposed to deliver her first child. Her death allegedly followed a time of 'torture … over demands for cash and goods in kind' (Supreme Court in *State Delhi (Administration) v Laxman Kumar*, 1985). The neighbours, who, upon hearing someone scream, had run into the house, found Goel burning and extinguished the fire by wrapping a blanket around her. When brought to a hospital, the severely injured woman accused her mother-in-law of setting her afire. Goel died the next day. Sudha Goel's husband, Laxman Kumar, her husband's brother, Subhash Chander and her mother-in-law, Shakuntala, were prosecuted on charges of murder. The defence claimed that Sudha Goel had been trying to light a kerosene stove when her saree caught fire. The sessions court found all the accused guilty and sentenced them to death. However, when the Delhi High Court, which had to confirm the sessions court's death sentence, engaged with the issue, it acquitted the accused (*Shakuntala and Others v The State*, 1983).

Women's groups had followed the proceedings of the case closely. Activists had sat in the courtroom and gathered outside the High Court when it was set to deliver its judgment. In fact, the High Court had anticipated protests against the decision it was about to deliver and foresaw that its judgment might be reversed at the next level. The judgment itself held that '[t]he verdict of acquittal, which we are about to deliver, is bound to cause flutter in the public mind, more particularly amongst women social bodies and organisations' (*Shakuntala and Others v The State*). It almost apologetically continued: 'Judges are human beings and can err. The satisfying factor is that we are not the final court and there is a court above us and if our judgment is wrong it shall be set right' (ibid).

And indeed, the High Court's acquittal of the accused 'was the spark that relit the ire of public opinion' (Sarkar et al, 1994, p 32). Women's organisations 'were

[30] On a large scale, the dowry boycott, according to Madhu Kishwar, did not have the desired effect. Kishwar, therefore, later changed her position on dowry. In 1988 she stated: 'To suggest that women refuse dowry and go emptyhanded to their marital homes is to suggest that they make even greater martyrs of themselves than society makes of them. Until we can ensure inheritance rights for daughters, we have no right to ask them to sacrifice the inadequate compensation they get by way of dowry' (Kishwar, 1988, p 10). 'We should forget the slogan, "Dahej mat do, dahej mat lo" ("Do not give the dowry; do not take dowry") and raise the slogan "Betiyon ko virasat do, Betiyan, apni virasat lo" ("Daughters must be given property rights; daughters must claim inheritance rights")' (Kishwar, 1988).

agitated in the extreme' and held a *dharna* ('protest') outside the High Court (Sarkar et al, 1994, p 32). The demonstrations outside the Court even resulted in a petition for contempt filed against three women's groups and a resolution of the Delhi High Court Bar Association condemning the demonstrations (Kumar, 1993, p 124; Jethmalani & Dey, 1995, p 59). A group of 12 women's organisations, among them the Indian Federation of Women Lawyers, the Centre for Women's Development Studies, Saheli and *Manushi*, came together to initiate a joint petition to the Supreme Court against the acquittals by the High Court (Sarkar et al, 1994, pp 59–60; Jethmalani & Dey, 1995).

Two years later, in 1985, the Supreme Court gave its verdict in the *Sudha Goel* case. It sentenced Shakuntala (Sudha Goel's mother-in-law) and Laxman Kumar (Sudha Goel's husband) to life imprisonment but acquitted the husband's brother Subhash Chander. The Court also used the opportunity to speak about the need for social change more generally, holding that '[e]veryone in the country whether an individual or an organisation should contribute to social metabolism' (*State Delhi (Administration) v Laxman Kumar and Others*).

Many saw this judgment as a direct outcome of the efforts of women's organisations and feminist lawyers (Sarkar et al, 1994, p 60; Jethmalani & Dey, 1995). Scholar-activists Lotika Sarkar, Usha Ramanathan and Madhu Mehra (1994, p 32) opined that the 'public pressure, and the uncomfortable knowledge that it was the cynosure of critical eyes, definitely made [a] difference to scrutiny, reappraisal and reinterpretation of the evidence' in the case. To be sure, the Supreme Court explicitly stressed its independence from the protests that had happened in front of the Court by stating in its judgment: 'What happens outside the Court room when the Court is busy in its process of adjudication is indeed irrelevant' (*State Delhi (Administration) v Laxman Kumar and Others*). Yet, as Sarkar et al (1994, p 32) stated, this statement carried 'the confession of a keen and immediate awareness of the watching public eye'.

The three women's organisations accused of contempt got off lightly. The Delhi High Court held that the groups' motivation 'to advance the cause of suffering women in this country' was 'of course unreservedly accepted' and therefore confined itself to expressing its disapproval of the groups' actions and asking the respondents to moderate their activities (*Shri VK Dutta v MDSCW and Others*, cited in Jethmalani & Dey, 1995, p 59).

While, so far, the story looks simple and promising – a regressive High Court judgment sparked a campaign by feminist activists, which led to a Supreme Court judgment in the feminist interest – a closer look at the two judgments shows that the picture is not so black and white. The *Sudha Goel* judgments are good examples of what Ratna Kapur (2016, p 750) might have had in mind when she spoke about cases in which something might be lost despite a court victory and something might be won despite a defeat. An analysis of the two cases' language and line of argumentation reveals why this is the case.

Though the Delhi High Court acquitted the accused, it seems to have considered and approved of the feminist arguments and activism on a large scale. The Court held in its judgment that: 'We appreciate the anxiety displayed by some of the women organisations in causes of wife burning – a crime to be condemned by one and all [and] if proved deserving the severest sentence' (*Shakuntala and Others v The State*, paragraph 134). 'The evil of dowry', according to the Court, was 'a matter of concern for the society as a whole' (ibid). It was part of broader 'social and economic conditions' that discriminated against women and had 'to be fought at different levels' (ibid).

The Supreme Court, on the other hand, although ultimately deciding in a manner that feminists had favoured, used a reasoning that deployed various gendered stereotypes. In its concluding remarks, for instance, the Court compared a young wife (the 'girl' in the Court's terminology) to a plant that needs particular care to flourish:

> Every marriage ordinarily involves a transplant. A girl born and brought up in her natural family when given in marriage, has to leave the natural setting and come into a new family. When a tender plant is shifted from the place of origin to a new setting, great care is taken to ensure that the new soil is suitable and not far different from the soil where the plant had hitherto been growing … When a girl is transplanted from her natural setting into an alien family, the care expected is bound to be more than in the case of a plant … In the growing years in the natural setting the girl – now a bride – has formed her own habits, gathered her own impressions, developed her own aptitudes and got used to a way of life. In the new setting some of these have to be accepted and some she has to surrender (*State Delhi (Administration) v Laxman Kumar and Others*).

Such reasoning does not see the wife as an equal partner to her husband and her freedom from harassment and ill-treatment as legal rights, but rather regards her as a weak creature in need of care and protection.

While this closer analysis of the judgment does not deny what has been said above about the women's movement's impact on the Court, it diminishes the positive evaluation of the Supreme Court's judgment and the narrative of linearity to a certain extent.

D. Law Reform

In the meantime, while the *Sudha Goel* case was before the Delhi High Court, feminists could celebrate some early successes of their campaigns at the level of law-making. In August 1983, the Law Commission of India published its 91st report, recommending several legal reforms regarding dowry and dowry violence. These included changes to the Indian Penal Code and the Indian Evidence Act. The Commission suggested that a provision 'should be inserted in the Indian Penal Code, punishing a person who, by persistent act[s] of cruelty, drives a member of the family living with him to commit suicide' and that 'persistent demands for dowry shall amount to persistent acts of cruelty for this purpose' (Law Commission of India, 1983b, p 10). Furthermore, it suggested a provision holding that in cases 'where a married woman dies within five years of her marriage of burns or injuries' sustained in her marital home and, when her husband does not inform the police about the death and when he has no reasonable explanation for the death (the burden of proof thereby lying on him), the husband shall be guilty of an offence punishable with imprisonment of up to three years and/or a fine (Law Commission of India, 1983b, p 10). In addition, the Commission suggested the insertion of a provision in the IEA providing that in the circumstances mentioned above if there was 'credible information that there had been persistent demands for dowry', it should be 'presumed' that the woman's death 'was the result either of suicide to which the woman was driven by such persistent demands of dowry, or homicide' (Law Commission of India, 1983b, p 10).

In December of the same year, shortly after the Delhi High Court judgment in the *Sudha Goel* case, the Parliament passed the Criminal Law (Second Amendment) Act, 1983, which introduced the changes the Law Commission had suggested. The Act introduced a new Section 498A into the Indian Penal Code to deal with cases where the husband or his relatives subject a woman to cruelty. Cruelty, according to the provision, meant any conduct that was 'likely to drive the woman to commit suicide or cause grave injuries or danger to life, limb or health' or harassment of a woman to have her or her family meet unlawful dowry demands. The offence was made cognisable and non-bailable.[31] The fact that this norm provided for the accused to be arrested without a warrant and held without bail, along with the fact that it recognised family (rather than just spousal) violence as a criminal offence, made the introduction of Section 498A 'groundbreaking' in the view of many feminists (Basu, 2015, p 179).

The Act further amended Section 174(3) CrPC, as demanded by feminists, so that it now ordered a mandatory post-mortem in cases where a woman had died an unnatural death within seven years of marriage. Furthermore, a new Section 113A IEA, entitled 'Presumption as to abetment of suicide by a married woman', ordered that in cases of a woman's suicide within seven years after her marriage where it was shown that her husband or his relatives had subjected her to cruelty, the court might 'presume … that such suicide had been abetted by her husband or by such relative of her husband'. The provision thus shifted the burden of proof to the accused.

In 1984 and 1986, two legislative reforms were passed to amend the Dowry Prohibition Act. The Dowry Prohibition (Amendment) Act, 1984 and the Dowry Prohibition (Amendment) Act, 1986 broadened the definition of dowry to include presents given at any time after the marriage, imposed a ban on dowry-related advertisements and inserted a new Section 8A into the Dowry Prohibition Act, compelling the government to appoint 'dowry prohibition officers' to monitor compliance with the Act. Notably, the Act of 1986 also introduced

[31] The CrPC made a distinction between 'bailable' (Section 436) and 'non-bailable' (Section 437(1)) offences. The Bharatiya Nagarik Suraksha Sanhita, 2023, maintains this distinction (Section 2(1)(c)). In the case of bailable offences, bail is 'a matter of right' (Satish, 2016, p 19). Upon arrest, if the person is willing to meet the conditions of bail, they can be immediately released by the police. In cases of non-bailable offences, on the other hand (generally the cases that are more serious in nature), bail is 'a matter of discretion' (Satish, 2016, p 19).

a new Section 304B into the Indian Penal Code, entitled 'dowry death'. This section defined dowry deaths as cases where the death of a woman is caused by 'burns or bodily injury' or where the woman has died under other unnatural circumstances within seven years of her marriage and where it is 'shown that soon before her death she was subjected to cruelty or harassment by her husband or any relative of her husband for, or in connection with, any demand for dowry'. It further provided that in such cases, the husband of the deceased or his relatives 'shall be deemed to have caused her death'. The section imposed a minimum penalty of imprisonment for seven years and a maximum of life imprisonment. It was accompanied by a new Section 113B IEA that introduced the presumption that the death of a woman within seven years of marriage amounted to dowry death if the existence of cruelty in connection with dowry demand could be proved.

Many commentators perceived these changes in the law as a direct response to the movement's campaign (Sarkar et al, 1994; Mehra, 1998; Singh, 2003). Sarkar et al (1994, p 16) opined that the women's movement's constant reporting about suicides and murders of young married women was 'a source of embarrassment to the government' and put the legislator under pressure to act. Most feminists welcomed the reforms of the early and mid-1980s, even though some flaws remained.[32] 'Through the criminalisation of dowry', wrote Madhu Mehra (1998, p 81), 'the law has censured and brought within state purview hitherto private conduct – this must be viewed as a strategic achievement of feminist engagement with the law'.

E. Evaluation and Further Developments

In terms of law-making, the feminist campaign against dowry violence can indeed be called successful. The campaign initiated three legislative reforms, the first only a few years after the movement's campaign began (1983), the other two following shortly after that (1984 and 1986). This is relatively quick – especially if we compare it to the campaigns regarding personal laws, where it often took decades until feminist activism resulted in legislation. The reforms introduced a new offence – dowry death (Section 304B) – into the IPC and shifted the burden of proof to the accused, making it much easier for cases to succeed in court. The reforms further introduced a new Section 498A into the IPC to deal with cases of cruelty towards the wife. They also amended Section 174(3) CrPC as demanded by feminists so that the section ordered a post-mortem in certain instances, and they introduced a new Section 113A IEA dealing with cases of abetment of suicide. Furthermore, reforms to the Dowry Prohibition Act broadened the definition of dowry, imposed

[32] One flaw that feminists and women's rights activists identified in the reformed law was the fact that not only the *taking* of dowry, but also the *giving* of dowry was criminalised. This meant that women or their families who attempted the prosecution of their in-laws would have to reveal that they themselves had given dowry and thus committed a criminal offence. This would make a woman and her relatives 'reluctant to sue her in-laws for fear of reprobation' (Vanita, 1984, p 30).

a ban on dowry-related advertisements and made the government appoint dowry prohibition officers to monitor compliance with the Act.

What led to these speedy law reforms? First, the movement's strength seemed to have been influential. The anti-dowry campaign was very vocal in the late 1970s and early 1980s, with hubs of protests in several cities. As in the anti-rape campaign, women used the stories of individual victims – such as Tarvinder Kaur or Sudha Goel – to point to the urgency of the matter and to stress the importance of their demands. The anti-dowry campaign drew on tactics of naming and shaming, such as protests in front of the houses of the families that had subjected women to maltreatment or in front of the police stations that had refused to file FIRs and in front of the courts where the accused were on trial. These forms of protest generated significant media responses, which helped the feminist campaign. Furthermore, concerning several demands, feminists had the Law Commission on their side. The feminist campaigns also benefitted from the fact that, at this time, there was little counter-mobilisation – this changed, however, after the law reforms.

The legal success was later reduced by a societal backlash that led the courts to undo some of the legislator's changes. After the law reforms, the narrative emerged that women would misuse the new laws, especially Section 498A IPC (Basu, 2015, p 177; Sen & Mandal, 2015, pp xxx–xxxi). Often, these accusations of misuse had a misogynist tone, alleging that irrational or greedy women would seek to imprison their innocent husbands. The debate around the misuse of Section 498A IPC gave authority by groups like Pirito Purush Pati Parishad ('Harassed Men and Husbands' Forum', Kolkata), Patni Atyachar Virodhi Manch ('Forum against Torture by Wives', Delhi) and Save the Indian Family (India-wide) (Basu, 2015, p 180).

The rhetoric also found its way into government institutions and the jurisprudence of the Supreme Court. The government's Committee on Reforms of the Criminal Justice System (2003, p 191), for instance, feared that an 'impulsive woman may lodge an FIR even on a trivial act', making 'innocent persons languish in custody'. When she later changed her mind, getting 'into the mood to forget and forgive', it would be too late: 'Even if she wishes to make amends by withdrawing the complaint, she cannot do so as the offence is non compoundable. The doors for returning to family life stand closed' (Committee on Reforms of Criminal Justice System, 2003, p 191). In 2005, the Supreme Court held that the misuse of Section 498A IPC can unleash 'legal terrorism'.[33] In 2010, the Court found that it was 'a matter of common experience that most of these complaints under Section 498-A IPC are filed in the heat of the moment over trivial issues without proper deliberations' and recommended 'a serious relook of the entire provision [Section 498A]' by the legislature (*Preeti Gupta and Another v State of Jharkhand*). In 2014, the Court held that Section 498A IPC was one of the provisions that were

[33] *Sushil Kumar Sharma v Union of India*. Ultimately, the Court, however, dismissed the public interest litigation asking that Section 498A IPC be declared unconstitutional. It held that the 'mere possibility of abuse of a provision of law does not per se invalidate a legislation'.

'used as weapons rather than shield[s] by disgruntled wives' so as 'to harass … the husband and his relatives', leading to cases where 'bed-ridden grand-fathers and grand-mothers of the husbands' got arrested (*Arnesh Kumar v State of Bihar*).

The Rajya Sabha (2011) and the Law Commission (2012) recommended that the offence under Section 498A IPC remain cognisable and non-bailable, but be made compoundable. As of 2026, however, the provision remains a non-compoundable offence. When the Indian Penal Code, 1860, was replaced by the BNS in 2024, the substance of Section 498A was retained in reorganised form as Sections 85 and 86 of the BNS. Yet, in several cases[34] the Supreme Court issued directions 'to prevent the misuse of Section 498A' (*Rajesh Sharma v The State of Uttar Pradesh*) and thus narrowed the section's scope.

Feminist scholars and women's rights activists have warned about changes to Section 498A IPC. For instance, Flavia Agnes (2015, p 12) stated that Section 498A must be saved 'from the shackles of adverse propaganda and "misuse" by the media'. The organisation Vimochana has conducted studies on the use of the provision in Bangalore to counter the 'myth of misuse' (Doddahatti, 2017). More empirical research is needed here to analyse the consequences of the law reforms. What is clear is that the debates around the misuse of Section 498A IPC impacted other feminist campaigns on gender-based violence that followed the anti-dowry campaign, as the next section will show.

III. 'To Give a Crime a Name': The Campaign for a Law on Domestic Violence

While dowry violence is one form of domestic violence, domestic violence also appears in many other forms of physical, sexual or psychological harm that women face in the domestic context, especially in the context of their marriage or intimate partnership. The campaign against domestic violence confronted society and the state with the fact that domestic violence was a systemic issue and with the problem that society and state institutions often shied away from dealing with cases of domestic violence by addressing them as 'private' matters.

Like the anti-dowry campaign and the anti-rape campaign, the campaign against domestic violence, too, began in the late 1970s, when women's groups and activists addressed the issue of wife beating and led boycotts and protests against the sale of alcohol, which they perceived as a driver of battering. From the early 1990s onwards, feminist interventions were channelled into the demands for a Domestic Violence Act. They succeeded in 2005 with the introduction of the Protection of Women from Domestic Violence Act.

[34] *Rajesh Sharma v State of Uttar Pradesh* (2017); *Social Action Forum v Union of India* (2018); *Kahkashan Kausar v State of Bihar* (2022); *Dara Lakshmi Narayana v State of Telangana* (2024).

A. No 'Private' Issues

Women who faced domestic violence had limited legal remedies at their disposal. Put simply, there were three options – at least in theory. Firstly, married women who faced violence by their husbands could seek divorce. Most personal laws (but not all, as the example of Christian personal law in Chapter four has shown) perceived 'cruelty' as a ground for divorce. Secondly, battered women could obtain a civil injunction in the form of a non-molestation order through the Civil Procedure Code, the Specific Relief Act, 1963 or (after 1984) the Family Courts Act, 1984. Such orders, however, often lacked enforcement (Keshwaar, 1991, p 7). Thirdly, women who had been subjected to violence could file criminal charges against the perpetrator. Different sections of the IPC were available, including Sections 323 (hurt), 324 (hurt by dangerous weapons or means), 325 (grievous hurt), 326 (grievous hurt by dangerous weapons or means), 337 (assault in order to confine a person), 342 (wrongful confinement), 346 (wrongful confinement in secret), 352 (assault), and 506 (criminal intimidation).

In practice, however, it was hard for battered women to use these legal frameworks, in particular because the police were often reluctant to file complaints by women against their abusive partners, because they perceived domestic violence as a 'private' matter in which the state should not interfere. A study conducted by Flavia Agnes in the early 1980s shows that:

> Very few of the wife beating cases actually reach the police station and the police take action on only a few of these. The usual form of action is to call the offender, the husband, to the police station and to 'give him advice or counselling'. Sometimes the man may be kept in the station to 'sober him down' (Agnes, 1984, p 21).

The introduction of Section 498A IPC in 1983 opened additional opportunities. Although the enactment of this Section was a reaction to the anti-dowry campaign and paragraph (b) dealt explicitly with cases of dowry harassment, paragraph (a) of the section had a broader scope and generally applied to cases where a husband or his relatives had subjected a woman to cruelty, ie any wilful conduct that was 'likely to drive the woman to commit suicide or to cause grave injury or danger to life, limb or health'. Feminists' experience in using this provision, however, was that the law was of little help in many cases because of its high evidential threshold and its narrow definition that only protected legally married women (Jaising, 2014, p 5). The existing legal framework was thus found to be 'ineffective' for women's protection (Agnes, 1984, p 21).

Stereotypes informing court decisions were another problem. In cases where domestic violence led to women's suicide, judges were, for instance, reluctant to see acts of domestic violence as causing the suicide when they found that the deceased woman had been overly 'sensitive' or temperamental or had been unable to 'adjust' herself in her in-laws' house (Mehra, 1998). For instance, in *Sharad Birdhi Chand Sarda v State of Maharashtra* (1984), the Supreme Court acquitted a husband accused of murder, holding that the deceased wife 'was a highly emotional and sensitive woman' and suffered 'out of sheer frustration'. In *Nilakantha Pati v State of Orissa* (1994), the Orissa High Court acquitted the accused husband on the basis that the wife had been 'unable to adjust herself in the family of the accused'. The Court concluded (at paragraph 29) that

> after a mild beating by the accused for some domestic quarrel in the morning in question, the possibility of the deceased putting an end to her life out of disgust being possessed of a temperament diametrically opposite to that of the accused cannot be altogether ruled out.

The reference to a 'mild beating' in this case also indicates how courts downplayed and normalised domestic violence.

In addition, as was the case with dowry violence, large parts of society regarded domestic violence in the 'private' sphere as less severe than violence between strangers, which is why individuals who knew about the violence, as well as state institutions, often refrained from interfering (Agnes, 1984; Saheli, 1987; Jaising, 2014, p 4). As one commentator noted:

> If a man beats up a woman on the street, the police, the people around and the courts would be prompt to intervene; but if a man beats up his wife, no one, neither the neighbours nor the police will intervene unless compelled to (Keshwaar, 1991, p 8).

In a similar vein, Saheli (1987) stated: 'While violence on the streets is at least recognised as a crime, wife battering has to result in grievous bodily harm before it is even perceived as a crime at all'. Domestic violence was 'seen by everybody' and yet 'unseen by anybody', as an MP would later put it in the debates on the Domestic Violence Act (D Puradeswari, Lok Sabha Debates, 23 August 2005, 14th series, Volume XII, No 20), to point to the fact that relatives and neighbours typically knew that a woman was being subjected to domestic violence, and yet nobody acted upon this. This was, of course, an argument that feminists were confronted with worldwide. Carole Pateman (1988) in her book *The Sexual Contract* from 1988 stated: 'The state as a male-dominated institution may seek to keep domestic violence as a private matter so as not to disrupt the gender order and broader "sexual contract"'.

Women who faced domestic violence and left the abusive environment were often rendered homeless (Agnes, 1984; Saheli, 2002a; Jaising, 2014, p 6). In cases where they were economically dependent on their husbands, they could not afford to live on their own, and even in cases where they *did* have independent sources of income, landlords often refrained from offering flats to single women. The women's natal families frequently persuaded the women to return to their violent partners rather than allowing them to move back in with their parents (Agnes, 1984; Jaising, 2014, p 10). In the few states where shelters for women existed, these were often poorly equipped; women were often practically locked in these homes without being allowed to go out to work, children were sometimes not admitted, and here, too, the staff tended to persuade women to return to the abusive relationships they had left (Agnes, 1984; Saheli, 1987). Saheli (1984b) noted that experience gained by women's organizations increasingly shows that no home belongs to a woman. Those of us working with battered women have shared with them the trauma of being thrown out with their children, in the middle of the night, with nowhere to go.

B. Politicising the Personal

Attempts to protest against domestic violence – then usually termed 'wife battering' – date back to the early days of the women's movement. Women's groups pursued different means to tackle the phenomenon. Consciousness-raising attempted to bring the 'private' topic 'out of the four walls of the home' (Saheli, 1987) by showing that it was a widespread phenomenon. It sought to 'reach out to a large segment of women' to make them recognise that domestic violence was 'a gross violation of human rights' (Saheli, 1987). No longer should domestic violence be treated as less severe than other forms of violence (Keshwaar, 1991, p 8). Women shared their experiences of violence in support groups (Saheli, 1987; Gangoli, 2007, p 101) and publications. Most prominently, in her autobiography *My Story … Our Story: Of Rebuilding Broken Lives*, Flavia Agnes (2014 [1984]) narrated her experience with domestic violence and her long way out of it.

Feminists also revealed common myths about domestic violence as untrue: that domestic violence was a problem only among the working class; that men only beat when they are drunk; that only men with severe psychological issues beat their wives; or that the wife's wrongful behaviour is the cause for the violence (Agnes, 1984). Instead, scholar and activist Flavia Agnes (1984, p 6), for instance, showed by drawing on interviews and surveys with domestic violence survivors that the phenomenon was widespread and 'cuts across all class barriers'.

Activists also helped domestic violence survivors on a practical level: they sheltered battered women, helped them to find employment, supported women in finding psychological assistance, confronted abusive husbands in their workplaces, and helped women retrieve their belongings from their marital homes (Saheli, 1987; Gangoli, 2007, p 101). Women's groups also produced legal manuals on domestic violence, informing women about the existing laws and providing advice on what women should do in cases of violence (Gangoli, 2007, p 103).

Seeing one cause for the problem of domestic violence in the fact that wives were frequently economically dependent on their husbands and therefore practically unable to leave violent relationships (Agnes, 1984, p 18), one feminist demand was that the state provide battered women with 'free legal aid' and ensure that legal representation was 'more committed', 'sympathetic and understanding' (Agnes, 1984, p 19). Another demand was that the state provide shelters for women on a large scale (Agnes, 1984, p 19; Saheli, 1988).

The demand for a 'Domestic Violence Act' had already been made in the early 1980s (Agnes, 1984, p 23). It became more vocal in the early 1990s (Keshwaar, 1991; Gangoli, 2007, p 103; Jaising, 2014). Indira Jaising and the Lawyers Collective played a central role in this campaign, the motive of which was not only to provide women with alternative legal remedies but also to make the law recognise the phenomenon of domestic violence, or, in the words of Indira Jaising (2011) 'to give a crime a name'. In 1991, the journal of the Lawyers Collective published a cover story addressing the 'crying need for a law against domestic violence' (Keshwaar, 1991). In the same issue of *The Lawyer*, it printed the first model law against domestic abuse based on suggestions made by women's rights activists, survivors of domestic violence, lawyers, and judges. Commentators made it clear that 'violence' should cover not only physical but also psychological violence, for instance, in cases of verbal abuse or situations where women were not allowed to leave the house or to meet friends or family members, or where women were deprived of food, clothing, medicine, and other necessities (Bakshi, 1994, p 13).

The early 1990s also witnessed essential developments in international law and its impact on Indian politics. India ratified CEDAW in 1993. In the same year, the United Nations General Assembly passed the Declaration on the Elimination of Violence Against Women. In 1994, the UN Human Rights Commission appointed the first Special Rapporteur to investigate the causes and consequences of violence against women. In 1995, the Fourth World Conference on Women in Beijing reiterated the understanding of violence against women as a human rights issue. In 1996, the United Nations Commission on Human Rights passed its framework for model legislation on domestic violence, providing comprehensive guidelines for states in drafting domestic violence laws. At the same time, many foreign states introduced laws on domestic violence. These developments gave significant impetus to the campaign and served as an argument for the feminist calls for a Domestic Violence Act (Keshwaar, 1991, p 9; Bakshi, 1994, p 13; Dutta, 1999).

In 1993, the feminist campaign achieved a first interim success. The NCW asked the Lawyers Collective to prepare a draft Bill on domestic violence (Jaising, 2009, p 52; 2014, p 7). In the following years, the organisation consulted with lawyers, women's organisations and other civil society groups nationwide and presented various Bills to the NCW (Jaising, 2009, 2014). Although there had been debates about making the law gender-neutral to extend its protection to men who faced violence in the home, the final version of the Domestic Violence Bill, as presented by the Lawyers Collective, remained gender-specific in order to adequately reflect that, statistically, domestic violence was predominantly committed by men against women (Jaising, 2014, p 11).

The Bill was based on the assumption that both the criminal and the civil justice systems were 'ineffective' in catering to the 'immediate needs of women in violent situations' and sought to fill this gap (Lawyers Collective, 1999; Lawyers Collective, 2001). The Bill's 'preamble' described domestic violence as 'a heinous crime against society that has operated as a severe form of oppression of women' and stressed the state's 'obligation under the Constitution of India and international commitments towards ending violence against women and children' (Lawyers Collective, 1999; Lawyers Collective, 2001).

The Bill gave the aggrieved woman a right to reside in the shared household – a right considered necessary, given that many women were thrown out of their houses with nowhere to go. It also established so-called 'protection officers', whose role was to provide a 'link between the aggrieved women and the legal system' and help the aggrieved women gather evidence to support their cases in court (Jaising, 2014, p 10).

C. A Women's Law

After the Lawyers Collective had submitted the final version of its Bill to the NCW, the Indian government reacted with an interesting move. On 8 March 2002 – International Women's Day – it introduced a separate Bill, the Protection from Domestic Violence Bill, 2002. This put feminists in a challenging situation. At one level, they supported the government's acknowledgement that domestic violence was a serious concern to be addressed by law (Saheli, 2002b; Jaising, 2014, p 13); at another level, however, feminists sought to oppose this specific Bill, as it fell short compared with the feminist suggestions. The difficult task was thus to oppose the problematic provisions in the government's Bill without having the overall project fail.

The scope of the government's Bill was much narrower than that of the Lawyers Collective's Bill, as it protected women only against violence by 'relatives', ie persons related by blood, marriage or adoption (Section 2(a) and (i) of the Bill), and not by intimate partners to whom the women were not married. The Bill further required that the assault was 'habitual' or that it made the 'life of the aggrieved person miserable by cruelty' (Section 4 of the Bill). Feminists, in contrast, argued that 'every single act of violence degrades the woman even if the abuser is not "habitual" in his behaviour' (Jaising, 2014, p 14). Women's groups also criticised the Bill because it contained no right for victims of violence to reside in the shared household (Saheli, 2002b). They also found fault with the Bill's emphasis on preserving the family. The Bill provided for mandatory counselling (Section 11), a provision that, according to women's groups, placed 'the victim and the abuser in an equal position', thereby leading to 'further disempowerment of the woman' (Saheli, 2002b). Women's groups thus termed the Bill 'disappointing' and 'dangerous in its implications for women victims' and demanded that the Law Ministry and the Ministry for Women and Child Development push for adequate changes (Saheli, 2002b).

In response to the discomfort expressed by women's groups, the government's Bill was referred to a standing committee, which allowed individuals and women's organisations to put forward their concerns with the Bill in writing and via oral presentations (Jaising, 2014, p 15). The report that the standing committee submitted in December 2002 adopted most of the suggestions made by the women's groups (Jaising, 2014), especially the one that the law should apply to intimate partnerships beyond marriage.[35] In 2004, after the elections, the Parliament took up the Bill again.

Speakers in the parliamentary debate largely praised the proposed law as an important, even historic piece of legislation. Some commentators thanked the women's organisations who had paved the way for the law (R Senthil, Lok Sabha Debates, 14th series, Vol XIII, No 21, 24 August 2005). A few MPs based their support for the Bill on a feminist standpoint and a critique of patriarchy.[36] Most supporters (male and female), however, referred to women's 'empowerment' instead,[37] thereby often deploying traditional gender roles,[38] paternalistic views on women's protection,[39] or the need for the country's modernisation and development.[40] Tejaswini Seeramesh, for instance, stated:

> Women are helpless human beings in this world. That is why, I would request you to correct the system, empower women with economic and social strength. Then only, we can bring equality and end all the violence that is perpetrated on the women. That is why, I would like to support this Bill (Lok Sabha Debates, 14th series, Vol XIII, No 21, 24 August 2005).

Kanti Singh, the then Union Minister of Human Resource Development, who had moved the Bill, said:

> A tormented and victimized woman sitting behind the closed doors and confined to the four walls of home can hardly play any role in the development of the society. Therefore, an effort has been made through this bill to empower and provide justice to

[35] The Committee's report states: 'The Committee is aware of the fact that in our society there are numerous cases where a man and a woman, though not legally married, live together as husband and wife and their relationship has got social sanction too. Moreover, the issue of domestic violence is more proximate with the basic human rights of a woman to live a dignified life. Therefore, providing relief under the present Bill to a woman whose marriage is not legally valid won't be in conflict with the existing laws and will not give any legal sanction to the illegal marriages. The Committee, therefore, suggests that Clause 2(i) should be suitably amended to include those women also who have been living in [a] relationship akin to marriages and in marriages considered invalid by law' (Department-Related Parliamentary Standing Committee on Human Resource Development, 2002, Section 4.3).

[36] Archana Nayak, for instance, stated: 'We need to strike at the root cause of such violence, which is: the feudal mentality of patriarchy', Lok Sabha Debates, 14th series, Vol XII, No 20, 23 August 2005.

[37] Sumitaa Mahajan, Lok Sabha Debates, 14th series, Vol XII, No 20, 23 August 2005; Tejaswini Seeramesh, Lok Sabha Debates, 14th series, Vol XIII, No 21, 24 August 2005.

[38] Sumitaa Mahejan stated that 'Women form the pivot of the entire family. The entire family is dependent on her, be it her role as a mother, a sister or a wife', Lok Sabha Debates, 14th series, Vol XII, No 20, 23 August 2005; Nivedita Mane perceived the woman as the 'honour of a family', Lok Sabha Debates, 14th series, Vol XIII, No 21, 24 August 2005.

[39] Tejaswini Seeramesh, Lok Sabha Debates, 14th series, Vol XIII, No 21, 24 August 2005; Krishna Tirath pointed to the need to 'protect the women who have fallen prey to domestic violence', Lok Sabha Debates, 14th series, Vol XIII, No 21, 24 August 2005.

[40] Kiran Maheshwari stated: 'The domestic violence was never treated as violence in this country. Now when it comes to modernity, we are forced to consider it as violence in the modern atmosphere, as it is the demand of the situation', Lok Sabha Debates, 14th series, Vol XII, No 20, 23 August 2005. See also the statements by Nivedita Mane, Lok Sabha Debates, 14th series, Vol XIII, No 21, 24 August 2005. Kanti Singh, the Minister who presented the Bill, stated: 'The domestic violence is a kind of violation of the human right and a great hindrance in the way of development', Lok Sabha Debates, 14th series, Vol XII, No 20, 23 August 2005.

> those women who are being victimized by their own family members behind the closed doors of their own house (Kanti Singh, Lok Sabha Debates, 14th series, Vol XIII, No 21, 24 August 2005).

Very few MPs invoked women's constitutional rights,[41] and rather than referring to equality, MPs referred to women's dignity. D Purandeswari, for instance, argued that 'this is one of the most important legislations which have been protecting women against the steps taken to assault on the women's most basic fundamental right, that is, to lead a life of honour and dignity' (Lok Sabha Debates, 14th series, Vol XII, No 20, 23 August 2005).

Several commentators supporting the Bill narrated examples of cases of violence against women that they had heard of or read in newspapers. And several female supporters of the Bill explicitly stressed that by supporting women's rights they were not 'against men' (Sumitaa Mahajan, Lok Sabha Debates, 14th series, Vol XII, No 20, 23 August 2005). Commentators also pointed out that other countries had passed similar laws[42] or referred to the UN's framework for model legislation on domestic violence.[43]

MPs who were sceptical towards the Bill feared that such legislation would 'promote the values and ethos of the Western Culture' (Shaleindra Kumar, Lok Sabha Debates, 14th series, Vol XII, No 20, 23 August 2005), stressed the danger that the Bill would be misused (Shaleindra Kumar, Lok Sabha Debates, 14th series, Vol XII, No 20, 23 August 2005), or argued that the state should not interfere in 'private' matters. Mitrasen Yadav, for instance, said:

> We have several social relations in which not law but the fraternal, maternal love are the guiding force. We will not find any father here who would tolerate torture on his daughter. When a girl is young she is treated as flesh and blood of the family and when she grows up she is married away under the protection of her husband. There also she gets the same love and affection and protection … My submission is that though law should certainly be formulated for their protection … we cannot do everything with the help of law (Lok Sabha Debates, 14th series, Vol XIII, No 21, 24 August 2005).

Yet, overall, there was ample support for the Bill and – to the delight of feminist activists – both Houses passed it in the second half of 2025. Indira Jaising recalls that when the Bill was passed in the Lok Sabha, she told her colleague: 'Our life's work is done' (Lawyers Collective, 2012).

[41] Minati Sen stressed that '[t]here are certain provisions in the articles 14, 15 and 21 of the Constitution. They should be properly implemented and that is the objective of this Bill'. A few commentators mentioned 'human rights', thereby potentially not only referring to international human rights, but also constitutional rights: Minati Sen stated that '[v]iolence against women is also an issue of human rights' (Lok Sabha Debates, 14th series, Vol XII, No 20, 23 August 2005) and Minister Kanti Singh stated that 'domestic violence is a kind of violation of the of the human right' (Lok Sabha Debates, 14th series, Vol XII, No 20, 23 August 2005).

[42] Kanti Singh said: 'Several countries have also formulated such laws', Lok Sabha Debates, 14th series, Vol XII, No 20, 23 August 2005.

[43] Veerendra Kumar, Lok Sabha Debates, 14th series, Vol XIII, No 21, 24 August 2005.

On 27 October 2006, the Protection of Women from Domestic Violence Act, 2005 (PWDVA) came into force. The stated goal of the Act was to 'provide for more effective protection of the rights of women guaranteed under the Constitution who are victims of violence of any kind occurring within the family'. Indira Jaising (2014, p 1) points out that this invocation of the Constitution was remarkable as it broke with the understanding that constitutional law had no place in the 'private' ambit of the home and the family – as was most prominently articulated in the *Harvinder Kaur* case, mentioned in Chapter three. The Bill's statement of objects and reasons invoked CEDAW and held that domestic violence is 'undoubtedly a human rights issue'.

The Act granted rights to women and children who had faced violence by male partners or family members and held that domestic violence included physical, sexual and mental violence (Section 3). Notably, the Act protected women in 'domestic' (rather than only marital) relationships (Section 2(f)). It gave the aggrieved woman a right to reside in the shared household (Section 17) and a right to obtain civil relief. The latter included protection orders to stop and prevent violence (Section 18), residence orders (Section 19), monetary relief to reimburse the woman for medical expenditure and the loss of earnings, as well as maintenance (Section 20), orders granting temporary custody of her children (Section 21) and compensation orders for mental torture and emotional distress (Section 22). The Act further provided for the government to install 'protection officers' (Sections 8, 9 and 30), whose duties (Section 9) included, among other things, assisting the magistrate with the case and helping the aggrieved woman in obtaining legal aid, finding a shelter home or undergoing medical examination. The establishment of protection officers has been termed a 'novel element' by scholars comparing domestic violence Acts internationally (De Silva de Alwis, 2012, p 228). The Act further provided duties for shelter homes and medical facilities.

The Act thus reflected many of the feminist demands and overlapped to a large extent with the Bill that the Lawyers Collective had drafted. It maintained gender-specificity, protected women in non-marital relationships, provided for a right to residence and civil remedies for the aggrieved women, and took up the institution of protection officers.

Yet, a few additions to the Act that had been included during the parliamentary process did not meet the feminist demands. These included the provision for joint counselling of the parties (Section 14) and the provision that allowed the magistrate to seek help from persons involved in 'promoting family welfare' (Section 15). Also, the Bill's provision that required State governments to monitor the functioning of the Act had been dropped in the law-making process (Jaising, 2014, p 17). The Lawyers Collective reacted to this by establishing its own monitoring procedures (Jaising, 2009). After the enactment of the PWDVA, several women's groups, including the Lawyers Collective and Majlis, also brought out handbooks, guidelines and compilations of case law to be used by aggrieved persons, activists, lawyers and judges.

In 2008, the PWDVA was challenged as unconstitutional before the Delhi High Court because it would discriminate against men – an argument that the Court, however, did not agree with (*Aruna Parmod Shah v Union of India*, 2008, paragraph 4). While cases in which men were subjected to domestic violence did occur, stated the Court, these were exceptions and would not require or justify the protection of men through an individual Act (ibid, paragraph 4). Against this backdrop, classifying women as a group in need of protection under the Act was not unconstitutional. The Court did not invoke Article 15(3) of the Constitution, which allows the state to make special provision for women, but placed women – as a particularly vulnerable group – in a different category to men, and therefore held that Article 14 of the Constitution was not violated. The Court then not only dismissed the petition but (in a rather unusual move) also stated that the petitioner had been 'needlessly wasting public time' and directed him to pay 3,000 rupees to the Delhi High Court's legal aid programme for women, children, scheduled classes and scheduled tribes (ibid, paragraph 8).

Later, several High Courts clarified that wives and female partners in live-in relationships could also file cases under the Act against *women*, recognising that domestic violence was frequently perpetrated by female in-laws (Abeyratne & Jain, 2012, p 345; Bhatia, 2016b). The Indian Parliament eventually reacted by adding a proviso to Section 2(q) of the Act, clarifying that a 'respondent' also includes an accused man's female relative (Abeyratne & Jain, 2012, p 345).

D. Evaluation

The story of the enactment of the PWDVA is a success story, and indeed one that is quite remarkable, as the women's movement largely shaped the law-making process, right from the initiative for a new law up until the final hearings in Parliament. Out of its many campaigns, the Lawyers Collective (n.d.-a) regards the enactment of the PWDVA in 2005 as its 'most successful' one. In the eyes of the organisation, the making of the PWDVA depicts 'a new era of law making in which the demand for a law is articulated by the civil society and the content of the law is arrived at through a consultative process directed at consensus building' (Lawyers Collective, n.d.-a). In this new form of law-making, the legislative process was 'no longer the sole preserve of the state' but a participatory process in which civil society played a key role (Lawyers Collective, n.d.-a).

However, the making of the law was not the only remarkable thing. The Act also marked a paradigm shift towards the acknowledgement of the structural dimension of domestic and gender-based violence. Indira Jaising, for instance, states:

> I remember one judge (who later became a judge of the Supreme Court) asking me in 1999, what I meant by 'domestic violence'. A concept unknown to the law as recently

as 2000, now forms part of legal tender and the new law is the primary protection for women from violence (Jaising, 2011, p 353).

Other organisations agreed with the evaluation that the enactment of the PWDVA brought about a crucial change for women who experience violence. An activist from Bharatiya Muslim Mahila Andolan, for instance, told me that the PWDVA was 'a very good law', 'a law which Muslim women also use in a big way to defend their rights. It's a law for everyone' (interview with the author on 29 December 2015).

Now, which factors impacted this success story? Constitutional rights, especially the right to equality, seemed to have played a marginal role. Little reference was made to Articles 14 and 15 in the law-making process. Yet women's dignity featured several times – probably, however, rather as a moral argument than a constitutional one.

Strategies of activism, however, played a central role. What certainly helped the law-making process was that one organisation with significant expertise, the Lawyers Collective, and Indira Jaising, as a prominent spokesperson, took the lead in making very concrete steps in the drafting process. Yet, they built strong alliances by including other organisations in the process. There was a broad consensus among the movement that the law was needed. Notably, the women's groups did not stop their activism when the government of India presented its own Bill. Instead, they united in protesting against the elements they thought should be amended. Furthermore, drafting the Bill was accompanied by the publication of opinion pieces that pointed out why a domestic violence Act was necessary. It is also noteworthy that the NCW gave women's groups a platform to articulate their opinions on the draft Bills.

Timing and international developments were also important to the campaign's success. That India had ratified CEDAW in 1993 was helpful for the campaign, as it put the government under pressure and gave feminists further support for their argumentation. Also, when India was debating the Domestic Violence Bill, other states had recently passed or were about to pass domestic violence laws, too – an aspect that featured in feminist writing and in the parliamentary debates. These developments gave impetus to the campaign since, by passing the law, India was following a worldwide trend and could present itself as a progressive state.

IV. 'You Call it Teasing; We Call it Harassment': The Campaign against Sexual Harassment at the Workplace

The last campaign that I consider in this chapter is the campaign against sexual harassment in the workplace, which began in the 1990s. The feminist campaign not only succeeded in establishing the term 'sexual harassment' for behaviour that had previously been downplayed as 'Eve teasing' or outraging women's 'modesty', but also brought about a landmark Supreme Court decision – the *Vishaka* judgment – and obtained a crucial new law, the Sexual Harassment of Women at Workplace (Prevention, Prohibition and Redressal) Act, 2013.

A. No 'Trivial Matters'

Similarly to domestic violence, sexual harassment was a phenomenon for which there existed no proper name and no specific legal redress when feminists began focusing on it. Society often trivialised sexual harassment as flirting or 'Eve-teasing'. The few laws that existed reflected an understanding that sexual harassment was not so much a violation of a woman's rights but rather a violation of her honour. Section 354 IPC criminalised assaults or criminal force against a woman with the intention to 'outrage her modesty'. Section 509 IPC prohibited words, sounds, gestures, or the exhibition of objects with the intent to insult a woman's modesty. Courts frequently relied upon these sections in cases of alleged rape where the evidence was not strong enough to convict the accused under Section 375 IPC. They did not, however, usually draw upon these sections in cases of other forms of sexual harassment.

Labour law or workplace rules also offered little help for women who faced sexual harassment at work. Although some workplaces had conduct rules and mechanisms for taking disciplinary action against employees in cases of misconduct, sexual harassment of women employees was usually not recorded as a type of misconduct (Jaising, 2015, p 135). The tenor of feminist commentators in the early and mid-1990s was thus that the laws offered 'little protection to women' (Nagasaila, 1991, p 1965). 'Despite the large numbers of women in the Indian workforce and the widespread nature of the problem [of sexual harassment], no serious attempt has been made towards effectively tackling it', stated one commentator (Nagasaila, 1991, p 1965).

Furthermore, there were practical hurdles to making use of the existing laws. Filing criminal complaints against co-workers or employers was particularly challenging due to the power structures in the workplace. Women frequently refrained from making a complaint because they were afraid of losing their jobs or facing hostility from co-workers. The organisation Saheli (1997b), for example, wrote: 'Protesting against sexual harassment is extremely difficult, because it most often results in a hostile work environment, delay in promotion, or even loss of one's job'. Madhu Kishwar stated that it was 'fairly common for a man accused of sexual harassment to start a counter campaign against the woman alleging sexual misconduct on her part' (Kishwar, 1992a, p 3) or that 'the authorities protect the culprit' and silence or punish the woman who made the misconduct public (Kishwar, 1992a, p 6).

In addition, on those occasions where women decided to take action against harassing behaviour, courts frequently used Section 95 IPC to quash their claims. The norm stipulated that there was no offence if the harm experienced was 'so slight that no person of ordinary sense and temper would complain of such harm'. Rupan Deol Bajaj's case, which ultimately ended before the Supreme Court, illustrates the application of this norm in the general context of trivialisation of sexual harassment.

Rupan Deol Bajaj was an officer of the Indian Administrative Service in the State of Punjab. In 1988, a senior police officer, Kanwar Pal Sigh Gill, had, in the presence of several other people, molested Bajaj and slapped her bottom at an official dinner party (Murthy & Dasgupta, 2011, p 69; Bajaj, 2018). Her complaint to the authorities, however, remained unanswered. When she approached the authorities to take executive action under conduct rules for moral turpitude against Gill, they told her 'that they will not do anything. The chief secretary said to me, "Rupan, these things keep happening. You are not diminished. Consider yourself lucky, it could have been worse"' (Bajaj, 2018). After this experience, Bajaj filed an FIR with the police, which she also made public in a newspaper, and approached the courts, lodging a complaint under Sections 354 and 509 IPC, only for it to be dismissed on the ground that hers was too trivial a matter to be considered as an offence (Bajaj, 2018).

B. Feminist Demands for Reform

As in other campaigns, the women's movement saw its first task in raising awareness by pointing to the widespread phenomenon of sexual harassment and by expounding the structural problems with it. Feminists pointed out that sexual harassment was a violation of fundamental rights and not harmless flirting or 'Eve-teasing'. Posters stated, for example: 'You call it teasing, we call it harassment. Recognise the difference and stop this violence'.[44]

Feminists and activists also addressed the lack of legislation on sexual harassment, and suggested law reforms. Some of them thereby invoked constitutional rights, such as the right to equality (Articles 14 and 15), the freedom to practise any profession or occupation (Article 19(1)(g)), the right to a dignified life (Article 21), and the right to work (Article 41) (Nagasaila, 1991, p 1965; Kishwar, 1992b, p 17). To support their call for legislative intervention, commentators referred to the US, where courts had regarded sexual harassment as a violation of fundamental rights and had granted damages to victims (Nagasaila, 1991, p 1965; Kishwar, 1992a, p 13; Vashney, 1998).

Making concrete suggestions on what needed to change, Madhu Kishwar (1992b, p 17), for example, demanded 'that every workplace install and follow a rigorous set of procedures that make sexual harassment an offence that might even result in the harasser losing his job and being subject to court action'. She thereby

[44] Poster reprinted in Murthy & Dasgupta (2011, p 72) and on *poster women*, available here: https://www.posterwomen.org/?p=503.

placed a focus on the employers' responsibilities, so that the burden did not solely lie on the woman who had been harassed. Kishwar (1992b, p 17) suggested that workplaces assign official bodies with 'the task of listening to complaints of sexual harassment, recording them in writing, … taking official note of each of them' and conducting enquiries into the allegations. She further stated that it should be the employer's duty to make every employee 'aware that sexual harassment is unacceptable within the firm and is a punishable offence' (Kishwar, 1992b, pp 17–18). If there was substantial evidence against an accused, there should be a possibility to temporarily suspend him from his job for the period of the investigation (Kishwar, 1992b, p 18). The report of the enquiry committee should be made public 'unless the woman complainant specifically requests … to keep it confidential' (Kishwar, 1992b, p 18). Many of these demands were later taken up in the *Vishaka* judgment and – much later – in the Sexual Harassment of Women at Workplace (Prevention, Prohibition and Redressal) Act. But let us proceed step by step.

C. The *Vishaka* Case

Apart from awareness raising and law reform campaigns, women's rights activists also turned to the courts to make their claims heard. The key case in this context was initiated by several women's groups, most prominently the organisation Vishaka. Interestingly, the incident that the group used to make its claim on sexual harassment was not one of the stereotypical cases of workplace harassment in an office in the city but a case of rape that had occurred in a rural part of Rajasthan.

The case that Vishaka brought before the Supreme Court dealt with the rape of Bhanwari Devi, a grassroots social worker (a so-called *sathin*) working for the Women's Development Programme run by the State of Rajasthan.[45] According to the petition that Vishaka and the other groups filed in the Supreme Court,[46] part of Bhanwari Devi's work as a *sathin* was to raise awareness about and persuade people against child marriage. When Bhanwari Devi had attempted to prevent the marriage of a one-year-old daughter of a higher caste man, Devi met with opposition and hostility from some people in the village and was subjected to an 'economic and social boycott' (petition, paragraph 17).

On 22 September 1992, a group of higher caste men attacked Devi and her husband, beat up her husband, raped Bhanwari Devi and threatened her with dire consequences if she were to speak about the incident (petition, paragraph 23). Devi faced severe difficulties when trying to register a complaint against the men.

[45] The Women's Development Programme came into existence in Rajasthan in 1984. The *sathins* (literally 'friends') were chosen from the underprivileged sections of society, especially the Dalit and tribal communities. Bhanwari Devi belonged to a pottery caste (*kumhar*). The work of the *sathins* included intervening in cases of rape or domestic violence, challenging the power of all-male caste *panchayats* and preventing child marriages (P Baxi, 2014, p 35).

[46] Writ Petition (Criminal) No 666 of 1992, reproduced in *Kali's Yug* of August 1998.

According to the petition, the police only filed an FIR after long arguments and the police kept the *sathin*'s clothes as 'evidence', so she was forced to walk home covered in her husband's bloodstained turban (petition, paragraphs 30–32). A first hospital refused her a medical examination, and a second hospital only conducted the examination 48 hours after the incident. The Rajasthan State criminal court later acquitted the five accused because, among other aspects, the judge found it implausible that upper-caste men would rape a lower-caste woman.[47] The case drew widespread attention and led to protests by women's groups (Sen, 2014, p 336; Jaising, 2015, p 2).

In their public interest litigation before the Indian Supreme Court, Vishaka and others used this case to challenge sexual harassment in the workplace. The petition was premised on the argument that although Bhanwari Devi had repeatedly reported the month-long harassment she had been subject to through her work, the state had made no attempts to protect her and had thereby violated Articles 14 and 21 of the Constitution. The organisations accused the State of Rajasthan and the Union of India of a 'failure to recognise' that women workers who are employed by the state 'are systematically vulnerable to various forms of sexual abuse' (petition, paragraph 8). The petitioners asked the Court 'to direct that a committee headed by the National Commission for Women in consultation with women's groups and individuals as well as lawyers be appointed to prepare and submit guidelines on sexual harassment' (petition, grounds). These guidelines should suggest 'preventive steps' against sexual harassment and remedies for women who have experienced harassment (petition, grounds). In addition, the petitioners asked the Court to issue an order directing the Indian state to pay compensation of 1 million rupees to Bhanwari Devi (petition, prayer).

Before the Supreme Court decided the *Vishaka* case, it gave a verdict in Rupan Deol Bajaj's case – the case of the officer who had been sexually harassed at an official dinner party. Bajaj had pushed her case through the hierarchy of the judicial system until it reached the Supreme Court, which gave its verdict seven years after the incident, on 12 October 1995. In *Rupan Deol Bajaj v Kanwar Pal Singh Gill*, the Court stated that

> it cannot but be held that the alleged act of Mr Gill in slapping Mrs Bajaj on her posterior amounted to 'outraging of her modesty' for it was not only an affront to the normal sense of feminine decency but also an affront to the dignity of the lady.

[47] Unreported judgment of the District and Sessions Court, Jaipur, in *The State v Ramkaran and Others*, dated 15 November 1995 (cited in Sood, 2008, p 867; P Baxi, 2014, p 36). The Court held that it was 'beyond comprehension that those who live in a rural culture, including Gyarsa [the accused], who Bhanwari Devi says is a respectable person and who some in the village listen to, would in this manner commit a rape. Particularly in collusion with someone who is forty years of age and that in broad daylight in the jungle in presence of other men. The court is of the opinion that Indian culture has not fallen to such low depths: that someone who is brought up in it; an innocent, rustic man; will turn into a man of evil conduct who disregards caste and age differences and becomes animal enough to assault a woman' (see the English translation provided by P Baxi, 2014, p 36).

The Court clarified that 'under no circumstances' was such an incident of sexual harassment a trivial matter in the sense of Section 95 IPC and it thus constituted an offence under Sections 354 and 509 IPC (ibid). Although the Court did not use the term 'sexual harassment' and though it focused on the plaintiff's 'dignity' rather than her right to equality, the judgment was an essential step in paving the way towards recognising sexual harassment as a rights violation. Rupan Deol Bajaj later stated that long before the #MeToo movement, her case set a 'precedent' that benefitted many other women (Bajaj, 2018).

Two years after *Rupan Deol Bajaj v Kanwar Pal Singh Gill*, in 1997, the Supreme Court gave its verdict in *Vishaka and Others v State of Rajasthan and Others*. *Vishaka* was a judgment that made history. To Zia Mody (2013), it was one of the '10 judgements that changed India'. The judgment was extraordinary in several ways. Firstly, it established the term 'sexual harassment' for the first time in Indian jurisprudence (Sen, 2014, p 340). Secondly, the Court held that each incident of sexual harassment was a 'clear violation of the rights under Articles 14, 15 and 21 of the Constitution' (*Vishaka*), thereby applying fundamental rights horizontally between private parties (Dam, 2005; Mody, 2013). Thirdly, the Court drew heavily on India's obligations under international human rights law, particularly on Articles 11 and 24 of CEDAW, which India had ratified in 1993. And lastly and most importantly, the Court, in this case, created a legislation-like list of guidelines on sexual harassment, which it declared binding 'at all workplaces or in other institutions until a legislation is enacted for the purpose' (*Vishaka*).[48] The Court thus went far beyond what the petitioners had requested, which was to direct that a committee be established to prepare guidelines on sexual harassment. The Court's reasoning was that while ensuring women's 'safety and dignity' in the workplace was primarily the task of the legislature and the executive, in the absence of adequate legislative measures, it was the Court's duty 'to find an effective alternative mechanism' to 'fill the legislative vacuum' (*Vishaka*).

The Court's guidelines read like a legal Act. They defined sexual harassment as 'unwelcome sexually determined behaviour', including physical contact, demands or requests for sexual favours, sexually coloured remarks, the showing of pornography or 'other unwelcome physical verbal or non-verbal conduct of sexual nature' (guideline 2). They stipulated that it was the 'duty of the employer' to prevent acts of sexual harassment (guideline 1). They required the employer to take preventive steps through an expression of prohibition of sexual harassment, the provision of appropriate penalties and the provision of appropriate work conditions (guideline 3). They further required the employer to initiate criminal proceedings and disciplinary actions against harassers (guideline 5). They demanded that the employer ensure that persons who experienced harassment

[48] This act of judicial law-making has not gone uncontested. The Supreme Court in a later case held with regard to *Vishaka*: 'Can the Court convert itself into an interim Parliament and make law until Parliament makes a law on the subject? I have grave doubts about this' (*University of Kerala v The Council of Principals of College in Kerala and Others*, 2009).

were 'not victimised or discriminated against' (guideline 4). They suggested the creation of appropriate complaint mechanisms (guideline 6), which should ideally be headed by a woman and have at least 50 per cent female members and should issue an annual report to the government (guideline 7).

D. The Aftermath of *Vishaka*

Ratna Kapur (2005b, p 38) summarises that the judgment was particularly 'significant at a symbolic level for its validation of the problem with sexual harassment, and its recognition of the fact that it is an experience many women are almost routinely subjected to in the workplace'. Naina Kapur (2013, p 28), who had acted as lead instructing counsel before the Supreme Court, stated:

> Vishaka made it impossible for us to slip back to the way things are. It gave us language. Women's experience of unwelcome sexual conduct was no longer a patronising transgression of her 'modesty', it was sexual harassment – a violation of her constitutional equality.

But feminists and women's rights activists also expressed the dire need to work on the implementation of the guidelines so that they would not 'remain mere rhetoric, but actually help women who have been sexually harassed' (Saheli, 1997b). Challenges to their implementation were sensed, particularly in the informal work sector (Saheli, 1997b). Women's groups also actively made the judgment public and disseminated the guidelines. Saheli wrote and performed a theatre play entitled '*mahaul badalna hai*' ('the atmosphere has to change') (Saheli, 2006a).

After *Vishaka*, several cases were brought before the High Courts (and occasionally before the Supreme Court) using the judgment as a reference point. These cases essentially sought the establishment of complaints committees or challenged orders of dismissal based on the decisions of these committees (Mody, 2013, p 196). The Supreme Court followed up on *Vishaka* in several cases, the first of which was *Apparel Export Promotion Council v AK Chopra* in 1999, where it held that physical contact was not a prerequisite of sexual harassment and reaffirmed that sexual harassment in the workplace was a form of gender discrimination.[49] In the meantime, several Indian States enacted laws or ordinances prohibiting sexual harassment.

On 19 October 2012, the Supreme Court in *Medha Kotwal Lele and Others v Union of India and Others* held that 15 years after *Vishaka*, 'many women still

[49] Ratna Kapur (2016, pp 753–54) points out that the judgment also contained problematic arguments and presumptions. In particular, she criticises the fact that the Court regarded the accused's conduct as unwelcome because the woman was unmarried and hence, in the Court's view, not familiar with or knowledgeable about sex. This reasoning draws on an understanding that the complainant's past sexual history can be used to assess whether or not sexual harassment had taken place, thus rendering only 'some kinds of women worthy of protection under the legal regime' (R Kapur, 2016, p 754).

struggle to have their most basic rights protected at workplaces' and that '[t]he belief of the Constitution framers in fairness and justice for women is yet to be fully achieved at the workplaces in the country' (ibid, paragraph 1). The Court demanded that 'the existing laws, if necessary, be revised and appropriate new laws be enacted by Parliament and the State Legislatures to protect women from any form of indecency, indignity and disrespect at all places' (ibid, paragraph 15). The Court directed those States that had not yet enacted adequate and appropriate legislation to do so within two months (ibid, paragraph 15). It demanded that '[t]he implementation of the guidelines in Vishaka has to be not only in form but substance' (ibid, paragraph 13). 'Lip service, hollow statements and inert and inadequate laws with sloppy enforcement', stated the Court, were 'not enough for true and genuine upliftment of our half most precious population – the women' (ibid, paragraph 15).

Meanwhile, several States enacted laws to combat sexual harassment. In the first decade of the new millennium, various stakeholders introduced Bills into Parliament to do justice to the demands of the *Vishaka* judgment. Only in 2010, however, did the process move significantly forward. The Prohibition of Sexual Harassment of Women at Workplace Bill, 2010 was introduced in Parliament in 2010, then referred to a parliamentary standing committee, which held consultations with the Ministry of Women and Child Development, the National Commission for Women, and several women's rights groups, as well as men's rights groups, and produced a report in December 2011 (Department-related Parliamentary Standing Committee on Human Resource Development, 2011).

Two common critiques that feminists articulated towards this and earlier Bills concerned, first, the exclusion of domestic workers from the purview of the Bills, and secondly, provisions that punished 'false and malicious complaints' by women (All India Democratic Women's Association, 2010; Saheli, 2011; N Kapur, 2013). In particular, the latter provision would, in the view of many women's organisations, create and reinforce 'the stereotype that complaints of sexual harassment and violence against women are often false and/or malicious, when the reality is quite to the contrary, and the struggle for justice is an uphill task for every woman' (Saheli, 2011).

On 3 September 2012, the Lok Sabha passed the Sexual Harassment of Women at Workplace (Prevention, Prohibition and Redressal) Bill. The Rajya Sabha passed it in February 2013. The Bill received the assent of the President of India in April 2013 and came into force in December 2013 as the Sexual Harassment of Women at Workplace (Prevention, Prohibition and Redressal) Act (later frequently referred to as the POSH (ie Prevention of Sexual Harassment) Act). On the same day, the Ministry of Women and Child Development issued the Sexual Harassment of Women at Workplace (Prevention, Prohibition and Redressal) Rules, 2013. The Act refers to Articles 14, 15 and 21 of the Indian Constitution and to 'internationally recognised human rights', particularly

CEDAW. Women's groups proudly perceived the Act's enactment as the result of their own 'relentless lobbying' (Saheli, 2014a).

The Act expanded the definition of workplaces to include the domestic space (Section 2(e)), as women's rights activists had demanded (Saheli, 2014a; Jaising, 2015, p 8). In line with the *Vishaka* judgment, Section 4 of the Act provided for the establishment of 'complaints committees', each presided over by a woman and required to send annual reports to the employer and the District Officer (Section 21). Where the employer failed to institute an internal committee or to take appropriate action, they could be punished with a fine (Section 26). Aggrieved women or someone else representing them could make a written sexual harassment complaint to the complaints committee (Section 9). During the pendency of an inquiry, the committee could recommend that the employer transfer either the aggrieved woman or the respondent to another workplace or grant leave to the woman (Section 12). Where the committee found that the allegation of sexual harassment had been proved, it was required to recommend that the employer take appropriate action and deduct an appropriate sum from the respondent's salary to be paid to the aggrieved woman (Section 13). The Act also stipulated that the employer's duty was to 'provide a safe working environment' and to organise regular workshops and awareness programmes to sensitise employees (Section 19).

One aspect where the feminist campaign remained unsuccessful was the provision on the punishment of false complaints. Section 14 of the Act allowed the committee 'to take action against the woman' in cases where it concluded 'that the allegation against the respondent is malicious' or that the aggrieved woman had made a false complaint (Section 14(1)). This provision was problematic from the point of view of many women's rights activists, as it fed into 'the public discourse about the misuse of pro-women laws' (Saheli, 2014a). Commentators also critically remarked that the Act would not do justice to cases where the employer himself was the accused, that it recommended conciliation before the initiation of an enquiry (Section 10(1)) and that it gave unilateral power to the employer in the nomination of the commission members (Section 4(2)) (John, 2014). Generally, however, feminists saw the Act as a long-awaited positive step and a 'significant event' (Jaising, 2015, p 135).

In addition to the passing of the POSH Act, the Criminal Law (Amendment) Act, 2013, which as I describe above came into being after the Delhi rape case, introduced a new Section 354A on 'Sexual Harassment' into the Indian Penal Code. The provision defined sexual harassment in the same terms as the *Vishaka* judgment and made the offence punishable with up to five years' imprisonment, a fine, or both. It also introduced new provisions criminalising sexual voyeurism (Section 354C IPC) and stalking (Section 354D IPC). Thus, women who experience sexual harassment in the workplace today have the option of pursuing two different routes: a complaint through the company's internal complaints mechanism, or the filing of a criminal complaint with the police. In practice, the internal route is used more frequently (Hatti & Ravi, 2021).

E. Evaluation

The campaign against sexual harassment was undoubtedly successful. The extraordinary verdict in the *Vishaka* case, which introduced legally-binding guidelines, practically surpassed the women's groups' expectations. The judgment played a crucial role in sensitising society at large about the phenomenon of sexual harassment and the need to tackle this phenomenon at various levels. The POSH Act also largely reflects feminist demands. Yet, the reform of the law did not happen remarkably quickly. After the *Vishaka* judgment, 16 years passed before these reforms came into force.

Concerning the *Vishaka* case, it seems that two aspects relating to the feminist actors' strategies helped bring about the landmark judgment: firstly, several different organisations worked together collaboratively, and secondly, the organisations expressly linked their petition to a specific case. The rape of Bhanwari Devi, the lack of adequate support by the police and the subsequent acquittal of the accused had provoked protests and widespread media attention. The petition elaborated in detail the physical and mental violence and subsequent injustices that Bhanwari Devi had experienced. Although the Supreme Court did not grant the damages that the group had demanded for Bhanwari Devi, the specific incident likely contributed to the Supreme Court perceiving the issue of sexual harassment as urgent and important. In the eyes of the Court, the 'brutal gang rape of [a] social worker in a village of Rajasthan' revealed 'the hazards to which a working woman may be exposed and the depravity to which sexual harassment can degenerate; and the urgency for safeguards by an alternative mechanism in the absence of legislative measures' (*Vishaka*).

Interestingly, however, Bhanwari Devi's situation differed starkly from that of the women who ultimately benefitted most from the *Vishaka* judgment. As Murthy and Dasgupta (2011, p 74) stress, it is not without irony that the rape of a lower-caste village woman in rural India was the trigger for a campaign for workplace safety whose gains were later mostly reaped by urban middle-class women.

International law, too, played a role in the campaign against sexual harassment, the *Vishaka* judgment and the following law-making process. Like the developments regarding the Domestic Violence Act, *Vishaka* and the POSH Act occurred in a context that was not independent of international developments. Law making processes in other countries and the international arena, as well as India's ratification of CEDAW in 1993, were helpful for feminist demands. In *Vishaka*, the Court held that the right to work with dignity was a 'universally recognised basic human right' and that international norms that stipulated the right to freedom from sexual harassment were 'of great significance in the formulation of the guidelines'. Similarly, the statement of objects and reasons of the Protection of Women Against Sexual Harassment at Workplace Bill, 2010, referred to Article 11 of CEDAW, which requires state parties to take measures to eliminate women's discrimination in the field of employment.

The #MeToo movement, a worldwide phenomenon that also occurred in India, would later build upon these debates and achievements. Bhanwari Devi saw herself as an early predecessor of the women decrying everyday sexism.

> MeToo is happening because I broke the silence. Today, women are speaking up because I spoke up nearly 30 years ago. I will get justice some day. And if I don't, then my daughters will get justice. And if they don't, then their daughters will. They will get it because women are no longer prepared to remain silent (Bhanwari Devi, cited in Bhandare, 2020, p 169).

V. Conclusion

All four campaigns portrayed in this chapter were successful. Feminists not only achieved significant law reform in all four areas, but they also managed to bring about some landmark decisions by the Indian higher judiciary.

The anti-rape campaign pushed the legislator to reform the rape law thrice, in 1983, 2002, and 2013. Women's groups were able to crush Section 155(4) IEA, thereby making a rape survivor's past sexual history legally irrelevant. They succeeded in bringing about a shift in the burden of proof in certain cases of sexual assault and in broadening the definition of rape. Similarly, concerning dowry-related violence, the law reforms came in stages, in 1983, 1984 and 1986. They introduced the offences of dowry death (Section 304B IPC) and spousal cruelty (Section 498A IPC) into Indian criminal law, shifted the burden of proof in certain cases of dowry-related violence, made post-mortems mandatory in specific cases (Section 174(3) CrPC), broadened the definition of dowry in the Dowry Prohibition Act, 1961, banned dowry-related advertisements, and introduced 'dowry prohibition officers' to monitor compliance with the law. In the area of domestic violence, feminist activism led to the enactment of the PWDVA in 2005, which protected women in 'domestic' (rather than marital) relationships and provided reliefs for women who faced violence. Lastly, concerning sexual harassment, feminist activism led to the passing of the POSH Act in 2013, which not only put the employer under the obligation to actively prevent sexual harassment but also established mechanisms to report acts of sexual harassment and seek redress for the same.

The reforms thus brought about changes in both substantive and procedural law. In some cases, explicitly discriminatory provisions, such as Section 155(4) IEA, were changed through the reforms. Most reforms brought about new provisions to supplement laws that were insufficient to tackle specific social phenomena. Many of the new provisions were gender-specific: they granted women special treatment and rights. With cases like *Sakshi*, *Sudha Goel*, and *Vishaka*, women's groups also brought about landmark judicial decisions.

A few shortcomings remain. Despite decade-long campaigns, feminists did not manage to bring about a law reform to criminalise marital rape. Other flaws in the reformed laws include the provision for joint counselling in the PWDVA and the provision on women's false and malicious complaints in the POSH Act. And some of the landmark judgments, such as *Sudha Goel*, still contain gender stereotypes. Yet, despite these flaws, feminists have overall been successful in their campaigns against gender-based violence. The following sub-sections seek to explain why this was the case.

A. Rights

The success of the feminist campaigns presented here is particularly astonishing when we consider that, from a constitutional law point of view, the chances of success were not particularly promising. Unlike family law, the laws concerning women rarely contained direct discrimination. The central question then is how, despite these challenging circumstances, feminists managed to bring about such significant reforms, and which success factors were important in the four campaigns scrutinised here.

B. Activism

Concerning movement-controlled factors, the women's movement's strategies were undoubtedly a key determinant of its success.

(i) The Movement's Strength, Prioritisation and Coherent Strategy

The campaigns concerning reform of the laws on rape and dowry violence seem to indicate that the women's movement was particularly successful when the issue had a high priority on the movement's agenda and when there was ample support from various movement actors. However, the campaign for the Domestic Violence Act was also successful, even though it was primarily led by one group – the Lawyers Collective (which, however, got other organisations on board when it came to drafting model legislation, etc). This indicates that rather than the sheer number of participants actively engaged in the campaign, it was more important that feminists had a clear goal, prioritised the issue at stake, and spoke with one voice.

(ii) Identifiable Victims

As in the campaigns regarding the personal law system, feminists were particularly successful when an identifiable victim featured as the focal point of the law reform demands. Activists could use the cases of Mathura, Sudha Goel and Jyoti Singh to point to the cruelties that women experienced at the hands of state officials, family members and strangers. In doing so, they emotionalised the debate and thereby intensified media attention. The aspect of the identifiable victim also played a role when it came to litigation. The *Vishaka* case is a prime example here. The three women's organisations who acted as petitioners in the case used the story of Bhanwari Devi to point to the state's failure in addressing sexual harassment. In the *Vishaka* case, like in the *Ahmedabad Women's Action Group* case (discussed in Chapter four), a women's group filed a petition to fight for a greater cause. *Vishaka*, however, was highly successful, while *Ahmedabad Women's Action Group* failed. It might have played a role here that Vishaka and the other organisations used a particular incident to make their broader claim, while the Ahmedabad Women's Action Group did not.

C. State Institutions

(i) International Law

Regarding the movement's environment, India's obligations under international human rights law might have contributed to the campaigns' successes regarding the Domestic Violence Act and the POSH Act. India ratified CEDAW in 1993. From then onwards, women's groups, judges, and parliamentarians could use CEDAW, in addition to the Indian Constitution, to support their arguments for law reform. In addition, transnational women's movements and the UN played a key role in promoting campaigns targetting violence against women and in disseminating an understanding of violence against women as a human rights violation (King & Sifaki, 2019).

(ii) Women's Policy Agencies

The National Commission for Women has played a role in advancing feminist campaigns, albeit a limited one. The NCW has been actively involved in the drafting processes of several laws. It served as a co-petitioner in cases such as *Sakshi*. It has consulted and actively involved feminist organisations such as the Lawyers Collective when drafting laws. Yet, compared to the competencies that the National Commission for Women Act of 1990 grants the organisation, the NCW failed to live up to its potential.

D. Society

Several societal factors were impactful in this area of activism.

(i) Counter-mobilisation

The early feminist campaigns certainly benefitted from the fact that in the first decade of activism there was no significant counter-mobilisation against the feminist campaigns. Counter-mobilisation only emerged after Section 498A IPC had been introduced and the notion of women's misuse of the law gained prominence. Challenges to feminist activism then came mainly from men's rights groups opposing feminist demands. Parliamentarians and judges took up the notion of the law's misuse, and it is also reflected in the outcome of judgments and legal Acts. This created hurdles for the feminist campaigns.

(ii) Public Opinion and the Media

Public opinion and the media have also impacted the outcomes of feminist legal activism, both positively and negatively. Several cases indicate that media coverage favouring the women's movement's goals has supported the feminist agenda. The widespread media coverage around the *Mathura* case, the anti-rape and anti-dowry campaigns, the *Vishaka* case and the Delhi rape case gave impetus to the feminist cause. On the other hand, the arguments that women misuse the laws and that feminists seek a Westernisation that endangers Indian culture have also found resonance in media discourses and thereby impeded the movement's success.

(iii) Legal Culture

Notions drawing on a public–private divide and holding that the state should not interfere in the private sphere were also articulated in certain areas concerning violence against women. Interestingly, however, they were not strong enough to impede the feminist campaigns regarding reforms of the laws on rape and domestic violence. The only topic where the argument of non-interference in the 'private' realm has been able to impact the state's action was marital rape. Here, courts and Parliament held on to the argument that criminalising marital rape would endanger the institution of marriage and thereby society at large.

6

Conclusion

While changes in the laws and their interpretation are ultimately brought about by parliaments and courts, it is often social movements, activists and cause lawyers who set processes of legal change in motion in the first place. This book has used feminist legal activism in India to demonstrate this. Indian feminists can proudly look back at a century of legal activism. They have been involved in the Constitution-making process, ensuring that women were granted equality before the law. They have also used this Constitution in campaigns for law reforms in the post-independence era. This activism is based on a belief in the law as a central vehicle for social change and in themselves as the motors who can set this vehicle in motion.

Indeed, feminists do not have blind trust in the power of legal change. They see the limitations of legal activism: the long and cumbersome procedures of bringing about legal change, the danger that in the law-making processes, feminist ideals are watered down, the lack of law enforcement, the incoherence in how judges decide similar cases, and the biases that women face in the courts and other state institutions. Despite these limitations, however, feminists and women's rights activists in India have, over the past 50 years, achieved several milestones in broadening gender equality. And they remain optimistic. Indira Jaising (2022), one of the key protagonists of feminist legal activism, states:

> Feminism has given me the lens through which I interpret the Constitution, and an approach to my advocacy and my life. There has been success on the way, and so-called failures as well. Yet, I don't consider any case as 'lost'. Each case leads to the next step in a spiral ladder climbing higher and higher. Every case is a precedent for the next one to be relied upon or undone. The avenue of legislative undoing has also been explored successfully. There are no full stops to judgments; every judgment is a conversation between stakeholders, enriching our contribution to the rule of law.

The actors involved in feminist struggles are diverse and range from small independent groups to large party-affiliated organisations, religious women's groups, feminist lawyers' organisations, individual lawyers, activists, writers, and journalists. They bring various areas of expertise to the women's movement. For this study, legal expertise and knowledge of religious law were particularly important.

Throughout the last five decades, feminist legal activism has succeeded with several campaigns. In reaction to feminist demands, the Indian national Parliament has passed new laws and legislative amendments in the areas of personal laws, sexual assault, dowry-related violence, and domestic violence. In addition, the Supreme Court and various High Courts have given multiple judgments on these issues, some of which have become landmark judgments reported all over the country and beyond and have changed the Indian legal landscape entirely. Yet, other campaigns failed or were only partly successful, in the sense that feminists only achieved a limited number of their demands and/or achieved these only after several decades of lobbying and litigating.

The study revealed a difference in the success rate of the campaigns in the two different issue areas: the movement was more successful with its activism concerning violence against women than concerning marriage and the family, even though in the latter area, the discrimination was far more evident than in the former. The book has demonstrated that the rights lens alone cannot explain this phenomenon. Instead, the impact of feminist legal activism can best be understood through a holistic lens, considering four different dimensions.

The research design of this study does not allow me to comment on *all* success factors that Chapter three introduced as potentially influential (studies comparing countries with different political or constitutional systems would be necessary here). Yet, the book can elaborate on several factors that prove particularly relevant in the Indian case, most notably the expertise and strategies of the feminist groups and actors, international law, the presence or absence of counter-mobilisation, and the role of religion and legal culture. Section I of this concluding chapter will briefly sum up these findings. Section II will then say a few words about the limits of law reform and the need for further action to translate legal into social reform before ending (in section III) with a few words on current political developments and challenges for feminist legal activism in India.

I. Success Factors

A. Rights

This study has shown that direct discrimination against women in a particular field of law – and hence a more blatant violation of the Constitution's equality provisions – does *not* translate into greater success rates for feminist legal activism.

Although family law in India contained manifestly discriminatory provisions and the Supreme Court and the High Courts, with their power to undertake judicial review, could easily have struck these provisions down as unconstitutional, feminist actors have obtained comparatively little success in this area. The judiciary has been reluctant to interfere in personal laws. In cases where the courts did intervene, they were highly cautious in positioning themselves on gender equality issues and instead frequently struck down the provisions in question on other grounds or re-interpreted the problematic clauses to make them less discriminatory. The Parliament, too, largely refrained from bringing about reform in family law. By contrast, concerning laws on violence against women, feminists achieved significantly more success, and the law reform processes were faster than in family law.

This contrast is astonishing. It means that India persistently maintains a system of unconstitutional personal laws. Drawing on arguments of the separation of powers, the doctrine of non-interference or the public–private divide, the Indian state avoids calling unconstitutional norms unconstitutional, and refrains from bringing family law into accordance with gender equality. The Indian Constitution in Article 25 makes the freedom of religion subject to other fundamental rights, including the right to equality. In practice, however, religious freedom has often been considered a 'trump card against any claim of equality by women' (Jaising, 2022).

A second important aspect is that where reform attempts were successful, Parliament and courts frequently preferred to justify their decisions with women's *dignity* than with reference to formal or substantive equality. Dignity plays a central role in the case law and parliamentary debates on personal laws as well as on violence against women. This resonates with scholarship analysing discourses in other areas of the law, such as abortion law (D Jain & Shah, 2020). One explanation here is that the concept of dignity may seem less 'foreign' than the concept of gender equality (and therefore potentially attracts less opposition from conservative forces). Indian jurisprudence has had a long tradition of focusing on dignity, at least since the early days of public interest litigation, when the Supreme Court read a right to a dignified life into the right to life in Article 21 of the Constitution. The danger, however, is that in drawing on the dignity argument, the courts and law-makers make a case on morality and decency rather than alluding to the law's perpetuation of systemic gender discrimination and the social hierarchies.

This is not to say that rights are unimportant or to contradict the scholarship finding that rights make a difference for feminist legal activism (Baldez, Epstein, & Martin, 2006; Lambert & Scribner, 2020, 2023). After all, feminist actors in India *did* have constitutional rights at hand and could claim them in court. How the outcome of their attempts would have looked had they had to work with a different Constitution remains an open question. Yet, the campaign examples presented in this book show that to have equality rights enshrined in the Constitution does not automatically guarantee success in challenging discriminatory laws. Other factors are (also) important.

B. Activism

Factors related to feminist activism are insightful in trying to explain why feminist activism has been so much more successful in the area of violence against women than in the area of marriage and the family. This study supports the scholarship arguing that the social movement's expertise and strategies are crucial for success.

I have shown that some organisations are repeat players in feminist legal activism. Indira Jaising and her organisation, Lawyers Collective, are the prime example here. But other groups, too, have shown that with expertise in certain areas of law, including religious law, experience in using the legal system, and skills in making (feminist) legal arguments, be it vis-à-vis the media or in court, they have the potential to bring about landmark decisions and impact legislative action.

A promising strategy was to combine legislative lobbying, litigation and broader legal tactics. Women's groups and activists have filed petitions in courts, sent letters to Members of Parliament suggesting reforms, drafted model laws, served as experts in consultations on parliamentary standing committees, and participated actively in the public debate about specific Bills. This has been a promising strategy. Notably, the significant legal changes discussed in this study were not all brought about by the Indian Supreme Court. Instead, the Indian High Courts and the Indian Parliament have been as important as, if not more important than, the Supreme Court.

Another successful strategy of feminist actors was to use specific cases of individual women directly affected by the law in question (or the lack of laws) to demonstrate the need for reform. This proved useful in the campaigns for reforms of rape and dowry laws, but also in litigation. Although public interest litigation (PIL) allows for cases to be filed in the broader interest and does not require that the claimant is directly concerned, feminists found it more challenging to be successful with an abstract claim. Cases where the claimant (or one of the claimants) was directly affected by the law in question or where the petitioning women's group used a specific incident to make its claim proved more successful.

Framing and bargaining were other essential aspects that impacted chances of success, particularly concerning family law. The campaign for a Uniform Civil Code (UCC) was presumably unsuccessful because, among other aspects, feminists sweepingly rejected religion and openly opposed the demands of religious community spokespersons. Later campaigns regarding personal laws, where feminist activists worked in collaboration with representatives of religious groups or where their arguments drew on religious scripts like the Quran, were more successful. These acts of collaboration sometimes included a process of bargaining, in which feminists gave up specific goals to achieve at least some degree of positive change.

C. State Institutions

Concerning external factors, state institutions have played a central role, too. The power of the Supreme Court and the High Courts to pursue judicial review and the institute of public interest litigation have somewhat benefitted feminist litigation, although not as much as one would think. Some of the landmark decisions came out of PIL cases or cases where feminist lawyers have intervened as amicus curiae. However, in several other cases filed as PIL, the courts refrained from taking action. This was especially the case where women's groups did not provide a specific example of a woman 'hurt' by the provision in question.

Women's policy agencies – first and foremost the National Commission for Women – have played a limited role. Regarding the law reform processes concerning violence against women, the NCW collaborated with women's groups. Overall, however, the organisation often remained invisible to reform debates and did not pride itself as a feminist institution. This strengthens the point made in Chapter three that women's policy agencies in India are 'symbolic' rather than 'insider' agencies.

International law also impacted the outcomes of feminist legal activism and explains why the movement was more successful with its campaigns regarding violence against women than family law. As the Indian state had made significant reservations to the international human rights conventions regarding personal laws, women's rights activists and state actors were limited in using arguments based on international law obligations. In contrast, regarding violence against women, there existed no such reservations, and state organs had to apply international human rights law to its full extent. After India ratified CEDAW in 1993, women's groups, judges and parliamentarians used the Convention to support their arguments, particularly in the campaigns regarding domestic violence and sexual harassment.

Whether more women (or more feminists for that matter) in Parliament or on the benches of the courts would have made a difference to the law reform campaigns discussed here is a question that must remain unanswered. The number of women (let alone feminists) was constantly low in the Indian Parliament and on the High Courts and the Supreme Court. It remains to be seen if the legal landscape changes when more women are appointed to the significant institutions in the future. In 2023, the Parliament passed a Bill requiring the Lok Sabha and the state Legislative Assemblies across the country to set aside one-third of their seats for women (The Constitution (One Hundred and Sixth Amendment) Act, 2023). The law has not yet come into force, but the developments should be of great scholarly interest when it does.

D. Society

The most crucial factors in explaining the different outcomes of feminist activism in the two focus areas were societal ones.

Public opinion and the media have impacted the outcomes of feminist legal activism in India, both positively and negatively. Several cases indicate that media coverage favouring the feminist goals has supported the respective campaigns. The widespread media coverage of cases such as the Supreme Court's decision in *Mathura*, the movement's anti-rape and anti-dowry campaigns, the Delhi rape case and the petition by Shayara Bano certainly gave impetus to the feminist demands and strengthened their cause. On the other hand, arguments that the state should refrain from interfering in family law, that women would misuse the laws against gender-based violence and that the law reform suggestions would endanger Indian culture were also articulated in the media and thereby impeded the movement's success.

Strong counter-mobilisation has been a hindering factor for feminist success. This is particularly visible in family law, where religious groups like the All India Muslim Personal Law Board strongly opposed state interference. With this opposition, they impacted the media discourse, law-makers and judges. Concerning the laws on violence against women, there have also been counter-movements, but they were weaker than the religious groups. Yet, this counter-mobilisation gave impetus to narratives about the misuse of the laws and an erosion of Indian culture – narratives that found repercussions in court decisions and parliamentary debates.

A legal culture that draws on the understanding that the state should not interfere with 'private' or religious matters is widely shared among law-makers, judges and the wider public – a fact that presents significant obstacles to feminist legal activism. However, this only partly explains why feminist activism has been more successful with campaigns concerning violence against women than concerning family law. Indeed, family law is largely perceived as a 'private' realm to be kept free from state interferences. But the argument of privacy could also be made about rape, domestic violence and dowry crimes. And indeed, arguments drawing on a public–private divide were articulated in the debates concerning these areas of law. Interestingly, however, they were not strong enough to impede the feminist campaigns.

One potential explanation here is that when rape is raised as a topic, people commonly think about atrocities committed by strangers (although we know from empirical data that in most rape cases the perpetrators are people whom the victim knows). Media coverage about brutal cases such as the rape of Bhanwari Devi or Jyoti Singh have perpetuated this narrative and taken it out of the 'private' realm. The focus here was on excess rather than on the structural dimension of gender-based violence. Regarding domestic violence, the international context seems to have been influential. Law reforms in other countries, pressure from the international community after CEDAW entered into force, and the Indian state's wish to present itself as modern and part of a global movement banning gender-based violence ultimately trumped the 'privacy' argument. Further, the framing of violence against women as a human rights violation also impacted the national culture in the sense that the privacy argument lost support.

Notably, the only area where the argument of non-interference in the 'private' realm has been able to impede the feminist campaign concerns marital rape. Here, courts and Parliament have held on to the argument that criminalising marital rape would endanger the institution of marriage and thereby society at large. I described some recent positive developments concerning the marital rape exception in Chapter five. It remains to be seen when this last bastion of gender-discrimination will fall.

The high degree of religiosity and the strong presence of religious community representatives (particularly from minority communities) has been another aspect that impeded feminist success in legal activism. In the campaigns regarding family law, spokespersons of religious communities significantly impacted the discourse on the personal laws in a way that disadvantaged the feminist agenda, and religious groups acted as counter-movements to feminist activism. The notion that personal law is somewhat 'sacrosanct' and thus immune to change (or only to be changed by religious experts) and that religion-based personal laws are crucial identity markers for the members of religious minority communities is strong, and even finds its way into court decisions and law-making processes. In contradistinction to this, there are no such notions concerning the laws related to violence against women, and society shares the understanding that it is undoubtedly the state's role to enact, amend and apply the secular rules in criminal law, criminal procedure law and the like.

A second, related, factor explains the state's reluctance to interfere in family law: the power dynamics between the state and influential non-state actors. The Indian state, argues Shalini Randeria (2002, p. 301), 'has never had a monopoly over the production, administration or interpretation of personal law'. Instead, it tolerates 'a multiplicity of "customary" and scriptural sources of norms' to be administered, adjudicated and reformed by non-state institutions (Randeria, 2002, pp 301–3). This situation might be explained by historical developments dating back to British colonialism. But there is another reason. Randeria describes the state's power-sharing as deliberate and strategic and terms the Indian state a 'cunning' state. The 'cunning state [...] *chooses* to exercise selective and partial sovereignty over its territory and citizens' (Randeria, 2002, p 308, emphasis added). Indeed, it is convenient for the state to 'outsource' some areas of law to non-state institutions to save state institutions, such as police offices and courts, from overburdening and a backlog of work. Furthermore, the Indian state might also refrain from interfering in family law because it wishes to avoid confrontation and conflict with religious groups and communities. The aftermath of the *Shah Bano* case in the mid-1980s demonstrated that any state interference with personal laws bears the risk of provoking a backlash.

This strategy, however, has led to problematic outcomes. In pushing religion-based personal laws into an extra-constitutional no-(wo)man's-land, where undemocratic non-state institutions apply them, the Indian state neglects its constitutional duties to protect the fundamental rights of its citizens.

II. After Law Reform

Chapter one pointed out that 'success' as per the understanding of this book was a positive response by the legislature or the judiciary to the feminist reform campaigns. The book has not analysed whether the law reforms that feminists initiated were ultimately translated into lived reality. I leave it to other scholars to deal with the circumstances that make laws effective. However, a few words should be said about the possibilities for social change that progressive law reforms may provide.

Rosenberg, Bail and Krishnaswamy (2019) point to the hurdles for translating legal change into social change on the ground in the Indian context: the 'often antagonistic relationship between the Supreme Court and the national government' might limit the government's willingness to promote Supreme Court orders (Rosenberg et al, 2019, p 345). The Indian state's resource constraints, inefficiency and corruption among state institutions create barriers to successful implementation (Rosenberg et al, 2019, p 345). And the heterogeneity among the federal States leads to differing willingness and capacity to implement Supreme Court orders (Rosenberg et al, 2019, p 345). Yet, the authors also state that legal change can make a difference for the people's lives, when government and courts favour it and when social movement groups and society pressurise state actors to implement it (Rosenberg et al, 2019).

Notably, Rosenberg et al do not address legal culture as an impediment to implementing legal change. Yet beliefs about the law, or what the women's rights activists I spoke to termed people's 'mindset' are of central importance in turning laws into reality. Law enforcement agencies and people at large must somehow identify with a law or acknowledge it as part of *their* legal culture in order to apply it and live according to it. Scholarship has pointed out that laws borrowed from foreign jurisdictions and incompatible with relevant local cultures are likely to fail in practice (Okoth-Ogendo, 1993; Wenzel, 2014).

Women's groups and feminist activists are central in both pressuring and monitoring state organs and changing people's 'mindset' on legal issues. The earlier chapters have shown that the work of women's groups, cause lawyers, and activists does not stop when they have achieved a progressive judgment or obtained new legislation. Instead, women's groups invest much time and energy into disseminating knowledge about such law reforms. They publish manuals and offer seminars for lawyers, activists and state personnel. They also actively engage in what I termed 'everyday litigation' in Chapter two, ie the support of individual women at the level of lower courts in realising their rights. Scholarship has also explained how in contexts where state institutions fail to protect women against violence, individual women and women's organisations do the work of the state themselves (Roychowdhury, 2021). Individual women are often 'strangely proactive' when the criminal justice system does not fulfil its role: they gather evidence themselves and round up witnesses (Roychowdhury, 2021, p 10). Women's organisations supported these women by coaching them in 'how to take the law into their own hands and get what they could out of it' (Roychowdhury, 2021, p 10).

III. Current Developments and Future Challenges

While this book has looked back at the contemporary history of feminist legal activism, focusing on a period of the 1970s til the 2010s, a few words on current developments are due before ending.

In the last decade, the Indian Supreme Court produced several judgments that were celebrated as progressive from a gender equality viewpoint. For instance, the Court struck down Section 497 IPC, which enabled a husband to file a criminal complaint of adultery against his wife's male lover (*Joseph Shine v Union of India*, 2019). The Court found that the provision treated women as 'chattels' and was based on 'sexual stereotypes that view women as being passive and devoid of sexual agency' and therefore found that it violated Article 15 (ibid). The Court furthermore allowed women to access the Sabarimala temple in Kerala, from which they had previously been excluded (*Indian Young Lawyers Association v The State of Kerala*, 2019). It declared a right to legal identity to transgender people (*National Legal Services Authority of India v Union of India*, 2014) and decriminalised consensual sex between adults, including same-sex couples (*Navtej Singh Johar v Union of India*, 2018). The Supreme Court also declared that unmarried women have the same right to access abortion as married women (*X v The Principal Secretary*, 2022). In addition, the Court also released a *Handbook on Combatting Gender Stereotypes* that 'offers guidance on how to avoid utilising harmful gender stereotypes, in particular those about women, in judicial decision making and writing' (Supreme Court of India, 2022, p 6).

Does this mean that India is headed towards a positive future in terms of gender equality? Scholars point out that there are also downsides to these judgments. Ratna Kapur (2025) holds that a close reading of the judgments reveals how some of these decisions subscribe to nationalist, anti-minority, right-wing politics. And Saptarshi Mandal (2025, p 197) argues that while LGBTIQ rights in India are not under attack as they are in other countries, the Supreme Court's 'tolerance' of the LGBTIQ community, 'does not translate into support for substantive legal rights' of the community.

The Hindu nationalist Bharatiya Janata Party, which has been governing India for over 10 years now, uses the advancement of women's rights to pursue an anti-Muslim agenda – a phenomenon that is not new and that Chapter four addressed when engaging with the discourse around the UCC and reforms in Muslim divorce law. In Ratna Kapur's (2025, p 166) words, the Hindu right

> embraces a formal approach to equality. In this approach all women are treated the same. Any difference in treatment between women of different faiths is regarded as a violation of the constitutional doctrine of formal equality. This position translates into treating all Muslim women the same as Hindu women, with the majority used as the (Hindu) norm against which others (Muslims) are judged.

Anti-Muslim politics have accompanied these developments. Muslims have been the target of legislation banning cow slaughter, placing limits on conversion from

Hinduism to Islam and providing pathways for Hindus and other non-Muslims who immigrated to India from other states to acquire Indian citizenship. Besides these political and legal developments, the societal climate, too, has changed. Anti-Muslim hate speech is on the rise, and nationalist violence is widespread (Human Rights Watch, 2024). The Muslim majority region of Kashmir has had its special status abrogated and the rights of the people living in the area have been significantly curtailed (Herklotz, 2023b).

The past decade's politics have also diminished civil society's spaces. NGOs, organised groups of individuals, and cause lawyers have had their funding cut, their licences withdrawn, their offices raided; they are labelled anti-nationals, or must defend themselves against criminal charges (Jaising, 2025). Furthermore, the freedom of expression, association and assembly have been curtailed, by law reforms allowing the state to crack down on those critical of the state and by internet shutdowns in certain regions (Amnesty International, 2024, pp 194 et seq). These developments have a chilling effect on civil society engagement.

Another worrying development is that the Indian government under Modi has 'incrementally and systemically' undermined mechanisms that seek executive accountability (Khaitan, 2020). Further, democratic discourse in Parliament is diminishing. The Indian government has been working on curbing parliamentary deliberation in the law-making process (A Jain, 2022). Today, Parliament refers significantly fewer Bills to parliamentary standing committees than in earlier decades, allowing for less critical discussion before legislative acts are passed and leading to a situation where the executive dominates the law-making processes (Verma, 2025).

These developments are not unique to India. Democratic backsliding is a global phenomenon, often going hand in hand with a backlash against women's rights and a backsliding on states' commitments to gender equality.

It is hard to end the book on a positive note while looking into a grim world. What remains to be said is that civil society is needed more than ever. Potentially, looking back at a century of feminist activism in India may also make us somewhat hopeful. Learning from Indian feminism means learning not to give up. Feminists in India, as elsewhere worldwide, have fought for equality and obtained significant success. They will continue to do so in the future.

BIBLIOGRAPHY*

Abeyratne, R, & Jain, D (2012) 'Domestic Violence Legislation in India: The Pitfalls of a Human Rights Approach to Gender Equality' 21(2) *Journal of Gender, Social Policy & the Law* 333–78.

Agarwal, B (1994) *A Field of One's Own: Gender and Land Rights in South Asia* (Cambridge/New York, Cambridge University Press).

—— (2002) *'Bargaining' and Legal Change: Toward Gender Equality in India's Inheritance Laws* (Brighton, Institute of Development Studies).

—— (2003) 'Gender and Land Rights Revisited: Exploring New Prospects via the State, Family and Market' 3(1/2) *Journal of Agrarian Change* 184–224.

Agarwal, B, Sivaramayya, B, & Sarkar, L (1998) *Report of the Committee for Gender Equality in Land Devolution in Tenurial Laws* (New Delhi, Government of India).

Agnes, F (1984) *Violence in the Family: Wife Beating* (Women's Centre, Bombay, November 1984).

—— (1986) 'For Better or for Worse – Till Death Do Us Part: Christian Women Speak Out Against Oppressive Divorce Laws' 3(1) *WomeNews* 7, 12.

—— (2001) 'Minority Identity and Gender Concerns' 36(42), *Economic and Political Weekly* 3973–76.

—— (2002) 'Law, Ideology and Female Sexuality' 37(9) *Economic and Political Weekly* 844–47.

—— (2004) 'Law and Gender Inequality: The Politics of Women's Rights in India' in F Agnes (ed), *Women and Law in India* (New Delhi, Oxford University Press) pp 1–250.

—— (2006) Making Laws Work for Women: The Potential of Existing Laws against Domestic Violence' 156 *Manushi* 25–31.

—— (2011a) *Family Law Volume I: Family Laws and Constitutional Claims* (New Delhi, Oxford University Press).

—— (2011b) *Family Law Volume II: Marriage, Divorce, and Matrimonial Litigation* (New Delhi, Oxford University Press).

—— (2012) 'Bargaining in the Shadow of Law: Negotiating Property Rights in Matrimonial Disputes' in F Agnes & S Venkatesh Ghosh (eds), *Negotiating Spaces: Legal Domains, Gender Concerns, and Community Constructs* (Delhi, Oxford University Press) pp 335–57.

—— (2014 [1984]) *My Story ... Our Story: Of Re-Building Broken Lives*, 6th edn (Mumbai, Majlis).

Agnihotri, I (2001) 'Re-Reading Histories'. *Seminar 505*.

Agnihotri, I, & Mazumdar, V (1995) 'Changing Terms of Political Discourse: Women's Movement in India, 1970-1990s' 30(29) *Economic and Political Weekly* 1869–78.

Aguiar-Aguilar, AA (2020) 'Beyond Justices: The Legal Culture of Judges in Mexico' *GIGA Working Papers*.

Ahmed, F (2019) 'The Problem with Personal Law in India' in S Choudhry & J Herring (eds), *The Cambridge Companion to Comparative Family Law* (Cambridge, Cambridge University Press) pp 225–53.

Al-Sharmani, M (2013) 'Reforming Egyptian Family Laws: The Debate about a New Substantive Code' in M Al-Sharmani (ed), *Feminist Activism, Women's Rights and Legal Reform* (London/ New York, Zed Books) pp 73–100.

Alikarami, L (2019) *Women and Equality in Iran: Law, Society and Activism* (London, IB Tauris).

All India Democratic Women's Association (2010) 'AIDWA Press Statement on Bill for Protection of Women against Sexual Harassment at the Workplace in India'. Retrieved from http://feministlawarchives.pldindia.org/wp-content/uploads/AIDWA-Press-Statement-on-Bill-for-Protection-of-Women-against-Sexual-Harassment-at-the-Workplace-2010.pdf.

* n.d. = undated document.

—— (n.d.) 'About Us'. Retrieved from https://www.aidwaonline.org/about-us.
All India Muslim Personal Law Board (n.d.-a) Aims & Objectives. Retrieved from https://aimplb.org/aims-objectives/.
—— (n.d.-b) 'Uniform Civil Code Unacceptable to the Muslim Community: Muslims are Bound to Follow Sharia in their Religious Matters'. Retrieved from http://aimplboard.in/images/media/Press13-10-2016%20ENGLISH.pdf.
Amenta, E, & Zylan, Y (1991) 'It Happened Here: Political Opportunity, the New Institutionalism, and the Townsend Movement' 65(2) *American Sociological Review* 250–65.
Amnesty International (2024) *The State of the World's Human Rights*. Retrieved from https://www.amnesty.org/en/documents/pol10/7200/2024/en/.
Anklesaria, S (n.d.) 'Law and Women's Status: Property Laws as Symbols of Sex Discrimination'. Retrieved from http://feministlawarchives.pldindia.org/wp-content/uploads/S.no-41-Shahnaz-Anklesaria-Law-and-Women%E2%80%99s-Status-Property-Laws-as-symbols-of-Sex-determination.pdf.
Annesley, C, Engeli, I, & Gains, F (2015) 'The Profile of Gender Equality Issue Attention in Western Europe' 54(3) *European Journal of Political Research* 525–42.
Arya, S (2010) *The National Commission for Women: Assessing Performance*. Retrieved from https://archive.nyu.edu/jspui/handle/2451/34241.
Baer, S (2009) 'Dignity, Liberty, Equality: A Fundamental Rights Triangle of Constitutionalism' 59(4) *University of Toronto Law Journal* 417–68.
Baines, B. (2005) 'Using the Canadian Charter of Rights and Freedoms to Constitute Women' in B Baines & R Rubio-Marin (eds), *The Gender of Constitutional Jurisprudence* (Cambridge, Cambridge University Press) pp 48–74.
Baines, B, & Rubio-Marin, R (2005) 'Introduction: Toward a Feminist Constitutional Agenda' in B Baines & R Rubio-Marin (eds), *The Gender of Constitutional Jurisprudence* (Cambridge, Cambridge University Press) pp 1–21.
Baird, RD (2005) 'Religion and Law in India: Adjusting to the Sacred as Secular' in RD Baird (ed), *Religion and Law in Independent India*, 2nd edn (New Delhi, Manohar) pp 8–34.
Bajaj, RD (2018) 'A Retired IAS Officer on How the #MeToo Movement Can Use Her Case Against KPS Gill/Interviewer: Chander Suta Dogra', *The Wire*, 15 October 2018. Retrieved from https://thewire.in/women/rupan-deol-bajaj-kps-gill-case-me-too.
Baker, CN (2008) *The Women's Movement Against Sexual Harassment* (New York, Cambridge University Press).
Bakshi, PM (1994) 'Legislative Response for Tackling Domestic Violence' 9(1) *The Lawyer* 13–14.
Balasubrahmanyam, V (1985) 'Women, Personal Laws and the Struggle for Secularism' 20(30) *Economic and Political Weekly* 1260–61.
Baldez, L, Epstein, L, & Martin, AD (2006) 'Does the U.S. Constitution Need an Equal Rights Amendment?' 35(1) *The Journal of Legal Studies* 243–83.
Ballakrishnen, SS, & Samuel, R (2021) 'India's Women Legal Academics: Who They Are and Where You Might Find Them' in U Schultz, G Shaw, M Thornton & R Auchmuty (eds), *Gender and Careers in the Legal Academy* (Oxford, Hart Publishing) pp 115–32.
Banaszak, LA (1996) *Why Movements Succeed or Fail: Opportunity, Culture, and the Struggle for Woman Suffrage* (Princeton NJ, Princeton University Press).
Bano, S (1995) 'Muslim Women's Voices: Expanding Gender Justice under Muslim Law' 30(47) *Economic and Political Weekly* 2981–82.
Baruah, P (2020) '(De)Valuing Dignity: Three Risks of Dignity Inflation in the Indian Supreme Court's Reasoning' 55(31) *Economic & Political Weekly* 33–38.
—— (2022) 'Human Dignity in Indian Constitutional Adjudication' in JC-S Hsu (ed), *Human Dignity in Asia: Dialogue between Law and Culture* (Cambridge, Cambridge University Press) pp 21–39.
Bashevkin, S (1994) 'Confronting Neo-Conservatism: Ango-American Women's Movements under Thatcher, Reagan and Mulroney' 15(3) *International Political Science Review* 275–96.
Basu, A (1995) 'Feminism and Nationalism in India, 1917–1947' 7(4) *Journal of Women's History* 95–107.

Basu, A, & Ray, B (1990) *Women's Struggle: A History of the All India Women's Conference 1927–1990* (New Delhi, Manohar).
Basu, S (2015) *The Trouble with Marriage: Feminists Confront Law and Violence in India* (Oakland CA, University of California Press).
Baxi, P (2014) *Public Secrets of Law: Rape Trials in India* (New Delhi, Oxford University Press).
Baxi, U (1985) 'Taking Suffering Seriously: Social Action Litigation in the Supreme Court of India' 4 *Third World Legal Studies* 107–32.
Baxi, U, Dhagamwar, V, Kelkar, R, & Sarkar, L (1979) *An Open Letter to the Chief Justice of India.* Retrieved from http://feministlawarchives.pldindia.org/wp-content/uploads/open-letter-to-cji-in-the-mathura-rape-case.pdf.
BBC (2017a) 'Triple Talaq: How Indian Muslim Women Fought, and Won, the Divorce Battle', *BBC News*, 22 August 2017. Retrieved from https://www.bbc.com/news/world-asia-india-40484276.
—— (2017b) 'Triple Talaq: India Court Bans Islamic Instant Divorce', *BBC News*, 22 August 2017. Retrieved from http://www.bbc.co.uk/news/world-asia-india-41008802.
Bebaak Collective & Centre for Study of Society and Secularism (2017) 'Written Submission on Behalf of Intervenors Bebak Collective and Centre for Study of Society and Secularism by Advocate Ms Indira Jaising'. Retrieved from https://www.lawyerscollective.org/wp-content/uploads/2017/05/Bebaak-Collective-Written-submission-.pdf.
Beiner, TM (2005) 'Female Judging', 36 *University of Toledo Law Review* 821–47.
Bhandare, N (2020) 'The Beast in Our Midst: How India's MeToo Movement Broke the Silence on Workplace Sexual Harassment' in S Kirpal (ed), *Sex and the Supreme Court: How the Law is Upholding the Dignity of the Indian Citizen* (Gurugram, Hachette) pp 163–205.
Bharatiya Muslim Mahila Andolan (2015a) *Letter to PM Demanding Codification of Muslim Family Law.* Retrieved from https://feministlawarchives.pldindia.org/wp-content/uploads/Letter-to-PM-Demanding-Codification-of-Muslim-Family-Law-by-BMMA-2015.pdf?.
—— (2015b) *Muslim Family Law* (Belgaum, Omega Publications).
Bhatia, G (2016a) 'Horizontal Discrimination and Article 15(2) of the Indian Constitution: A Transformative Approach' 11(1) *Asian Journal of Comparative Law* 87–109.
—— (2016b) 'The Invalidation of S. 2(q) of the Domestic Violence Act: A Comment' *Constitutional Law and Philosophy*, 11 October 2016. Retrieved from https://indconlawphil.wordpress.com/2016/10/11/the-invalidation-of-s-2q-of-the-domestic-violence-act-a-comment/.
—— (2019) *The Transformative Constitution: A Radical Biography in Nine Acts* (Noida, Harper Collins Publishers).
—— (2022) 'Equality under the Indian Constitution' in U Davy & A Flüchter (eds), *Imagining Unequals, Imagining Equals: Concepts of Equality in History and Law* (Bielefeld, Transcript).
Bhuwania, A (2014) 'Courting the People: The Rise of Public Interest Litigation in Post-Emergency India' 34(2) *Comparative Studies of South Asia, Africa and the Middle East* 314–35.
—— (2017) *Courting the People: Public Interest Litigation in Post-Emergency India* (Cambridge/ New York/ Delhi, Cambridge University Press).
Bohra, N (1992) 'Marital Rape Exemption and the Equal Protection Clause' 7(1) *The Lawyer* 16–20.
Boneparth, E, & Stoper, E (1988a) 'Introduction: A Framework for Policy Analysis' in E Boneparth & E Stoper (eds), *Women, Power and Policy: Towards the Year 2000*, 2nd edn (New York, Pergamon Press) pp 1–25.
—— (eds) (1988b) *Women, Power and Policy: Towards the Year 2000*, 2nd edn (New York, Pergamon Press).
Bonilla Maldonado, D (ed) (2013) *Constitutionalism of the Global South: The Activist Tribunals of India, South Africa, and Colombia* (Cambridge, Cambridge University Press).
Burstein, P (1991) 'Legal Mobilization as a Social Movement Tactic: The Struggle for Equal Employment Opportunity' 96(5) *American Journal of Sociology* 1201–25.
Butalia, U (2005) 'Confrontation and Negotiation: The Women's Movement's Responses to Violence Against Women' in M Khullar (ed), *Writing the Women's Movement* (Delhi, Zubaan) pp 325–55.

—— (2017) 'Queer and Trans Women are Essential to Indian Feminism', *The Guardian*, 29 May 2017. Retrieved from https://www.theguardian.com/lifeandstyle/2017/may/29/indian-transgender-feminism-urvashi-butalia.
Chandhoke, N (2011) 'Civil Society in India' in M Edwards (ed), *The Oxford Handbook of Civil Society* (Oxford, Oxford University Press) pp 171–81.
Chandra, A, Hubbard, W, & Kalantry, S (2018) 'From Executive Appointment to the Collegium System: The Impact on Diversity in the Indian Supreme Court' 51(3) *World Comparative Law* 273–89.
Chandra, A, Sen, J, & Chaudhary, R (2021) 'Introduction: the Indian Feminist Judgements Project' 5(3) *Indian Law Review* 261–64.
Chappell, L (2002) *Gendering Government: Feminist Engagement with the State in Australia and Canada* (Vancouver, UBC Press).
Chatterji, J (1984a) 'Introduction' in Joint Women's Programme (ed), *Changes in Christian Personal Law* (JWP, New Delhi) pp 7–12.
—— (1995) *Letter to the Law Minister*. Retrieved from http://feministlawarchives.pldindia.org/wp-content/uploads/32.pdf?.
—— (n.d.-a) *Changes in Christian Personal Laws: A Brief Account of the Advocacy Process*. Retrieved from http://feministlawarchives.pldindia.org/wp-content/uploads/19.pdf.
—— (n.d.-b) *Christian Personal Law Reform*. Retrieved from http://feministlawarchives.pldindia.org/wp-content/uploads/32.pdf?.
—— (ed) (1984b) *Changes in Christian Personal Law* (New Delhi, Joint Women's Programme). Retrieved from http://feministlawarchives.pldindia.org/wp-content/uploads/Part-1.pdf?.
Cichowski, RA (2007) *The European Court and Civil Society: Litigation, Mobilization and Governance* (Cambridge, Cambridge University Press).
Cichowski, R, & Stone Sweet, A (2003) 'Participation, Representative Democracy and the Courts' in BE Cain, RJ Dalton & SE Scarrow (eds), *New Forms of Democracy? Reform and Transformation of Democratic Institutions* (Oxford, Oxford University Press).
Collins, PM (2004) 'Friends of the Court: Examining the Influence of Amicus Curiae Participation in U.S. Supreme Court Litigation' 38(4) *Law & Society Review* 807–32.
—— (2008) *Friends of the Supreme Court: Interest Groups and Judicial Decision* (New York, Oxford University Press).
Committee on Reforms of Criminal Justice System (2003) *Report, Volume 1*. Retrieved from http://feministlawarchives.pldindia.org/wp-content/uploads/Malimath-Commitee-Report.pdf.
Committee on the Status of Women in India (1974) *Towards Equality: Report of the Committee on the Status of Women in India*. Retrieved from https://pldindia.org/wp-content/uploads/2013/04/Towards-Equality-1974-Part-1.pdf.
Cotterrell, R (2008) 'Comparative Law and Legal Culture' in M Reimann & R Zimmermann (eds), *Comparative Law* (New York, Oxford University Press) pp 709–37.
Crenshaw, KW (1989) 'Demarginalizing the Intersection of Race and Sex: A Black Feminist Critique of Antidiscrimination Doctrine, Feminist Theory and Antiracist Politics' *The University of Chicago Legal Forum, 1989*, 139–67.
—— (1991) 'Mapping the Margins: Intersectionality, Identity Politics, and Violence Against Women of Color' 43 *Stanford Law Review* 1241–99.
Dahlgren, S (2013) 'Reajusting Women's Too Many Rights: The State, The Public Voice, and Women's Rights in South Yemen' in M Al-Sharmani (ed), *Feminist Activism, Women's Rights and Legal Reform* (London/ New York, Zed Books) pp 48–72.
Dam, S (2005) 'Lawmaking Beyond Lawmakers: Understanding the Little Right and the Great Wrong' 13 *Tulane Journal of International and Comparative Law* 109–40.
Dann, P (2011) 'Federal Democracy in India and the European Union: Towards Transcontinental Comparison of Constitutional Law' 44(2) *World Comparative Law* 160.
—— (2023), 'Southern Turn, Northern Implications: Rethinking the Meaning of Colonial Legacies for Comparative Constitutional Studies', 1(2) *Comparative Constitutional Studies*, pp 174–196.

Dann, P, Riegner, M & Bönnemann, M (2020) 'The Southern Turn in Comparative Constitutional Law: An Introduction' in P Dann, M Riegner & M Bönnemann (eds), *The Global South and Comparative Constitutional Law* (Oxford, Oxford University Press), pp 1–38.

—— (2024) 'The Southern Turn in Comparative Constitutional Law', in Av Bogdandy & E Schmidt-Aßmann (eds) *Theorising Comparative Public Law*, pp 131–174.

Das, M (1979) 'Women Against Dowry' 3 (July-August) *Manushi* 15–17. Retrieved from https://manushi.in/wp-content/uploads/2022/11/pdfs_issues/PDF%20files%203/14.%20Women%20Against%20Dowry.pdf.

Datta, K (2007) *Women's Studies and Women's Movement in India since the 1970s: An Overview* (Kolkata, Asiatic Society).

Davis, S, Haire, S, & Songer, D (1993) 'Voting Behavior and Gender on the United States Courts of Appeals' 77 *Judicature* 127–33.

De Aquino, S (2013) 'Organizing to Monitor Implementation of the Maria de Penha Law in Brazil' in M Al-Sharmani (ed), *Feminist Activism, Women's Rights and Legal Reform* (London/New York, Zed Books) pp 177–202.

De Silva de Alwis, R (2012) 'Domestic Violence Lawmaking in Asia: Some Innovative Trends in Feminist Lawmaking' 29(2) *UCLA Pacific Basin Law Journal* 176–233.

De Souza, SP, & Srivastava-Kehrer, M (2021) 'The Lack of Women in the Indian Judiciary: The Inadequacies of the Judicial Appointment Process' in T Herklotz & SP De Souza (ed), *Mutinies for Equality: Contemporary Developments in Law and Gender in India* (New York, Cambridge University Press) pp 38–56.

Department-related Parliamentary Standing Committee on Home Affairs (2013) *167th Report on the Criminal Law (Amendment) Bill, 2012.* Retrieved from https://sviproject.org/wp-content/uploads/2014/06/167th-Report-of-Standing-Committee-on-Home-Affairs-The-Criminal-Law-Amendment-Bill-2012.pdf.

Department-related Parliamentary Standing Committee on Human Resource Development (2002) *124th Report on the Protection from Domestic Violence Bill, 2002.*

—— (2011) *239th Report on the Protection of Women Against Sexual Harassment at Workplace Bill, 2010.* Retrieved from https://prsindia.org/files/bills_acts/bills_parliament/2010/SCR_Protection_of_Women.pdf.

Dequen, J-P (2016) 'Reflections on the Shayara Bano Petition: A Symbol of the Indian Judiciary's Own Evolution on the Issue of Triple Talak and the Place of Muslim Personal Law within the Indian Constitutional Frame?' 6 *Südasien-Chronik* 37–60.

Derichs, C, & Fennert, D (eds) (2014) *Women's Movements and Countermovements: The Quest for Gender Equality in Southeast Asia and the Middle East* (Newcastle upon Tyne, Cambridge Scholars Publishing).

Desai, N (2006) *Feminism as Experience: Thoughts and Narratives* (Mumbai, Sparrow).

Devenish, A (2019) *Debating Women's Citizenship in India, 1930–1960* (New Delhi, Bloomsbury Publishing).

Dhagamwar, V (1989) *Towards the Uniform Civil Code* (Bombay, Tripathi).

Dhingra, A (2022) 'Gender Discourses and the Making of the Indian Constitution' 29(1) *Indian Journal of Gender Studies* 33–54.

Dixon, R, & Nussbaum, MC (2012) 'Abortion, Dignity, and a Capabilities Approach' in B Baines, D Barak-Erez & T Kahana (eds), *Feminist Constitutionalism: Global Perspectives* (New York, Cambridge University Press) pp 64–81.

Dobrowolsky, A (2000) *The Politics of Pragmatism: Women, Representation, and Constitutionalism in Canada* (Oxford, Oxford University Press).

Dobrowolsky, A, & Hart, V (2003) 'Introduction: Women, New Politics and Constitutional Change' in A Dobrowolsky & V Hart (eds), *Women Making Constitutions: New Politics and Comparative Perspectives* (Basingstoke/ New York, Palgrave Macmillan) pp 1–19.

Doddahatti, BN (2017) 'The Dangerous, False Myth That Women Routinely Misuse Domestic Cruelty Laws', *The Wire*, 11 August 2017. Retrieved from https://thewire.in/gender/section-498a-domestic-cruelty-laws.

Dür, A (2008) 'Measuring Interest Group Influence in the EU: A Note on Methodology' 9(4) *European Union Politics* 559–76.
Dür, A, & Mateo, G (2013) 'Gaining Acces or Going Public? Interest Group Strategies in Five European Countries' 52 *European Journal of Political Research* 660–86.
Dusche, M (2017) 'Butas and Daivas as Justices in Tulu Nadu: Implications for the Philosophy of Law' 6 *Südasien-Chronik* 11–36.
Dutta, N (1999) 'Domestic Violence: Tolerating the Intolerable?' 14(1) *The Lawyer* 4–9.
Eberhard, C, & Gupta, N (2005) 'Legal Pluralism in India: An Introduction' 31 *Indian Socio-Legal Journal* 1–10.
Eckert, J (2004) 'Urban Governance and Emergent Forms of Legal Pluralism in Mumbai' 50 *Journal of Legal Pluralism* 29–60.
El Masry, I (2014) 'Women's Movements and Countermovements in Tunisia' in C Derichs & D Fennert (eds), *Women's Movements and Countermovements: The Quest for Gender Equality in Southeast Asia and the Middle East* (Newcastle upon Tyne, Cambridge Scholars Publishing) pp 107–35.
Ennaji, M (2014) 'Women's NGOs and Social Change in Morocco' in C Derichs & D Fennert (eds), *Women's Movements and Countermovements: The Quest for Gender Equality in Southeast Asia and the Middle East* (Newcastle upon Tyne, Cambridge Scholars Publishing) pp 137–50.
Entman, RM (1993) 'Framing: Toward Clarification of a Fractured Paradigm' 43(4) *Journal of Communication* 51–58.
Epp, CR (1998) *The Rights Revolution: Lawyers, Activists, and Supreme Courts in Comparative Perspective* (London, The University of Chicago Press).
Epstein, L, & Kobylka, JF (1992) *The Supreme Court and Legal Change: Abortion and the Death Penalty* (Chapel Hill NC/ London, The University of North Carolina Press).
Ertürk, Y (2019) 'Feminist Advocacy for Family Law Reform: Cross-Country Overview' in M Afkhami, Y Ertürk & AE Mayer (eds), *Feminist Advocacy, Family Law and Violence Against Women: International Perspectives* (Abingdon/ New York, Routledge) pp 11–29.
Evrard, AY (2014) *The Moroccan Women's Rights Movement* (New York, Syracuse University Press).
Farhang, S, & Wawro, G (2004) 'Institutional Dynamics on the U.S. Court of Appeals: Minority Representation under Panel Decision-Making' 20(2) *Journal of Law, Economics and Organization* 299–330.
Farris, SR (2017) *In the Name of Women's Rights: The Rise of Femonationalism* (Durham NC/ London, Duke University Press).
Feminism in India (2021) *Intersectional Feminism-Desi Style*, Retrieved from https://feminisminindia.com/2021/12/23/podcast-the-importance-of-books-ft-urvashi-butalia/.
Ferree, MM, Gamson, WA, Gerhards, J, & Rucht, D (2002) *Shaping Abortion Discourse: Democracy and the Public Sphere in Germany and the United States* (Cambridge, Cambridge University Press).
Forbes, G (1996) *Women in Modern India* (Cambridge, Cambridge University Press).
Forum Against Oppression of Women (1989) *Towards a Uniform, Secular and Non Sexist Civil Code.* Paper presented at the Workshop on Social Movements, Human Rights and the Law in India (December 1989), Bombay. http://feministlawarchives.pldindia.org/wp-content/uploads/Towards-a-uniform-secular-and-non-sexist-civil-code.pdf.
Franceschet, S (2010) 'Explaining Domestic Violence Policy Outcomes in Chile and Argentina' 52(3) *Latin American Politics and Society* 1–29.
Freeman, J (1975) *The Politics of Women's Liberation: A Case Study of an Emerging Social Movement and Its Relation to the Policy Process* (New York, David McKay Company).
Friedman, LM (1987 [1975]) *The Legal System: A Social Science Perspective* (New York, Russell Sage Foundation).
Fuchs, G (2013) 'Strategic Litigation for Gender Equality in the Workplace and Legal Opportunity Structures in Four European Countries' 28(2) *Canadian Journal of Law and Society* 189–208.
Galanter, M (1974) 'Why the "Haves" Come out Ahead: Speculations on the Limits of Legal Change' 9(1) *Law & Society Review* 95–160.

Gandhi, N (2011) 'Feminist Thoughts from Here and There'. Retrieved from https://www.posterwomen.org/?p=5488.
Gandhi, N, & Shah, N (1992) *The Issues at Stake: Theory and Practice in the Women's Movement in India* (New Delhi, Kali for Women).
Gangoli, G (1996) 'The Right to Protection from Sexual Assault: The Indian Anti-Rape Campaigns' 6(4) *Development in Practice* 334–40.
—— (2007) *Indian Feminisms: Law, Patriarchies and Violence in India* (Aldershot, Ashgate).
Gargarella, R, Roux, T, & Domingo, P (eds) (2006) *Courts and Social Transformation in New Democracies: An Institutional Voice for the Poor?* (Aldershot, Ashgate).
Gauri, V, & Brinks, D (eds) (2008) *Courting Social Justice: Judicial Enforcement of Social and Economic Rights in the Developing World* (Cambridge, Cambridge University Press).
Gelb, J, & Palley, ML (1982) *Women and Public Policies* (Princeton NJ, Princeton University Press).
George, TE, & Epstein, L (1991) Women's Rights Litigation in the 1980s: More of the Same' 74(6) *Judicature* 314–21.
Goel, U (2015) 'The Delhi Rape Case and International Attention: An Interview with Urvashi Butalia' in NC Schneider & F-M Titzmann (eds), *Studying Youth, Media and Gender in Post-Liberalisation India* (Berlin, Frank & Timme) pp 133–39.
Goetz, AM, & Jenkins, R (2018) 'Feminist Activism and the Politics of Reform: When and Why Do States Respond to Demands for Gender Equality Policies?' 49(3) *Development and change* 714–34.
Gordon, L (2014) 'The Women's Liberation Movement' in DS Cobble, L Gordon & A Henry (eds), *Feminism Unfinished: A Short, Surprising History of American Women's Movements* (New York, Liveright Publishing Corporation) pp 69–145.
Griffith, J (1986) What is Legal Pluralism? 18(24) *Journal of Legal Pluralism* 1–55.
Grødeland, AB, & Miller, WL (2015) *European Legal Cultures in Transition* (Cambridge, Cambridge University Press).
Guerrero, M (2020) *Strategic Litigation in EU Gender Equality Law* (Brussels, European Commission).
Guruswamy, M, & Aspatwar, B (2013) 'Access to Justice in India: The Jurisprudence (and Self-Perception) of the Supreme Court' in D Bonilla Maldonado (ed), *Constitutionalism of the Global South: The Activist Tribunals of India, South Africa, and Colombia* (Cambridge, Cambridge University Press) pp 329–59.
Guruswamy, M, & Katju, A (2020) 'From Adultery to Sexual Autonomy: The Constitutional Potential of Joseph Shine' in S Kirpal (ed), *Sex and the Supreme Court: How the Law is Upholding the Dignity of the Indian Citizen* (Gurugram, Hachette) pp 136–59.
Hariharan, G (1999) 'Githa Hariharan & Another vs. Reserve Bank of India & Another' Retrieved from https://githahariharan.com/wp-content/uploads/write_up_on_case.pdf.
Hark, S, & Villa, P-I (2017) *Unterscheiden und herrschen: ein Essay zu den ambivalenten Verflechtungen von Rassismus, Sexismus und Feminismus in der Gegenwart* (Bielefeld, Transcript).
Hasan, Z (2018 [1994]) 'Introduction: Contextualising Gender and Identity in Contemporary India' in Z Hasan (ed), *Forging Identities: Gender, Communities and the State of India* (London/ New York, Routledge).
Hatti, P, & Ravi, A (2021) 'Towards an Egalitarian Workplace: Developments in Anti-Sexual Harassment Law' in T Herklotz & S De Souza (eds), *Mutinies for Equality: Contemporary Developments in Law and Gender in India* (New Dehli, Cambridge University Press).
Haussman, M, & Sauer, B (2007) 'Introduction: Women's Movements and State Restructuring in the 1990s' in M Haussman & B Sauer (eds), *Gendering the State in the Age of Globalization: Women's Movements and State Feminism in Postindustrial Democracies* (Lanham MD, Rowman & Littlefield) pp 19–33.
Hawkesworth, M (1994) 'Policy Studies within a Feminist Frame' 27(2/3) *Policy Sciences* 97–118.
Helferich, B, & Kolb, F (2001) 'Multilevel Action Coordination on European Contentious Politics: The Case of the European Women's Lobby' in D Imig & S Tarrow (eds), *Contentious Europeans: Protest and Politics in an Emerging Policy* (Lanham MD, Rowman and Littlefield) pp 143–61.

Herklotz, T (2016) 'Dead Letters? The Uniform Civil Code through the Eyes of the Indian Women's Movement and the Indian Supreme Court' 49(2) *World Comparative Law* 148–74.
—— (2017a) 'Shayara Bano versus Union of India and Others: The Indian Supreme Court's Ban of Triple Talaq and the Debate around Muslim Personal Law and Gender Justice' 50(3) *World Comparative Law* 300–11.
—— (2017b) 'Walking a Tightrope: Balancing Law, Religion and Gender Equality in the Aftermath of the Indian Supreme Court's Triple Talaq Ban' 9 *Zeitschrift für Recht und Islam* 179–204.
—— (2021) 'Armed with the Constitution: Feminist Litigation on Indian Family Law' in T Herklotz & SP De Souza (eds), *Mutinies for Equality: Contemporary Developments in Law and Gender in India* (New York, Cambridge University Press) pp 115–32.
—— (2023a) 'Feminist Constitutional Activism in India' 56(1) *World Comparative Law* 153–74.
—— (2023b) 'Kashmir, Minority Rights and Indian Constitutionalism: Introduction to the Special Issue' 56(4) *World Comparative Law* 667–74.
Hirschl, R (2007) *Towards Juristocracy: The Origins and Consequences of the New Constitutionalism* (Cambridge MA, Harvard University Press).
Hong Tschalaer, M (2017) *Muslim Women's Quest for Justice: Gender, Law and Activism in India* (Cambridge, Cambridge University Press).
Htun, M (2003) *Sex and the State: Abortion, Divorce, and the Family under Latin American Dictatorships and Democracies* (Cambridge, Cambridge University Press).
Htun, M, & Weldon, SL (2010) 'When Do Governments Promote Women's Rights? A Framework for the Comparative Analysis of Sex Equality Policy' 8(1) *Perspectives on Politics* 207–16.
—— (2012) 'The Civic Origins of Progressive Policy Change: Combating Violence against Women in Global Perspective, 1975–2005' 106(3) *The American Political Science Review* 548–69.
Hull, GT, Bell Scott, P & Smith, B (eds) (1982) *All the Women Are White, All the Blacks Are Men, But Some of Us Are Brave: Black Womens' s Studies* (New York, The Feminist Press).
Human Rights Watch (2024) 'India: Hate Speech Fueled Modi's Election Campaign'. Retrieved from https://www.hrw.org/news/2024/08/14/india-hate-speech-fueled-modis-election-campaign.
Irudayam, A, Mangubhai, JP, & Lee, JG (2011) *Dalit Women Speak Out: Caste, Class and Gender Violence in India* (New Delhi, Zubaan).
Irving, H (2008) *Gender and the Constitution: Equity and Agency in Comparative Constitutional Design* (New York, Cambridge University Press).
Jagori (2009) *Marching Together: Resisting Dowry in India* (New Delhi, Jagori).
—— (n.d.) [no title]. Retrieved from http://feministlawarchives.pldindia.org/wp-content/uploads/Urgent-for-Comments-from-the-jagori-Group.pdf.
Jain, A (2022) 'Democratic Decay in India: Weaponising the Constitution to Curb Parliamentary Deliberation' 34(1) *National Law School of India Review* 246–75.
Jain, D, & Shah, PK (2020) 'Reimagining Reproductive Rights Jurisprudence in India: Reflections on the Recent Decisions on Privacy and Gender Equality from the Supreme Court of India' 39(2) *Columbia Journal of Gender and Law* 1–53.
Jaising, I (2005a) 'From "Colonial" to "Constitutional", Gender Justice and Governance' in I Jaising (ed), *Men's Laws, Women's Lives: A Constitutional Perspective on Religion, Common Law and Culture in South Asia* (New Delhi, Women Unlimited) pp 323–38.
—— (2005b) 'Gender Justice: A Constitutional Perspective' in I Jaising (ed), *Men's Laws, Women's Lives: A Constitutional Perspective on Religion, Common Law and Culture in South Asia* (New Delhi, Women Unlimited) pp 1–22.
—— (2009) 'Bringing Rights Home: Review of the Campaign for a Law on Domestic Violence' 44(44) *Economic and Political Weekly* 50–57.
—— (2011) 'An Outsider, Inside' in R Menon (ed), *Making a Difference: Memoirs from the Women's Movement in India* (New Delhi, Women Unlimited) pp 347–69.
—— (2013) 'Gender Justice and the Indian Supreme Court: The Post-Colonial Project' in O Vilhena, U Baxi & F Viljoen (eds), *Transformative Constitutionalism: Comparing the Apex Courts of Brazil, India and South Africa* (Pretoria, Pretoria University Law Press) pp 230–43.

—— (2014) 'Bringing Rights Home: Review of the Campaign for a Law on Domestic Violence' in K Kannabiran (ed), *Women and Law: Critical Feminist Perspectives* (New Delhi, Sage) pp 1–31.

—— (2015) *Sexual Harassment at Workplace*, 2nd edn (Gurgaon, Lexis Nexis).

—— (2022) 'Feminist Lawyering: The Other Side of the Independence Movement' *The Leaflet*, 15 March 2022. Retrieved from https://theleaflet.in/feminist-lawyering-the-other-side-of-the-independence-movement/.

—— (2025) 'Civil Society and its Engagement with the Constitution' in A Jain & T Herklotz (eds), *Indian Constitutionalism at Crossroads: 2014-2024* (Berlin, Verfassungsbooks) pp 69–81.

Jethmalani, R, & Dey, PK (1995) 'Dowry Deaths and Access to Justice' in R Jethmalani (ed), *Kali's Yug: Empowerment, Law and Dowry Death* (Delhi, Har-Anand) pp 36–78.

Jha, S (2008) 'Rights versus Representation: Defending Minority Interests in the Constituent Assembly' in R Bhargava (ed), *Politics and Ethics of the Indian Constitution* (New Delhi, Oxford University Press).

John, M (2014) 'Fears and Furies of Sexual Harassment: Time to Go Beyond Vishaka', 49(15) *Economic and Political Weekly* 29–32.

John, ME (2005) 'Feminism, Poverty, and the Emergent Social Order' in R Ray & M Fainsod Katzenstein (eds), *Social Movements in India: Poverty, Power and Politics* (Lanham MD Rowman & Littlefield Publishers) pp 107–34.

Joint Action Committee Against Rape and Sexual Harassment (n.d.) 'Memorandum'. Retrieved from http://feministlawarchives.pldindia.org/wp-content/uploads/S.no-15-Memorandum-from-Joint-Action-Committee-against-Rape-and-Sexual-Harassment-New-Delhi-circa-1980s.pdf.

Joint Women's Programme (1986) *Need for a Uniform Civil Code*. Retrieved from http://feministlawarchives.pldindia.org/wp-content/uploads/S.no-59-Need-for-uniform-civil-court-recommendation-of-meeting-at-constitution-club-deputy-chairmen-hall-14.10.1986.pdf.

Juyal, P (2005) 'Introduction' in P Juyal (ed), *Women's Studies in India: Some Contemporary Contours* (Seoul, Asian Center for Women's Studies) pp 19–50.

Kali's Yug (2000) 'A Point of Debate: The Christian Marriage Act', *Kali's Yug* (July) 49–51.

Kalpagam, U (2004) 'Perspectives for a Grassroots Feminist Theory' in M Chaudhuri (ed), *Feminism in India* (Delhi, Kali for Women) pp 334–48.

Kamenitsa, L (2001) 'Abortion Debates in Germany' in D McBride Stetson (ed), *Abortion Politics, Women's Movements, and the Democratic State: A Comparative Study of State Feminism* (Oxford, Oxford University Press) pp 111–34.

Kandiyoti, D (1988) 'Bargaining with Patriarchy', 2(3) *Gender and Society* 274–90.

Kannabiran, K (2010) 'Feminist Deliberative Politics in India' in A Basu (ed), *Women's Movements in the Global Era: The Power of Local Feminisms* (Boulder CO, Westview Press) pp 119–56.

Kapur, D, & Mehta, PB (2006) *The Indian Parliament as an Institution of Accountability* (Geneva, UN Research Institute for Social Development).

Kapur, N (2013) 'The Way Things Are: Workplace Sexual Harassment', 48(24) *Economic and Political Weekly* 27–29.

Kapur, R (2005a) *Erotic Justice: Law and the New Politics of Postcolonialism* (New York, Routledge).

—— (2005b) 'Subversive Sites: Feminist Engagements with the Law in India' in M Khullar (ed), *Writing the Women's Movement: A Reader* (New Delhi, Zubaan) pp 152–74.

—— (2016) 'Gender Equality' in S Choudhry, M Khosla & PB Mehta (eds), *The Oxford Handbook of the Indian Constitution* (Oxford, Oxford University Press) pp 742–55.

—— (2017) 'Triple Talaq Verdict: Wherein Lies the Much Hailed Victory?', *The Wire*, 28 August 2017. Retrieved from https://thewire.in/171234/triple-talaq-verdict-wherein-lies-the-much-hailed-victory.

—— (2025) 'Gender, Equality, and the Predicaments of Faith' in A Jain & T Herklotz (eds), *Indian Constitutionalism at Crossroads: 2014–2024* (Berlin, Verfassungsbooks) pp 161–172.

Kapur, R, & Cossman, B (1996) *Subversive Sites: Feminist Engagements with Law in India* (New Delhi, Sage Publications).

—— (2013) 'On Women, Equality and the Constitution: Through the Looking Glass of Feminism' in N Menon (ed), *Gender and Politics in India* (New Delhi, Oxford University Press) pp 197–261.

Karat, B (1995) 'Uniformity vs Equality: The Concept of Uniform Civil Code', *Frontline*, November 1995, 82–84.

Kashyap, G (2024) 'Representation of Women Judges in High Courts has Improved only by 3 percent in three years' *Supreme Court Observer*, 31 August 2024. Retrieved from https://www.scobserver.in/journal/representation-of-women-judges-in-high-courts-has-improved-only-by-3-percent-in-three-years-august-2024/.

Katzenstein, MF (1989) 'Organizing Against Violence: Strategies of the Indian Women's Movement', 62(1) *Pacific Affairs* 53–71.

Kaur, N (1982) 'Mobilizing Against Dowry Murders', 13 *Manushi* 41–42.

Keating, C (2011) *Decolonizing Democracy: Transforming the Social Contract in India* (Pennsylvania, Penn State University Press).

Keck, ME, & Sikkink, K (1999) 'Transnational Advocacy Networks in International and Regional Politics', 51(159) *International Social Science Journal* 89–101.

Keshwaar, S (1991) '"Scream Silently, or the Neighbours Will Hear": The Crying Need for a Law Against Domestic Violence', 6(4) *The Lawyer* 4–9.

Khaitan, T (2020) 'Killing a Constitution with a Thousand Cuts: Executive Aggrandizement and Party-state Fusion in India', 14(1) *Law & Ethics of Human Rights* 49–95.

Khan, H (2017) 'Ending Instant Divorce is a Victory. But Indian Women Have a Fight Ahead', *The Guardian*, 25 August 2017. Retrieved from https://www.theguardian.com/commentisfree/2017/aug/25/islamic-instant-divorce-victory-india-talaq-women-harmful-practices.

Khilnani, S (2012 [1997]) *The Idea of India* (Gurgaon, Penguin Books).

King, S, & Sifaki, E (2019) 'Ending Domestic Violence: The Politics of Global Norm Diffusion' in S Nazneen, S Hickey & E Sifaki (eds), *Negotiating Gender Equity in the Global South: The Politics of Domestic Violence Policy* (London, Routledge) pp 44–63.

Kishwar, M (1986a) 'Dowry: To Ensure Her Happiness or to Disinherit Her?', 34 *Manushi* 2–13.

—— (1986b) 'Pro Women or Anti Muslim? The Shah Bano Controversy', 32 *Manushi* 4–13.

—— (1988) 'Rethinking Dowry Boycott', 48 *Manushi* 10–13.

—— (1992a) 'Sexual Harassment and Slander as Weapons of Subjugation', 68 *Manushi* 2–15.

—— (1992b) 'Sexual Harassment: Ways to Obtain Redressal at the Workplace', 69 *Manushi* 17–18.

—— (1993) 'Breaking the Stalemate: Uniform Civil Code vs. Personal Law', 77 *Manushi* 2–5.

—— (1994) 'Codified Hindu Law: Myth and Reality', 29(33) *Economic and Political Weekly* 2145–61.

—— (2005) *Strategies for Combating the Culture of Dowry and Domestic Violence in India*. Retrieved from http://www.un.org/womenwatch/daw/egm/vaw-gp-2005/docs/experts/kishwar.dowry.pdf.

—— (n.d.) 'Destined to Fail: Inherent Flaws in the Anti Dowry Legislation', 148 *Manushi* 3–12.

Kitschelt, HP (1986) 'Political Opportunity Structures and Political Protest: Anti-Nuclear Movements in Four Democracies', 16(1) *British Journal of Political Science* 57–85.

Klare, KE (1998) 'Legal Culture and Transformative Constitutionalism', 14(1) *South African Journal on Human Rights* 146–88.

Kokal, K (2020) *State Law, Dispute Proceeding and Legal Pluralism: Unspoken Dialogues from Rural India* (London, Routledge).

Kolb, F (2007) *Protest and Opportunities: The Political Outcomes of Social Movements* (Frankfurt/New York, Campus Verlag).

Krishnakumari, NS, & Geetha, AS (1983) 'Dowry: Spreading Among More Communities', 16 *Manushi* 31–32.

Krishnan, JK (2006) 'Lawyering for a Cause and Experiences from Abroad', 94 *California Law Review* 575–616.

Kumar, R (1993) *The History of Doing: An Illustrated Account of Movements for Women's Rights and Feminism in India 1800–1990* (New Delhi, Kali for Women).

Lambert, PA, & Scribner, DL (2020) 'Constitutions and Women's Rights Advocacy: Strategic Uses of Gender Provisions in Argentina, Chile, Botswana, and South Africa', 8(2) *Politics, Groups, and Identities* 228–47.

—— (2023) *Gender, Constitutions, and Equality: A Global Comparison* (New York, Routledge).

Law Commission of India (1960) *15th Report on Law Relating to Marriage and Divorce Amongst Christians in India.* Retrieved from https://cdnbbsr.s3waas.gov.in/s3ca0daec69b5adc880fb464895726dbdf/uploads/2022/08/2022080534.pdf.

—— (1980) *84th Report on Rape and Allied Offences: Some Questions of Substantive Law, Procedure and Evidence.* Retrieved from https://cdnbbsr.s3waas.gov.in/s3ca0daec69b5adc880fb464895726dbdf/uploads/2022/08/2022080544.pdf.

—— (1983a) *90th Report on Grounds of Divorce amongst Christians in India: Section 10 Indian Divorce Act.* Retrieved from https://cdnbbsr.s3waas.gov.in/s3ca0daec69b5adc880fb464895726dbdf/uploads/2022/08/2022080892.pdf.

—— (1983b) *91st Report on Dowry Deaths and Law Reform: Amending the Hindu Marriage Act, 1955, the Indian Penal Code, 1860 and the Indian Evidence Act, 1872.* Retrieved from https://cdnbbsr.s3waas.gov.in/s3ca0daec69b5adc880fb464895726dbdf/uploads/2022/08/2022080815.pdf.

—— (1989) *133rd Report on Removal of Discrimination Against Women in Matters Relating to Guardianship and Custody of Minor Children and Elaboration of the Welfare Principles.* Retrieved from https://cdnbbsr.s3waas.gov.in/s3ca0daec69b5adc880fb464895726dbdf/uploads/2022/08/2022080845.pdf.

—— (2000a) *172nd Report on Review of Rape Laws.* Retrieved from https://cdnbbsr.s3waas.gov.in/s3ca0daec69b5adc880fb464895726dbdf/uploads/2022/08/2022082487.pdf.

—— (2000b) *174th Report on Property Rights of Women: Proposed Reforms Under the Hindu Law.* Retrieved from https://cdnbbsr.s3waas.gov.in/s3ca0daec69b5adc880fb464895726dbdf/uploads/2022/08/2022082470.pdf.

—— (2009) *217th Report on Irretrievable Breakdown of Marriage – Another Ground for Divorce.* https://cdnbbsr.s3waas.gov.in/s3ca0daec69b5adc880fb464895726dbdf/uploads/2022/08/2022081084-2.pdf.

—— (2012) *243rd Report on Section 498A IPC.* Retrieved from https://cdnbbsr.s3waas.gov.in/s3ca0daec69b5adc880fb464895726dbdf/uploads/2022/08/2022081023.pdf.

—— (n.d.) 'Post-Independence Developments'. Retrieved from https://lawcommissionofindia.nic.in/post-independence-developments/.

Lawyers Collective (1999) 'Domestic Violence Against Women (Protection) Bill, 1999: Second Draft'. Retrieved from http://feministlawarchives.pldindia.org/wp-content/uploads/14.pdf?.

—— (2012) *Staying Alive: 5th Monitoring & Evaluation 2012 on the Protection of Women from Domestic Violence Act, 2005* (New Delhi, Lawyers Collective).

—— (1996) 'Bhanwari Devi: Betrayed by the Judicial System', 11(1) *The Lawyer* 4–28.

—— (2001) 'Prevention of Domestic Violence', *Kali's Yug* (March), 72–82.

—— (n.d.-a) 'Women's Rights'. Retrieved from https://lawyerscollective.org/index.php/womens-right/.

—— (n.d.-b) 'About Us'. Retrieved from https://lawyerscollective.org/index.php/about/.

—— (n.d.-c) *Recent Changes in Laws Relating to Women* (Bombay, Bharat Printers), Retrieved from https://feministlawarchives.pldindia.org/wp-content/uploads/S.no-14-Lawyers-Collective-Recent-Changes-in-Laws-Relating-to-Women.pdf.

Legrand, P (1997) 'The Impossibility of "Legal Transplants"' 4(2) *Maastricht Journal of European and Comparative Law* 111–24.

Leslie, AN (2006) *Social Movements and Democracy in Africa: The Impact of Women's Struggle for Equal Rights in Botswana* (New York/ London, Routledge).

Lovenduski, J (2005a) 'Introduction: State Feminism and the Political Representation of Women' in J Lovenduski (ed), *State Feminism and Political Representation* (Cambridge, Cambridge University Press) pp 1–19.

—— (ed) (2005b) *State Feminism and Political Representation* (Cambridge, Cambridge University Press).

Lovenduski, J, Baudino, C, Guadagnini, M, Meier, P, & Sainsbury, D (2005) 'Conclusion: State Feminism and Political Representation' in J Lovenduski (ed), *State Feminism and Political Representation* (Cambridge, Cambridge University Press) pp 260–93.

MacKinnon, CA (1979) *Sexual Harassment of Working Women: A Case of Sex Discrimination* (New Haven CT/London, Yale University Press).

—— (2006) 'Sex Equality Under the Constitution of India: Problems, Prospects and "Personal Laws"', 4(2) *International Journal of Constitutional Law* 181–202.
Majlis (2020) *Transforming Victims into Survivors: Annual Report of Activities April 2019–March 2020.* Retrieved from https://majlislaw.com.
Mandal, S (2025) 'The Fabulous and the Fascist: LGBT Rights in Modi's India' in A Jain & T Herklotz (eds), *Indian Constitutionalism at Crossroads: 2014-2024* (Berlin, Verfassungsbooks) pp 189–201.
Manfredi, CP (2004) *Feminist Activism in the Supreme Court: Legal Mobilization and the Women's Legal Education and Action Fund* (Vancouver, UBC Press).
Manuh, T, & Dwamena-Aboagye, A (2013) 'Implementing Domestic Violence Legislation in Ghana: The Role of Institutions' in M Al-Sharmani (ed), *Feminist Activism, Women's Rights and Legal Reform* (London/ New York, Zed Books) pp 203–34.
Manushi (1980) 'Rape: The Victim is the Accused', 4 *Manushi* 42–46.
—— (1981a) 'Letters That Came in Response to Our Call for Boycotting Dowry Marriages', 7 *Manushi* 11–12.
—— (1981b) 'The New Rape Bill: Legislating Rape "Out of Existence"!', 7 *Manushi* 38–45.
—— (1981c) 'Pledges in Response to Manushi's Call for Boycotting Dowry Marriages', 8 *Manushi* 5.
—— (1984) 'A Christian Woman Demands Equal Succession Rights', 25 *Manushi.*
—— (1986) 'Is A Father A "Natural" Guardian? Hindu Guardianship Act Challenged', 35 *Manushi* 32–36.
Martin, PY, Reynolds, JT, & Keith, S (2002) 'Gender Bias and Feminist Consciousness among Judges and Attorneys: A Standpoint Theory', 27 *Signs* 665–701.
McBride, DE, & Mazur, AG (2013) 'Women's Policy Agencies and State Feminism' in G Waylen, K Celis, J Kantola & SLW Weldon (eds), *The Oxford Handbook of Gender and Politics* (Oxford, Oxford University Press) pp 654–78.
McBride Stetson, D (2001a) 'Conclusion: Comparative Abortion Politics and the Case for State Feminism' in D McBride Stetson (ed), *Abortion Politics, Women's Movements, and the Democratic State: A Comparative Study of State Feminism* (Oxford, Oxford University Press) pp 267–95.
—— (2001b) 'US Abortion Debates 1959–1998: The Women's Movement Holds On' in D McBride Stetson (ed), *Abortion Politics, Women's Movements, and the Democratic State: A Comparative Study of State Feminism* (Oxford, Oxford University Press) pp 247–66.
—— (ed) (2001c) *Abortion Politics, Women's Movements, and the Democratic State: A Comparative Study of State Feminism* (Oxford, Oxford University Press).
McCammon, HJ, Campbell, KE, Granberg, EM, & Mowery, C (2001) 'How Movements Win: Gendered Opportunity Structures and U.S. Women's Suffrage Movements, 1866 to 1919', 66(1) *American Sociological Review* 49–70.
McCammon, HJ, Moon, M, Hearne, BN, & Robinson, M (2020) 'The Supreme Court as an Arena for Activism: Feminist Cause Lawyering's Influence on Judicial Decision Making', 25(2) *Mobilization: An International Quarterly* 221–44.
McCann, M (1994) *Rights at Work, Pay Equity Reform and the Politics of Legal Mobilization* (Chicago IL, The University of Chicago Press).
—— (2006) 'Law and Social Movements: Contemporary Perspectives', 2 *Annual Review of Law and Social Science* 17–38.
McCormick, P, & Job, T (1993) 'Do Women Judges Make a Difference? An Analysis of Appeal Court Data', 8(1) *Canadian Journal of Law and Society* 135–48.
McCrudden, C (2008) 'Human Dignity and Judicial Interpretation of Human Rights', 19(4) *The European Journal of International Law* 655–724.
Mehra, M (1993) *Paper on Status of Dowry in India.* Retrieved from http://feministlawarchives.pldindia.org/wp-content/uploads/2.pdf.
—— (1998) 'Exploring the Boundaries of Law, Gender and Social Reform', 6(1) *Feminist Legal Studies* 59–83.
Menon, N (1998) 'Women and Citizenship' in P Chatterjee (ed), *Wages of Freedom: Fifty Years of the Indian Nation-State* (Delhi, Oxford University Press) pp 241–66.
—— (2012) *Seeing Like a Feminist* (New Delhi, Zubaan/Penguin).

Menon, R (2011) 'Introduction' in R Menon (ed), *Making a Difference: Memoirs from the Women's Movement in India* (New Delhi, Women Unlimited).

Merry, SE, Rosen, MS, Levitt, P, & Yoon, DH (2010) 'Law From Below: Women's Human Rights and Social Movements in New York City', 44 *Law & Society Review* 101–28.

Mirchandani, M (2017) 'Triple Talaq and Marital Rape: Politics and Patriarchy Trump Gender Justice'. Retrieved from https://thewire.in/law/triple-talaq-marital-rape-patriarchy-politics-gender-justice.

Mody, Z (2013) *10 Judgements that Changed India* (Gurgaon, Shobhaa Dé Books).

Mohanty, CT (1991) 'Introduction: Cartographies of Struggle: Third World Women and the Politics of Feminism' in CT Mohanty, A Russo & L Torres (eds), *Third World Women and the Politics of Feminism* (Bloominton IN, Indiana University Press).

Mohanty, M (2001) 'Dowry and the Indian Woman: The Need for a Two Pronged Attack', *Kali's Yug* (March) 29–32.

Monteiro, R (1992) 'Belief, Law and Justice for Women: Debate on Proposed Christian Marriage and Matrimonial Causes Bill 1990', 27(43–44) *Economic and Political Weekly* WS 74–WS 80.

Moon, M, & Pawar, U (2008) *We Also Made History: Women in the Ambedkarite Movement* (New Delhi, Zubaan Books).

Morton, FL, & Allen, A (2001) 'Feminists and the Courts: Measuring Success in Interest Group Litigation in Canada', 34(1) *Canadian Journal of Political Science* 55–84.

Murthy, L, & Dasgupta, R (2011) *Our Pictures, Our Words: A Visual Journey Through the Women's Movement* (New Delhi, Zubaan).

Nagasaila, D (1991) 'Sexual Harassment as Sex Discrimination', 26(34) *Economic and Political Weekly* 1965–67.

Narain, V (2008) *Reclaiming the Nation: Muslim Women and the Law in India* (Toronto, University of Toronto Press).

Narrain, A (2014) 'Sexual Violence and the Death Penalty: A Tale of Two Judgments', 49(3) *Economic and Political Weekly* 38–42.

Nazneen, S (2013) 'Men Aboard? Movement for a Uniform Family Code in Bangladesh' in M Al-Sharmani (ed), *Feminist Activism, Women's Rights and Legal Reform* (London/ New York, Zed Books) pp 101–24.

Nazneen, S, & Hickey, S (2019a) 'Beyond the Inclusion-to-Influence Debate: The Politics of Negotiating Gender Equity' in S Nazneen, S Hickey & E Sifaki (eds), *Negotiating Gender Equity in the Global South: The Politics of Domestic Violence Policy* (Abingdon, Routledge) pp 3–20.

—— (2019b) 'How does Politics Shape the Negotiation of Gender Equity in the Global South? A Comparative Analysis' in S Nazneen, S Hickey & E Sifaki (eds), *Negotiating Gender Equity in the Global South: The Politics of Domestic Violence Policy* (Abingdon, Routledge) pp 191–213.

Nazneen, S, Hickey, S, & Sifaki, E (eds) (2019) *Negotiating Gender Equity in the Global South: The Politics of Domestic Violence Policy* (Abingdon, Routledge).

Nelken, D (2014a) 'Legal Cultures' in DS Clark (ed), *Comparative Law and Society* (Cheltenham, Edward Elgar Publishing).

—— (2014b) 'Thinking About Legal Culture', 1 *Asian Journal of Law and Society* 255–74.

Niaz, NS, & Soman, Z (2015) *Seeking Justice Within Family: A National Study on Muslim Women's Views on Reforms in Muslim Personal Law* (Belgaum, BMMA).

—— (2016) 'The Fight for Reform by Muslim Women Needs the Support of Muslim Men Too', *The Wire*, 11 May 2026. Retrieved from https://thewire.in/gender/seeking-change-muslim-men-must-support-muslim-womens-fight-for-reform.

Notz, G (2015) *Kritik des Familismus: Theorie und soziale Realität eines ideologischen Gemäldes* (Stuttgart, Schmetterling Verlag).

O'Connor, K, & Epstein, L (1983) 'Beyond Legislative Lobbying: Women's Rights Groups and the Supreme Court', 67(3) *Judicature* 134–43.

Okoth-Ogendo, H (1993) 'Constitutions without Constitutionalism: Reflections on an African Political Paradox' in D Greenberg, SN Katz, MB Oliviero & SC Wheatley (eds), *Constitutionalism and Democracy: Transitions in the Contemporary World* (New York/ Oxford, Oxford University Press) pp 65–82.

Omvedt, G (1993) *Reinventing Revolution: New Social Movements and the Socialist Tradition in India* (New York, East Gate).
Pai, S, & Kumar, A (eds) (2014) *The Indian Parliament: A Critical Appraisal* (Hyderabad, Orient Black-Swan).
Parashar, A (1992) *Women and Family Law Reform in India: Uniform Civil Code and Gender Equality* (New Delhi, Sage Publications).
—— (2013) 'Religious Personal Laws as Non-State Laws: Implications for Gender Justice', 45(1) *The Journal of Legal Pluralism and Unofficial Law* 5–23.
Parashar, A, & Dhanda, A (eds) (2008) *Redefining Family Law in India: Essays in Honour of B. Sivaramayya* (New Delhi, Routledge).
Partners for Law in Development (n.d.) 'About Us'. Retrieved from https://pldindia.org/about-us/.
Patel, V, & Khajuria, R (2016) *Political Feminism in India: An Analysis of Actors, Debates and Strategies*, (New Delhi, Friedrich-Ebert-Stiftung). Retrieved from http://library.fes.de/pdf-files/bueros/indien/12706.pdf.
Pateman, C (1988) *The Sexual Contract* (Stanford CA, Stanford University Press).
Peresie, JL (2005) 'Female Judges Matter: Gender and Collegial Decisionmaking in the Federal Appellate Courts', 114(7) *The Yale law journal* 1759–90.
Pillai, S (1986) 'Women's Victory', *India Today*, 31 March 1986, p 149.
Rahman, A (1990) 'Religious Rights Versus Women's Rights in India: A Test Case for International Human Rights Law', 28 *Columbia Journal for Transnational Law* 473–98.
Rai, S (2007) 'Emerging State Feminism in India: A Conversation with Vina Mazumdar, Member Secretary to the First Committee on the Status of Women in India', 9(1) *International Feminist Journal of Politics* 104–11.
Rai, SM, & Spary, C (2019) *Performing Representation: Women Members in the Indian Parliament* (New Delhi, Oxford University Press).
Rajagopal, B. (2007) 'Pro-Human Rights but Anti-Poor? A Critical Evaluation of the Indian Supreme Court from a Social Movement Perspective', 18(3) *Human Rights Review* 157–87.
Rajan, A (2019) 'India's Marital Rape Problem', *International Policy Digest*, 14 February 2019. Retrieved from https://intpolicydigest.org/2019/02/14/india-s-marital-rape-problem/.
Rajvanshi, A (2022) 'Marital Rape Isn't a Crime in India. This Lawyer Is Fighting to Change That', *Time*, 27 March 2022. Retrieved from https://time.com/6160414/marital-rape-india-karuna-nundy-interview/.
Rajya Sabha Committee on Petitions (2011) *140th Report on Petition Praying for Amendments in Section 498A of Indian Penal Code, 1980*. Retrieved from http://164.100.47.5/newcommittee/reports/EnglishCommittees/Committee%20on%20Petitions/140.pdf.
Ramanathan, U (2002) 'Of Judicial Power', 19(6) *Frontline*.
Randeria, S (2002) 'Entangled Histories of Uneven Modernities: Civil Society, Caste Solidarities and Legal Pluralism in Post-Colonial India' in Y Elkana, I Krastev, E Macamo & S Randeria (eds), *Unraveling Ties: From Social Cohesion to New Practices of Connectedness* (Frankfurt am Main/New York, Campus) pp 284–311.
Ray, R, & Katzenstein, MF (2005) 'Introduction: In the Beginning, There Was the Nehruvian State' in R Ray & MF Katzenstein (eds), *Social Movements in India: Poverty, Power, and Politics* (Lanham MD, Rowman & Littlefield Publishers) pp 1–31.
Rein, M, & Schön, D (1991) 'Frame-Reflective Policy Discourse' in P Wagner, CH Weiss, B Wittrock & H Wollmann (eds), *Social Sciences and Modern States: National Experiences and Theoretical Crossroads* (Cambridge, Cambridge University Press) pp 262–89.
Reuterswärd, C, Zetterberg, P, Thapar-Björkert, S, & Molyneux, M (2011) 'Abortion Law Reforms in Colombia and Nicaragua: Issue Networks and Opportunity Contexts', 42(3) *Development and change* 805–31.
Robinson, N (2016) 'Judicial Architecture and Capacity' in S Choudhry, M Khosla & PB Mehta (eds), *The Oxford Handbook of the Indian Constitution* (Delhi, Oxford University Press) pp 330–48.
—— 'The Structure and Functioning of the Supreme Court of India' in GN Rosenberg, S Krishnaswamy & S Bail (eds), *A Qualified Hope: The Indian Supreme Court and Progressive Social Change* (Cambridge, Cambridge University Press) pp 23–42.

Rosenberg, GN (1991) *The Hollow Hope: Can Courts Bring About Social Change?* (Chicago/London, The University of Chicago Press).

Rosenberg, GN, Bail, S, & Krishnaswamy, S (2019) 'Conclusion: Neither a Silver Bullet Nor a Hollow Hope' in GN Rosenberg, S Krishnaswamy & S Bail (eds), *A Qualified Hope: The Indian Supreme Court and Progressive Social Change* (Cambridge/ New York, Cambridge University Press) pp 345–57.

Rosenberg, GN, Krishnaswamy, S, & Bail, S (2019) 'Introduction: The Indian Supreme Court and Progressive Social Change' in GN Rosenberg, S Krishnaswamy & S Bail (eds), *A Qualified Hope: The Indian Supreme Court and Progressive Social Change* (Cambridge/ New York, Cambridge University Press) pp 1–19.

Roy, M (1999) 'Three Generations of Women', 6(2) *Indian Journal of Gender Studies* 203–19.

Roychowdhury, P (2021) *Capable Women, Incapable States: Negotiating Violence and Rights in India* (New York, Oxford University Press).

Rubio-Marin, R (2005) 'Engendering the Constitution: The Spanish Experience' in B Baines & R Rubio-Marin (eds), *The Gender of Constitutional Jurisprudence* (Cambridge, Cambridge University Press) pp 156–277.

Ruibal, A (2014) 'Movement and Counter-Movement: A History of Abortion Law Reform and the Backlash in Colombia 2006–2014', 22(44) *Reproductive Health Matters* 42–51.

Saberin, Z (2018) 'India: Triple Talaq or Instant Divorce Now a Criminal Offence' *Al Jazeera*. Retrieved from https://www.aljazeera.com/news/2018/09/india-triple-talaq-instant-divorce-criminal-offence-180919073349658.html.

Sadiqi, F, & Ennaji, M (2006) 'The Feminization of Public Space: Women's Activism, the Family Law, and Social Change in Mororro', 2(2) *Journal of Middle East Women's Studies* 86–114.

Saheli (1984a) 'About Ourselves': Newsletter March 1984. Retrieved from https://sites.google.com/site/saheliorgsite/about-us/about-ourselves.

—— (1984b) 'Violence Against Women: Newsletter March 1984'. Retrieved from https://sites.google.com/site/saheliorgsite/violence/domestic-violence/violence-against-women.

—— (1986a) 'The National Conference: Perspectives for an Autonomous Women's Movement in India: December 23–26th 1985 Bombay: Newsletter March 1986'. Retrieved from https://sites.google.com/site/saheliorgsite/conferences/autonomous-womens-conferences/the-national-conference-perspectives-for-an-autonomous-womens-movement-in-india.

—— (1986b) 'Towards a Uniform Civil Code: Newsletter March 1986'. Retrieved from https://sites.google.com/site/saheliorgsite/communalism/personal-law-debates/towards-a-uniform-civil-code.

—— (1987) 'Wife Battering: Issues Facing the Women's Movement: Newsletter October 1987'. Retrieved from https://sites.google.com/site/saheliorgsite/violence/domestic-violence/wife-battering-issues-facing-the-womens-movement.

—— (1988) 'Resolution of the Third Nari Mukti Sangharsh Sammelan in Patna'. Retrieved from https://sites.google.com/site/saheliorgsite/conferences/autonomous-womens-conferences/third-nari-mukti-sangharsh-sammelan-patna-1988-resolutions.

—— (1989) 'National Conference on Women, Religion And Family Laws: Newsletter December 1989'. Retrieved from https://feministlawarchives.pldindia.org/wp-content/uploads/National-Conference-on-Women-Religion-And-Family-Laws-Saheli-1989.pdf.

—— (1995) 'Egalitarian Civil Code: An Issue of Gender Justice: Newsletter January 1995'. Retrieved from https://sites.google.com/site/saheliorgsite/communalism/personal-law-debates/egalitarian-civil-code-an-issue-of-gender-justice.

—— (1997a) 'Egalitarian Civil Code: Every Woman's Basic Right: Newsletter March 1997'. https://sites.google.com/site/saheliorgsite/communalism/personal-law-debates/egalitarian-civil-code-every-womans-basic-right.

—— (1997b) 'Sexual Harassment at the Workplace: Finally, the Supreme Court Acknowledges the Problem: Newsletter Sept 1997'. Retrieved from https://sites.google.com/site/saheliorgsite/violence/sexual-harassment/sexual-harassment-at-the-workplace_1.

—— (1997c) 'The Stranglehold of State Patriarchy: Newsletter March 1997'. Retrieved https://sites.google.com/site/saheliorgsite/communalism/personal-law-debates/the-stranglehold-of-state-patriarchy.

—— (1997d) 'Women Unite! Break the Shackles of Tradition and Custom! 8th March 1997: Newsletter March 1997' Retrieved from https://sites.google.com/site/saheliorgsite/celebrations/international-womens-day/women-unite-break-the-shackles-of-tradition-and-custom.

—— (1999) 'Capital Punishment for Rape: Can it Tackle the Growing Violence Against Women?: Newsletter February 1999' Retrieved from https://sites.google.com/site/saheliorgsite/violence/rape-sexual-assault/capital-punishment-for-rape.

—— (2002a) 'Looking at Domestic Violence: A Saheli Presentation: Newsletter Jan–Apr 2002'. Retrieved from https://sites.google.com/site/saheliorgsite/violence/domestic-violence/looking-at-domestic-violence.

—— (2002b) 'Update on Domestic Violence Bill: New Scenario Poses New Challenges: Newsletter May–Aug 2002' Retrieved from https://sites.google.com/site/saheliorgsite/violence/domestic-violence/campaign-update-on-domestic-violence-bill.

—— (2005a) 'Hindu Succession Amendment Bill: Women's Groups Join to Plug Loopholes: Newsletter Jan–Apr 2005'. Retrieved from https://sites.google.com/site/saheliorgsite/communalism/personal-law-debates/hindu-succession-amendment-bill-womens-groups-join-to-plug-loopholes.

—— (2005b) 'Legislative Reforms in the Hindu Succession Act: Newsletter Sept–Dec 2005'. Retrieved from https://sites.google.com/site/saheliorgsite/legislative-reforms-in-hindu-succession-act.

—— (2006a) '25 Years of Saheli: Celebration and Struggle: Strengthening Autonomous Politics: Newsletter Dec 2006'. https://sites.google.com/site/saheliorgsite/about-us/25-years-of-saheli-celebration-and-struggle-strengthening-autonomous-politics.

—— (2006b) 'Towards a Politics of Justice: Afforming Diversities, Resisting Divisiveness: The Seventh National Conference of Women's Movements: Kolkata, 9–12 September 2006: Newsletter Dec 2006'. Retrieved from https://sites.google.com/site/saheliorgsite/conferences/autonomous-womens-conferences/towards-a-politics-of-justice-affirming-diversities-resisting-divisiveness.

—— (2011) 'Sexual Harassment at the Workplace: Still Struggling for an Effective Legislation: Newsletter Jan–Aug 2011'. Retrieved from https://sites.google.com/site/saheliorgsite/sexual-harrassment-at-the-workplace-still-struggling-for-an-effective-legislation.

—— (2014a) 'Looking at the Law(s) on Sexual Harassment at the Workplace: Newsletter Sept 2013-Aug 2014'. Retrieved from https://sites.google.com/site/saheliorgsite/violence/sexual-harassment/working-out-the-tensions-new-laws-on-sexual-harassment-at-the-workplace.

—— (2014b) 'Not Quite the Commission We Had Sought: Consistently Campaigning for a Better NCW!: Newsletter Sep 2013–Aug 2014' Retrieved from https://sites.google.com/site/saheliorgsite/other-issues/ncw-not-quite-the-commission-we-sought.

—— (2018) 'Triple Talaq. The Ban and the Bill. Debates and Updates: Newsletter Mar–Aug 2018'. Retrieved from https://sites.google.com/site/saheliorgsite/communalism/personal-law-debates/triple-talaq-the-ban-and-the-bill-debates-and-updates.

Samuels, H (2005) 'Feminist Activism, Third Party Interventions and the Courts', 13(1) *Feminist Legal Studies* 15–42.

Sangari, K (1995) 'Politics of Diversity: Religious Communities and Multiple Patriarchies', 30(52) *Economic and Political Weekly* 3381–89.

Sarat, A, & Scheingold, SA (eds) (2001) *Cause Lawyering and the State in a Global Era* (Oxford, Oxford University Press).

—— (eds) (2004) *Something to Believe In: Politics, Professionalism, and Cause Lawyering* (Stanford CA, Stanford University Press).

—— (2006) *Cause Lawyers and Social Movements* (Stanford CA, Stanford University Press).

Sarkar, L, Ramanathan, U, & Mehra, M (1994) *Gender Bias in Law: Dowry*. Retrieved from feministlawarchives.pldindia.org/wp-content/uploads/gender-bias-in-law.pdf

Sathe, SP (2002) *Judicial Activism in India: Transgressing Borders and Enforcing Limits*, 2nd edn (New Delhi, Oxford University Press).

Satish, M (2016) *Discretion, Discrimination and the Rule of Law: Reforming Rape Sentencing in India* (Cambridge, Cambridge University Press).

Sauer, B, Haussman, M, & McBride, DE (2007) 'Conclusion: State Feminism and State Restructuring since the 1990s' in M Haussman & B Sauer (eds), *Gendering the State in the Age of*

Globalization: Women's Movements and State Feminism in Postindustrial Democracies (Lanham MD, Rowman & Littlefield) pp 271–96.

Schneider, NC (2005) *Zur Darstellung von 'Kultur' und 'kultureller Differenz' im indischen Mediensystem: Die indische Presse und die Repräsentation des Islams im Rahmen der Zivilrechtsdebatte, 1985–87 und 2003* (Berlin, Logos).

—— (2009) 'Islamic Feminism and Muslim Women's Rights Activism in India: From Transnational Discourse to Local Movement – or Vice Versa?', 11(1) *Journal of International Women's Studies* 56–71.

—— (2015) 'Introduction' in NC Schneider & F-M Titzmann (eds), *Studying Youth, Media and Gender in Post-Liberalisation India* (Berlin, Frank & Timme) pp 9–16.

Sen, I (2012) 'Women's Polititics in India' in R Ray (ed), *Handbook of Gender* (New Delhi, Oxford University Press) pp 519–38.

Sen, J (2017) 'The Gender Question', *Frontline*, 15 September 2017. Retrieved from http://www.frontline.in/the-nation/the-gender-question/article9834658.ece.

Sen, R (2014) 'Mapping Women's Activism in India: Resistances, Reforms and (Re)-Creation' in L Fernandes (ed), *Routledge Handbook of Gender in South Asia* (Abingdon, Routledge) pp 333–46.

Sen, R, & Mandal, S (2015) 'Editorial Note: Indian Feminisms, Law Reform and the Law Commission of India: Special Issue in Honour of Lotika Sarkar', 6 *Journal of Indian Law and Society* vi-xxxvii.

Serajuddin, AM (2015) *Cases on Muslim Law of India, Pakistan and Bangladesh* (New Delhi, Oxford University Press).

Sharafi, M (2014) *Law and Identity in Colonial South Asia: Parsi Legal Culture, 1772–1947* (New York, Cambridge University Press).

Sharma, B (2017) 'Interview: Triple Talaq Ruling Fails to Address the Real Suffering of Muslim Women, Says Indira Jaising', *Huffington Post*, 25 August 2017. Retrieved from https://www.huffpost.com/archive/in/entry/why-the-triple-talaq-ruling-fails-to-address-the-real-suffering-of-muslim-women_in_5c10c6c4e4b09dcd67fc2717.

Shehada, N (2013) 'Debating Islamic Family Law in Palestine: Citizenship, Gender and "Islamic" Idioms' in M Al-Sharmani (ed), *Feminist Activism, Women's Rights and Legal Reform* (London/New York, Zed Books) pp 23–47.

Sheikh, S (2016) 'Why I Took on Triple Talaq and Why I Oppose the Uniform Civil Code', *Indian Express*, 16 November 2016. Retrieved from http://indianexpress.com/article/opinion/columns/triple-talaq-uniform-civil-code-indian-constitution-4377532/.

Shikhare, D (1986) 'Talaq Mukti Morcha in Maharashtra', 32 *Manushi* 23.

Sieder, R, Schjolden, L, & Angell, A (eds) (2005) *The Judicialization of Politics in Latin America* (New York, Palgrave Macmillan).

Sindhu, J, & Narayan, V (2018) 'Institution Matters: A Critical Analysis of the Role of the Supreme Court of India and the Responsibilities of the Chief Justice' 51(3) *World Comparative Law* 290–331.

Singh, K (2003) 'Dowry and the Law' in All India Democratic Women's Association (ed.) *Expanding Dimensions of Dowry* (Delhi, AIDWA) pp 28–34.

Sivaramayya, B (1997) 'Of Daughters, Sons and Widows: Discrimination in Inheritance Laws' 100 *Manushi* 27–32.

Solanki, G (2011) *Adjudication in Religious Family Laws: Cultural Accommodation, Legal Pluralism, and Gender Equality in India* (Cambridge, Cambridge University Press).

Sood, AM (2008) 'Gender Justice through Public Interest Litigation: Case Studies from India' 41(3) *Vanderbilt Journal of Transnational Law* 833–906.

Stearns, N (1988) 'Roe v. Wade: Our Struggle Continues', 4 Berkeley Women's Law Journal 1 (1–11).

Subramanian, N (2014) *Nation and Family. Personal Law, Cultural Pluralism, and Gendered Citizenship* (Stanford CA, Stanford University Press).

Sunder Rajan, R (2003) *The Scandal of the State: Women, Law and Citizenship in Postcolonial India* (Durham NC/ London, Duke University Press).

Supreme Court of India (2022) *Handbook on Combating Gender Stereotypes* (updated November 2023). Retrieved from https://cdnbbsr.s3waas.gov.in/s3ec0490f1f4972d133619a60c30f3559e/uploads/2024/01/2024012544.pdf.

Tarrow, S (2011) *Power in Movement: Social Movements and Contentious Politics* (Cambridge/ New York, Cambridge University Press).

Tate, CN, & Vallinder, T (eds) (1995) *The Global Expansion of Judicial Power* (New York, New York University Press).

Teltumbde, A (2017) 'Justice or Revenge in "Nirbhaya" Verdict?' 52(22) *Economic and Political Weekly* 10–11.

Thiruvengadam, AK (2017) *The Constitution of India: A Contextual Analysis* (Oxford, Hart Publishing).

UN Women (2017) 'Why and How Constitutions Matter for Advancing Gender Equality: Gains, Gaps and Policy Implications'. Retrieved from https://www.unwomen.org/en/digital-library/publications/2017/2/why-and-how-constitutions-matter-for-advancing-gender-equality.

United Nations (2006) *Declarations, Reservations, Objections and Notifications of Withdrawal of Reservations Relating to the Convention on the Elimination of All Forms of Discrimination against Women*, CEDAW/SP/2006/2, 23 June 2006. Retrieved from https://documents-dds-ny.un.org/doc/UNDOC/GEN/N06/309/97/PDF/N0630997.pdf?OpenElement.

Valiente, C (2007) 'The Women's Movement, State Feminism, and Unemployment Reform in Spain, 2002–2003' in M Haussman & B Sauer (eds), *Gendering the State in the Age of Globalization: Women's Movements and State Feminism in Postindustrial Democracies* (Lanham MD, Rowman & Littlefield Publishers) pp 210–24.

Valiramani, S (2017) 'Women's Rights Groups Speak Out Against Centre's Decision to "Criminalise Muslim Men" With Triple Talaq Bill', *The Wire*, 22 December 2017. Retrieved from https://thewire.in/gender/triple-talaq-criminalised-bill-womens-rights.

Vanita, R (1983) 'Two Bills to Amend the Rape and Dowry Laws: Mending or Marring?', 16 *Manushi* 27–30.

—— (1984) 'Nominal Changes', 24 *Manushi* 29–31.

—— (2011) '"More Lives than One": Manushi and the Women's Movement' in R Menon (ed), *Making a Difference: Memoirs from the Women's Movement in India* (New Delhi, Women Unlimited) pp 21–36.

Vashney, R (1998) 'Sexual Harassment at the Workplace' *Kali's Yug*(August), 2–9 http://feministlawarchives.pldindia.org/wp-content/uploads/Kali-1.pdf.

Vatuk, S (2005) 'Moving the Courts: Muslim Women and Personal Law' in Z Hasan & R Menon (eds), *The Diversity of Muslim Women's Lives in India* (New Brunswick/ London, Rutgers University Press) pp 18–58.

—— (2008a) 'Divorce at the Wife's Initiative in Muslim Personal Law: What are the Options and What are their Implications for Women's Welfare?' in A Parashar & A Dhanda (eds), *Redefining Family Law in India: Essays in Honour of B Sivaramayya* (New Delhi, Routledge) pp 200–35.

—— (2008b) 'Islamic Feminism in India: Indian Muslim Women Activists and the Reform of Muslim Personal Law', 42(2/3) *Modern Asian Studies* 489–518.

—— (2013) 'The "Women's Court" in India: An Alternative Dispute Resolution Body for Women in Distress', 45(1) *The Journal of Legal Pluralism and Unofficial Law* 76–103.

Verma, JS, Seth, L, & Subramanium, G (2013) *Report of the Committee on Amendments to Criminal Law*. Retrieved from https://archive.nyu.edu/bitstream/2451/33614/2/J_S_VermaCommitteReport.pdf.

Verma, M (2025) 'Amending the Constitution Without Deliberation: The Contemporary Indian Constitutionalism Experience' in A Jain & T Herklotz (eds), *Indian Constitutionalism at Crossroads: 2014-2024* (Berlin, Verfassungsbooks) pp 55–68.

Vimochana (n.d.) 'When Homes are Torture Chambers: Vimochana's Work with Victims of Domestic Violence', 110 *Manushi* 17–24.

Walters, M (2005) *Feminism: A Very Short Introduction* (Oxford, Oxford University Press).

Watson, A (1983) 'Legal Change: Sources of Law and Legal Culture', 131 *University of Pennsylvania Law Review* 1121–469.

Waylen, G (2007) 'Women's Mobilization and Gender Outcomes in Transitions to Democracy: The Case of South Africa', 40(5) *Comparative Political Studies* 521–46.

Weldon, SL (2002) *Protest, Policy, and the Problem of Violence Against Women: A Cross-National Comparison* (Pittsburgh PA, University of Pittsburgh Press).

Weldon, SL, & Htun, M (2013) 'Feminist Mobilisation and Progressive Policy Change: Why Governments Take Action to Combat Violence Against Women', 21(2) *Gender and Development* 231–47.

Wenzel, NG (2010) 'Constitutional Culture in Japan and the Philippines: Success and Failure in Post-War Constitutional Choice', 25(3) *Pacific Focus* 396–416.

—— (2014) 'Lessons from Constitutional Culture and the History of Constitutional Transfer: A Hope for Constitutionally Limited Government?', 20 *International Advances in Economic Research* 213–26.

Westergren, S (2004) 'Gender Effects in the Court of Appeals Revisited: The Data since 1994', 92 *Georgetown Law Journal* 689–708.

Williams, RV (2006) *Postcolonial Politics and Personal Laws: Colonial Legacies and the Indian State* (New Delhi, Oxford University Press).

Working Group on Women's Rights (1996) 'Reversing the Option: Civil Codes and Personal Laws', 31(20) *Economic and Political Weekly* 1180–83.

World Bank Group (2024) 'Proportion of Seats Held by Women in National Parliaments'. Retrieved from https://data.worldbank.org/indicator/SG.GEN.PARL.ZS.

Wrase, M (2020) 'Anti-Discrimination Law and Legal Culture in Germany' in B Havelková & M Möschel (eds), *Anti-Discrimination Law in Civil Law Jurisdictions* (Oxford, Oxford University Press) pp 136–54.

Zippel, KS (2006) *The Politics of Sexual Harassment: A Comparative Study of the United States, the European Union, and Germany* (Cambridge, Cambridge University Press).

Zuhur, S (2014) 'Women's Quest for Equality in Post-Revolutionary Egypt' in C Derichs & D Fennert (eds), *Women's Movements and Countermovements: The Quest for Gender Equality in Southeast Asia and the Middle East* (Newcastle upon Tyne, Cambridge Scholars Publishing) pp 27–53.

INDEX

www.ingramcontent.com/pod-product-compliance
Ingram Content Group UK Ltd.
Pitfield, Milton Keynes, MK11 3LW, UK
UKHW020813290926
15470UKWH00003B/1123

9 781509 985685